City Life

For Alan and Philip

City Life

Adrian Franklin

Los Angeles | London | New Delhi
Singapore | Washington DC

First published 2010

SAGE Publications Ltd
1 Oliver's Yard
55 City Road
London EC1Y 1SP

SAGE Publications Inc.
2455 Teller Road
Thousand Oaks, California 91320

SAGE Publications India Pvt Ltd
B 1/I 1 Mohan Cooperative Industrial Area
Mathura Road, Post Bag 7
New Delhi 110 044

SAGE Publications Asia-Pacific Pte Ltd
33 Pekin Street #02-01
Far East Square
Singapore 048763

Library of Congress Control Number 2009934247

British Library Cataloguing in Publication data

A catalogue record for this book is available from the British Library

ISBN 978-0-7619-4475-1
ISBN 978-0-7619-4476-8 (pbk)

Typeset by C&M Digitals (P) Ltd, Chennai, India
Printed in India at Replika Press Pvt Ltd
Printed on paper from sustainable resources

Contents

Acknowledgements

Excerpt from *Auto da Fay*, copyright © 2002 by Fay Weldon. Used by permission of *Grovel* Atlantic, Inc.
Excerpt from *Auto da Fay*, copyright © 2002 by Fay Weldon. Used by permission of Harper Collins Publishers Ltd.

Introduction

> The bombsites remained for decades. Nature quickly took them over, the split-apart houses, wild willow herb and buddleia creeping over ruined walls … Stray cats abounded, the ones who ran away when the bombs fell and never saw home again or had no homes or owners to return to. Old ladies fed them their rations, and they bred and became plentiful, but weren't keen on stroking.
>
> Fay Weldon, *Auto Da Fay*, 2002: 157

Most of us live in cities, our lives are city lives. This book investigates the life rather than the structures, buildings, policies, systems, human taxonomies and sociologies that normally comprise investigation of the city. Of course all of the above are part of the life of cities, a very important part, but actually, only a part. These descriptive traditions of urban studies have a tendency to reduce cities to abstractions of systems, whether social or physical (though seldom both together, regrettably), to empirical descriptions of their capabilities or failures (scorecards of progress or scandal), to their putative social and environmental problems (the driver of so much research, knowledge and perception of the city) and, most importantly, to mostly one-dimensional, single-discipline-based approaches (though I note with much pleasure Amin and Thrift's *Cities – Reimagining the Urban*, 2002), which have a tendency, a serious one in my view, to replicate all of the problems associated with the Great Divide between science and the humanities. So, we produce works on the city that emphasise one of its human or non-human features (its cultures, building, architecture, traffic, its risk from natural disaster, its air quality, its standard of housing) and very seldom tackle the city as if it is an assemblage of all of these things; we seldom see it as a totality of human and non-human networks of texts, software, culture, behaviour, architecture and trees and gardens. For this reason, it is very hard, actually, to say anything meaningful about the life of cities. And the life of cities is of course a critical variable in our lifestyle-rich cultures and affects the location of key workers and employers. Their lifestyle considerations span the Great Divide by being as concerned with environmental and ecological conditions as they are with culture, services, architecture and ambiance (and we do hear a lot about buzz, atmosphere, 'aliveness', excitement). We hear that successful cities are *tolerant* cities, but that tolerance is not just cultural and ethnic tolerance: it is a generalised tolerance and a genuine interest in and concern for such things as nature, the past, hybrids, new (and old) technologies, the hinterlands and neighbouring countries, the producers of our food and our clothes and our impact on their lives. This book suggests that all of these postmaterialist and posthumanist themes constitute the new ecological culture of contemporary Western and other modernising cities.

Even if we don't live in the great city itself (although increasingly the world has become urbanised) all of us live in its shadow, are held in place by its gravity and, actually, most of us long to live under its spell at certain moments of our lives. There is a lot of magic, phantasmagoria, ritual and transcendent content to city life that only occasionally surfaces in urban studies (for an exception see Pile, 2005) but which is crucial to understand if we are to fathom city life properly. Many of us long to leave the safe, predictable, humdrum places we were reared in (suburbs, little towns and rural backwaters) for the city lights; we long to spend time there shopping, where the shops are better and where the things sold are astonishing. Their very possession confers an aesthetic zing unavailable elsewhere. There is also something about their great works of public art and architecture that interpellate us, hail us, irrespective of whether they are nation-building shrines, whether they embody art or style movements or whether they are merely celebrity landmarks. In various ways these things define who we are, where we have come from and often where we are going. And, increasingly, we need to immerse ourselves in its transformative atmospheres because for many of us the city also promises to fulfil our potential, whatever that may be; a place to find oneself outside of those places where tradition and conservative cultures still hold some sway; the city as place of experimentation and self-making. This book is all about how cities, or many of them at any rate, came to be such central elements of our lives and why they take the form they do.

Can anyone doubt the suggestive orientation that Norman Foster's giant Gherkin gives to the London skyline, or Piano's anticipated Shard of Glass? We long for the theatre, music and cultural productions of the city and pay homage to its celebrity and genius. And we long for the potential, multiple possibilities that the city offers us in order to make ourselves in different ways. There has been a great deal of innovation in city life, both human and non-human: I like the idea of city farms, of city forests, of hawks who have learned to patrol its air and nest high in its buildings, and of foxes and badgers raising families under garden sheds.

If village, community and suburb offer us norms to comply with and follow, then the city offers us alternatives, multiple paths and becomings. If small places of community and belonging offer you judgement and certainty, cities offer, as Simmel (1997b) suggested, the freedom to explore and the giddiness of adventures into the unknown.

Image 0.1 An exciting city: Sydney, Australia (photo Adrian Franklin)

Paradoxically, what I have just written is both widely acknowledged and controversial, but mainly controversial. In recent years as in most times of modernity, the city has come in for some pretty harsh criticism. It has been made responsible for a whole host of bad things, from the destruction of tradition, community and the family to the emergence of anomie, individualism, blasé cosmopolitanism, consumerism and marketisation, and the denial and destruction of the natural world in favour of a world of humans among themselves. Cities are seen to swallow up their hinterlands and regions. Their commuters become a destructive curse to greenfield sites and traditional rural villages; their paradoxical enthusiasm for nature combined with their mobility continues to threaten wild borderlands. There is a widespread feeling of impending doom: that the world may one day become a *totalopolis*.

As with all such fears, however, the city is merely a new scapegoat, a new repository for our fears of change and our sense of insecurity. If we look closer at cities what we see is also exciting potential, pure potentiality, unfoldings, not all doom.

Cities then are magnificent and exciting places, and in my view are becoming more, not less so. All around the world cities are growing in human and cultural diversity and it is cities more than any other spaces that are benefiting in these ways from globalisation. Migrants to the city often keep their diverse cultural and ethnic forms intact, much as they were before they arrived. Parents keep up the old ways, the practices and principles of the old country. Why on earth not? But then eventually their children or grandchildren get fed up with being *other*, even when the city is just a mix of others. Often they want to hitch a ride on the modern zeitgeist, be a part of new eras of modernity and the unfolding modernity is rarely orientated to the preservation of tradition and ethnicity as an invariant form. Typically it is the opposite: the creation of hybrid worlds, fusion tastes and the liquefaction of difference, but at the same time the upholding of generalised tolerance to do so. This is understandable because cities are too complex and dynamic to hold still; they have to be in permanent flux, always becoming something else; something better (hopefully). After all, insisting on freezing time and culture goes against the spirit of city life. So diversity then becomes an endless future of fusions. Cultures don't disappear in cities, they bleed into one another. And as they do so, and I am thinking of the history of the mixing of black culture through the form of jazz for example, they do not disappear but transform, they challenge and create fusions and assemblages – often in the most surprising and hard-to-predict manner.

For example, we are all using, playing with and changing the use of English; we all dance to beats and tempos with origins far from our own shores and borders; but we all benefit from 'what the Romans did for us', from the socio-technical exploration of Victorian England, from Indian cuisine (now Britain's favourite take-away food for example), from American literature and French notions of *égalité* and we respect John Mortimer's reminders to look after trial by jury, the presumption of innocence and the upholding of civil liberties after he has gone (see his *Where There's a Will*, 2003). Authenticity is always an illusive quality, often born in periods of anxiety about change, but history teaches that city life is about the creation of hybrid cultural forms.

However, the speed at which different cultures have been thrown together in cities and the circumstances that have led to their cohabitation are not always conducive to the interpenetration of city cultures. Indeed, Zygmunt Bauman suggests in his *Globalisation* (1998) that insufficient time now elapses to allow the process of cultural familiarisation and accommodation to take place. In a 2003 interview (Franklin, 2003), he argued that 'the city environment continually generates a curious blend of mixophilia and mixophobia'. In Bauman's view, in the past there was more time for familiarisation, through a slow mutual accommodation with otherness, but today only those young people and young adults thrown together in mutual poverty, often in city centres or university campuses, are in a position to gaze at, explore and learn – to engage and develop their mixophilia.

Residential segregation and suburbanisation, on the other hand, make sure that we inhabit only a limited space of the city while others remain mysterious, inaccessible – other worlds kept apart through mixophobia. In time, there will be the slow churning of human cultural hybridisation; more immediately there will be turf wars, racisms, ghettoism, 'gated' living. It is therefore life affirming to notice how often some (though not all) of the buzzier, atmospheric places in cities are quarters with an 'edge', those with a little transgressive excitement, where multiple cultures find a way of cohabitation, which excite students and artists and which get woven into the more dream-like tales of an age. These places have often been the epicentre of the re-emergence and spread of a more tolerant, carnivalesque, culture-driven city life. In many ways these places are the inspiration of this book and the hope of cities. They can teach us a lot about where we might try to change things. This book is not a policy utopia but a means of commencing a new dialogue about city life; it tries to diagnose what that life is composed of and created by.

But these fusions are no longer merely human, cultural hybrids because another dynamic that makes cities even more exciting are the endless possible relationships we can have, make and remake with machines. Last night on my TV, Jeremy Clarkson told us (on his *Great Inventions* series) that the average English home now has twenty computers in it. They are in our cars, our washing machines, our food mixers and breadmakers, our televisions and DVDs, our cameras, mobile phones, heating systems, and of course we have increased the number of personal computers in family homes. Just how these interweave with our lives, what they enable us to do and become, and what *becomes* as a result of our interaction with them and those of other people (and their machines) in our lives would take up the space of many books. One member of my family has recently taken an interest in his family tree. It turns out that unknown to him, others sharing the same unusual surname were also putting together genealogies in their parts of the world, but over the past year or so, the Internet, seemingly with a life of its own, made connections between them without this ever being part of their individual projects. Now this relative has been connected to, writes to and intends to visit a perfect stranger in the USA on the basis of their recently discovered kinship. He is excited about this visit, in part because the trip enables him to see for the first time another exciting city, Chicago.

In this way cities are all connected in routine and unexpected ways, but because they are all also the result of very specific becomings, have come together from very diverse and different contexts, histories, cultures and opportunities, they are not all the same. To be a Londoner is not the same as being a Chicagoan; to live in one is not the same as living in the other and they are not becoming more similar. They have their own lines of flight. Those who see only standardised global retail chains reproduced in every world city see only a very small part of city life. Cities do not have to become drab, repetitive clones of each other, something that was feared by the first generation of urban theorists to consider the new global industrial cities, but rather they can venture out into new extensions, they can change course and they can copy and add things they like from elsewhere. We have to understand that city life is created by the peoples, natures and objects of specific cities; it is not something that can be planted in from elsewhere. We can nurture those conditions that enable people to create their own city culture but we cannot dictate its content or style.

But the diversity and excitement of cities is not restricted to the human, machine or cyborg. Cities teem with other non-humans from microbes to plants and animal species and these too are not a residuum; they are not merely the decorative additions we make in our gardens and the bits and scraps of non-human organisms that we have somehow missed in our attempt to sanitise a purely human space. In a way they have always been there, not always seen, not always appreciated. It is only in recent times that we have come to appreciate how much 'natural' life there is in cities and this is partly because we have begun to look with new posthumanist eyes.

Humans have pursued rather contradictory ambitions for city life. A group that we might call city builders, those responding to the threat of risk from non-humans of all kinds, have dreamed the dream of a human citadel, where all others were banished by rules and regulations, by barriers and membranes, by chemical toxicity and chemical regimes and by removal of niches and habitat. This group has triumphed rather less than they imagine, but their rhetoric has produced the widespread view that cities belong, properly, to humans, or its variant, that cities exclude non-human life. Both are wrong and lead to serious consequences that limit the possible richness and diversity of city life. Another group, who seldom act as a group, have been responsible, wittingly and unwittingly, for undoing the work of the city builders.

First there are those, and they are legion, from London to Hong Kong, who have wanted to share their lives with non-human others. They have acclimatised a wide range of non-humans into life in the city. Plants brought in from exotic climes to decorate city gardens in lavish, expensive but controlled ways have escaped all over the world – even in the exotic places of origin themselves. Australia, for example, has imported thousands of plants and hundreds of animals. Often, in league with gardeners, new strains/hybrids of plant that manage better in new climates emerged as a result of trials, experimentation, competition among gardeners and chance crossings in the unique and largely unplanned heterotopias of the Victorian garden. It was then possible for them to make their escape attempts, to wait their opportunity to spread and thrive. Buddleia (*Buddleia davidii*), named after the early eighteenth century English botanist the Reverend Adam Buddle, was introduced into the UK in 1890 from China. It was noted for its astonishing capacity to attract many butterflies otherwise not seen in the English city garden, and became therefore a significant reason why so many butterflies like the Red Admiral, the Peacock and the Comma were able to lead city lives subsequently. In Australia and New Zealand it enrolled the Australian Admiral (*Vanessa itea*) to the antipodean suburb, collaborating with the accidentally imported English nettle, which supplied food for its caterpillars. In the USA it brought in hummingbirds.

Initially, it was a prized shrub seen only in the most elegant British city gardens, but it took advantage of any lapse in the otherwise orderly sealed, sanitised and managed modern urban landscape. Buddleia was naturally adapted to poor, almost soil-less rocky mountainsides. Urban industrial ruins, when they occurred, were very much to its taste. Buddleia was first noticed (as a runaway city vagrant) in the crumbling ruins of abandoned country houses and slum districts in the 1930s. Then, as Fay Weldon makes clear, it took up residence in the thousands of urban bomb sites created by the Second World War. These were less concentrated than slums and as a result they spread over a wider range. As a denizen of human decline, buddleia was next noticeable in the waste grounds and embankments created by the decommissioned railway lines of the 1960s. In this way buddleia now transected Britain in the systematic manner of a railway network and as a result of this it very quickly established itself in the ruins of Thatcher's deindustrialisation programme of the 1980s. And, as local city councils lost income and the ability to maintain urban infrastructure in the 1980s to 1990s, buddleia cropped up wherever the hand of human urban maintenance hesitated. Buddleia, railway networks and deindustrialisation created a network, became intertwined and created a new nature and a new urban look. Buddleia's own network of insects were thus enrolled into new urban spaces.

So, in a buddleia-like manner, nature is interleaved into city life and is always potentially waiting to become more so. There are shy, previously much-hunted birds in Australia that the first settlers hardly ever saw, so they had to confine them in aviaries in zoological gardens. Once there and confined they began to learn the ropes of city life. How doors work for example; how humans *like* birds generally speaking and like to offer them food, or where humans will often dump unwanted food, seemingly without a further care. They learned that most of their carnivorous enemies gave cities a wide birth and how, despite everything, cities made pretty good nesting sites. But all this takes time and shows that cities are always likely to be 'becoming something else'.

Just as Brisbane and Sydney gained exotic city birds, London lost others that had been familiar Londoners for a very long time. First to go were the storks that were common in the seventeenth century, as John Philips records in his Georgic poem *Cyder*:

> Twill profit, when the Stork, sworn Foe of Snakes,
> Returns, to shew Compassion to thy Plants,
> Fatigued with Breeding. ...
>
> [*Cyder* (1708), Book 1, ll. 375–7]

Their annual migrations from Africa terminated as building changed and as more marshes close to cities were drained for agriculture and building. More recently, as gentrification and new building techniques closed most entrances to roof and gutter spaces, the English sparrow, long a symbol of Londoners, went into a steep and much-lamented decline. As we will see in Chapter 8, however, nature and humanity are not closed off to each other ecologically and there are aesthetic, sentimental, moral, ethical and symbolic relationships that mediate many relationships and outcomes. The sparrow, for example, has made a comeback because people have provided nest boxes on the sides of their homes, in quite staggering numbers. The stork has not nested in London again, but right in the heart of the West End there is a noisy and vibrant heron colony and they have entered the city to take advantage of cleaner water and more nutritious urban wetland ecologies. Key workers stop on their way into the city to admire and check progress of the new season's chicks. Workers and heron chicks both comprise city life but their combined trajectories, their intertwining and their becoming together, need to be part of what we count as the city.

In this way cities still have a cultural and performative coherence and have not been dissolved by liquid modernity, globalisation, the 'spaces of flows', electronic media and communications. On the other hand, all of these *have* had an impact on city life, but mainly by increasing the net in- and outflows of peoples, information and things that were always the defining features of cities: we still experience city life much as Virginia Woolf did in the 1920s using natural metaphors of flows, currents, growth, expansion and death. As then, city life always overwhelms us; there is always far more of it than we can ever possibly cope with and, as Bauman (2002) argues, there are now many movements of new peoples (and things) whom it is impossible to fix in any order of things.

We have moved quietly, but certainly not undramatically, into what Steve Crook (1999) called 'neoliberal regimes of risk management'. City and national states can no longer manage risk on our behalf and the number of risks and insecurities proliferates as the world becomes more mobile, liberal and flexible. Cities that were once bastions and havens of safety and hygiene are now as wide open to disease as they are to terrorist attack, racism, crime and (other) disorders and this too will have implications for city life, a point Touraine (2000) makes in his *Can We Live Together?* Despite that, more of us are more connected and more widely a part of and informed of this life. This book will argue that while this changes what it is to live in a city, it tends to add more life to, rather than move more life away from metropolitan centres. In sum, as both cities and their troubles grow in significance, the city has never been more relevant to global society.

This book investigates city life in its two main aspects. First, as we have just seen, in respect of the *ecological* relationships established in cities, between humans, machines and buildings (which were once called 'machines for living') and 'natures'. And second, in terms of its social and cultural composition, particularly the often noted (and sometimes lamented) sense of vibrant and fulfilling city life. Increasingly, competing global cities seek to instil or revive a sense of city life as 'buzz' or 'aliveness' and they often follow formulaic developmental methodologies in order to do so without knowing quite what this city life is in ontological terms or how it is generated as a social and cultural artefact. This book aims to analyse this special quality of successful cities and to describe its peculiar social and cultural content. In doing so it is necessary to trace the development of the city historically and so the early part of the book traces, briefly, the transition from the early, so-called traditional cities to the planned modern cities of the nineteenth and twentieth centuries and then, in rather more detail, their biographies from the mid-twentieth century until the present. The chapters thus fall into two sections, Part One: Becoming Cities and Part Two: Making City Life.

Part One: Becoming Cities

Chapter 1 commences with the birth of the city of Canterbury, England, when the centre of the tribal life of the Cantiaci became focused into a fully fledged Roman city. We can learn a lot from this brief exercise if only because it tells us a lot about the focal points and content of city life for most of their history. In this respect I beg to differ from Max Weber's (1958) view that the city's historic function was primarily one of defence. Unlike the modern city, which placed emphasis on the city as a place of work and residence, the Roman city and later medieval and early modern iterations placed great emphasis on cities as places of religious, ritual, trade, leisure and political life. Trade, meeting and rituals had been combined at special places prior to their elevation to cities from at least the Iron Age in the UK and Europe. In many respects, as we will see, the successful contemporary city has found ways to restore this transactional and ritual convergence in new contexts, whereas many people living in less successful cities still languish between the boredom of suburban residency and the indifference of the modern industrial estate. These 'non-places' are often compounded by city centres reduced to a nine-to-five retail and office function.

Chapter 2 considers the transformation of the traditional city into the machinic, spontaneous, and often unplanned city of the early nineteenth century. Again, an attempt is made to try to understand a newly urbanised working and industrial class alongside (and interpellated by) the strange and powerful new machines that dominated their landscape and created yet more possible ways of life in cities. This was by necessity an experimental period in modern planning, new urban technologies, politics and social transformation, in which microbes and an increasingly diverse amount of global natural resources were pulled into these cities for manufacture and consumption. Whereas Canterbury formed the focus for the traditional city, it was the large and affluent port cities like Bristol that were poised to become what Lewis Mumford (1961) characterised as 'Coketown'.

In Chapters 3 and 4 the transformation of Coketowns into planned, rationalised modern cities, epitomising what Zymunt Bauman calls 'solid modernity', will be analysed in relation to processes made world-famous in Paris and London. The Paris of Haussmann is essential to analyse for its effects, a lot of them completely unintended, on the nature of social and cultural life in the city. Here the important elements are the new spaces that were created and the momentum and content of the cultural practices. Paris became a model place not only because of its beautiful architecture and shops but because of the city life it made possible. It could be the city of love because it contained new and aestheticised places of assignation and lingering; places for meeting, slowing down, eating and drinking, promenading, dancing and play. From a very early example of a square in the Place des Vosges to the heroic boulevards and their socially sophisticated consideration of residential life in the city, Paris provides a good laboratory for the understanding of vibrant cities. However, it was only one model and beautiful though it was its birth and history has been tempered by accusations of exclusivity and intolerance, particularly of the urban poor who were displaced in vast numbers to make way for its new centre. Chapter 4 therefore considers the other possible 'solid modern' urban solution, one that has become more widely followed around the globe. For this, I turn my attention to London, to the USA and other British colonial cities, particularly in Australia, for this is where the garden city and suburban city life developed and grew to dominate entire cultures.

The problem with both forms of solid modern city was their basis in the belief that a good city could be planned much like a good water supply, drainage and sewerage system. It encouraged the granting of extensive powers and authority to experts, Bauman's (1992) 'legislators', who were given unparalleled control to lay down what was considered to be the true *scientific* path of human development. Life was not to be a matter of taste, tradition or culture (all of which are relative and ethnocentred) but the appliance of science; to find the most perfectible way, delivered in the most rational of schemes. It led to the generalisation of the mantra 'form follows function' and human city life tended to lose all semblance of its aesthetic, ludic, ritual and spiritual traditions in favour of the identification of core functions (housing, work, communications, health and so on). Periods of austerity and the ubiquitous spectre of poverty encouraged this attention to the *basics* of life (Inglehart, 1997 identifies this as a politics of materialism) at best banishing the aesthetic and pleasurable as foppish luxuries but at worst creating uncharted sociological spaces of rejection and despair (de Botton, 2006; Raban, 1974). Such critical thoughts gathered apace in the 1970s and were joined by others focused on an emerging environmental/ ecological critique of the modern city. Together they formed what might be called the 'dysfunctional city' discourse and this provided the critical material and catalyst for urban regeneration and efflorescence over the past thirty years. This is the subject of Chapter 5: The Dysfunctional City. It marked a turning point of a kind and provides the basis for the second part of the book in which cities become less dominated by all-powerful legislators, less concerned with producing a narrow range of functionality for the industrial 'workerist' city, and less focused around the city as a humanist citadel. Instead, new city cultures emerged that would be more reflexive (more interested in their cultural and environmental impacts, for example); they became more democratised through urban social movements and a good deal more performative as new city spaces were created for a range of new *cultural* innovations and institutions. In many ways cities came to reflect the shift from modern societies dominated by work, industry and workerism to those in which consumption, leisure and consumerism were to play a leading part. It dawned on people across the world that the city was no longer just a means to an end but an end in itself. That end was city life itself, but it had to be *made*.

Part Two: Making City Life

The dysfunctional modern city created significant cultural, political and policy-focused critiques and these paved the way for an emerging reflexivity that was to change the entire nature of the city. In searching for an apt metaphor for this transformation one has to combine a greater willingness to reflect on the wider impacts of cities as well as on the fact that this also involved creating far more relationships between people and between people, machines and other non-humans. It also alludes to the growing *complexity* of the city and a retreat from the one-dimensionality of solid modernity (see Urry, 2003a). For this reason Chapter 6 has been given the title 'The Ecological City', and it is significant that a common mentality informed both the greater emphasis given to ethnic and cultural understanding and tolerance (including a greater empathy for history and past cultures as is evident in gentrification and heritage-type activities) as well as to recognising more complex intertwinings with machinic and natural systems (Haraway, 2008; Law and Mol, 2002).

Chapter 7, 'City Lifestyle', looks more closely at how consumption, both as new forms of social movement and as consumerism itself, came to restructure the contemporary city as a cultural and a performative space. The performance of 'lifestyle' was new and took place through new consumer movements, through creating new ways of restoring and inhabiting older properties and neighbourhoods, through creating new urban markets and other exchange and performance spaces.

In these ways the distinction between residency and work in the city was blurred and broken down, both in spatial and performative terms. However, these new activities also transformed the public spaces of cities and created new forms of 'Spectacle and Carnival', which is the title of the next chapter.

Chapter 8 reconnects with earlier historical chapters to identify long-established traditions of spectacle and carnival in the city. The chapter traces how such activities were suppressed and discouraged by puritanical and Victorian cultures and how they resurfaced, often in undergound ways, in the early twentieth century. Jazz is highlighted as an early role model for others to follow and the efflorescence of new spectacles and the carnivalesque (through street carnivals and festivals) are documented and analysed in some detail as a means of understanding what it is that constitutes the new buzz and atmosphere that contemporary city dwellers, employees and developers are so keen to find/create.

Chapter 9, 'City Natures', takes a look at another efflorescence in the contemporary city: a new enthusiasm to share it with non-humans. Relationships with wildlife, birds, companion animals and plants in addition to the relationship cities have with larger natural forces such as extreme weather, volcanic activity and bushfires, form the basis of this chapter. Again, the emphasis is on the city as a post-human entity, which is both encouraged by people who have developed and wish to exercise strong ecological sentiments and is a result of the agency of non-humans. While some may argue that the city still represents an ecological threat to the planet, such anxieties need to be tempered by the fact that cities also seem to produce strong cultures of environmentalism and a keen sense of ethical responsibility to non-humans.

Part One

BECOMING CITIES

1 The Traditional City

> I am standing on the battlements of the impressive Norman-built city walls looking into the city of Canterbury, Kent, in the south of England. The walls, constructed by an organised system of civic contributions (murage) in the eleventh century, were placed there to protect its citizens and preserve the local faction of Norman power. The walls were made of flint and each flint was carefully shaped to expose would-be assailants to its many razor-sharp edges. It is hard to think of any modern material that could be more effective – and last so long – for these flints still have a keen edge. (*City Life* observation notebooks)

This massive effort and expense by the citizens of Canterbury was not excessive. It relates to a long-term investment in safety and risk management. But it also points to something important. Premodern towns like Canterbury might be linked to wider social formations but they existed first and foremost, as Max Weber (1958) argued, *for themselves*: cities were independent, tightly linked economic, administrative, ritual and political *associations*.

Most of the inhabitants had important stakes in the city; they held privileges and in return they owed duties to the collective body. They gave service in key areas of social life: ritual and religious ceremony, administrative and political office and military and defensive forces. They were required to contribute to the upkeep of their collective defensive walls. To its citizens Canterbury was the centre and repository of economic, political and social life and we can see it as a culmination and a concentration of a social corporation that had existed in this area for millennia, from the tribal times of the powerful Cantiaci, through Iron Age warfare with neighbouring kingdoms, their Romano-British experience as a thriving town and through the dangerous times of the Dark Ages. This provides a good baseline to measure just how much city life changed in our modern period.

Roman Canterbury

Before the Norman invasion of 1066, the Romans had also built a fortification of approximately one hundred acres of land across this good bridging point on the River Stour, and some of their fortifications can be seen within a short walk from my viewpoint here on the wall. In fact they are still a part of the defensive structure. The Roman-built fortress town was called Durovernum Cantiacorum and it was the hub town for the defence of the important coastal region of Romano-British Kent. The Roman name for this place suggests in an even stronger way that these early cities were places built by, and for, very specific people. Before the Romans invaded Britain this region was the kingdom of a powerful tribe, the Cantiaci.

The style of Roman imperial expansion was not to replace defeated neighbours by Roman citizens or colonists but to Romanise the inhabitants, or at least assimilate them while not undermining their own culture and religion. And indeed we know that Roman invaders often assimilated to styles of local culture, taste and religion. Thus, according to www.romanbritain.org, 'The Romano-British name for Canterbury then, could be translated as 'the Enclosed Settlement of the *Cantiaci* near the Alder Swamp'. It was emphatically not a city made and renamed anew – not New Rome or New Herculaneum, after the style of later European imperialists.

Image 1.1 The medieval city wall around Canterbury, UK (photo Adrian Franklin)

Prior to the Romano-British period, this settlement was the Cantiaci's military defensive hub built against other Iron Age neighbours with whom war was an on-going state of affairs. It did not prove much of a defence against the Romans, but with Roman help and know-how, it became impregnable. In the third century AD, when Roman Britain came under threat from across the North Sea, there is evidence of rebuilding and strengthening of this wall at around the same time that coastal sea forts were constructed.

Romano-British Canterbury became an *oppidum*, a town with its own mint, temples, basilica, bath house, forum and (two) theatres, one of which held an estimated audience of 3000 (to put this in perspective, the present day Marlowe Theatre seats 1000). The computer graphics of the town that followed the major archaeological digs of the past five years probably do not overdo the precision, planned lines and rationalisation of the original buildings, straight roads and urban infrastructures. Here was a highly organised town, built to last and building considerable stores of wealth. Archaeologists have found substantial caches of coins buried under the postholes of new buildings which are believed to be part of a ritual blessing of the new home by affluent merchants or administrators. The most important houses had impressive tiled floors, underground heating and luxurious plumbing.

Medieval Canterbury

The transition from Roman to medieval Canterbury was relatively peaceful and it thrived as a semi-independent, autonomous social entity. Max Weber's *The City* (1958) demonstrated how the occidental cities of the Mediterranean and northern Europe grew to become powerful independent social institutions in the absence of a rational administration of superordinate political associations such as the modern state/nation (Weber, 1958: 106). As Weber argued:

> In the middle ages the emergence of the autonomous and autocephalous city association with its administrative sponsor and its 'konsul' or 'Majer' or 'Burgermaster' at its head is an occurrence differentiating it from both Asiatic and ancient civic development. ... [w]here the polis first developed its characteristic features, the urban constitution represents a transformation of the power of the city king on the one hand and the clan elders on the other into a reign of notable persons from 'families' fully qualified for military service. (1958: 107)

City life in medieval times was not merely defined by location, residence or current occupation; it was the origin and locus of one's very life chances, one's self-identity, and the basis of one's religious cult and social network. True, there was an important degree of immigration and recruitment to such cities but to stay put carried with it many advantages and privileges as well as duties. The medieval city sensibility, whilst orientated to trade and economy, was in cultural terms and in terms of its social relations, relatively inward-looking.

Canterbury was no *ordinary* place however. Cities seldom are. It had been a political, ritual and religious centre for thousands of years and this was considerably strengthened through the ties between the merging nation-state and organised religion. Through the original patronage of the early Christian missionary Augustine by its local Anglo-Saxon king, Aethelred, and his Christian queen, Bertha, Canterbury acquired a very sophisticated medieval religious apparatus, including the cathedral, St Augustine's abbey, and two other monastic orders within the city wall. Aside from their religious functions these were also the loci of major landholdings, the accumulation of wealth and the organisation of labour markets and industry.

Canterbury later benefited considerably from the close relationship between its cathedral and the monarchy. Its archbishops were chosen from among the country's elite and this brought valuable other connections and ties. But perhaps the greatest asset Canterbury was to possess was the martyrdom of one of its archbishops, Thomas Becket, in 1170. He rapidly became very prominent in the cult of saints in medieval Europe and the astonishing movements of pilgrims to their shrines. Pilgrimage to Canterbury was one of the most important in Britain and northern Europe and

> for the next several centuries his tomb was the destination of vast numbers of pilgrims ... The holy blissful martyr – Englishman, soldier, priest, and saint – symbolized for medieval Christians the manliness, goodness, grace, and mercy that were possible for them all. Three centuries later Chaucer's countrymen – including his king – were making frequent and devout pilgrimages to Thomas's tomb. They went in search of a cure for physical or spiritual illness, in search of guidance, in search of peace. (www.the-orb.net/textbooks/anthology/beidler/becket.html)

According to the cathedral's own records, the numbers visiting Canterbury at any one time were on an unprecedented scale and were a spectacle in their own right. In 1470, for example, it was estimated that over 100,000 pilgrims moved on their knees through the nave to the Pilgrim's Steps (www.historylearningsite.co.uk/canterbury_cathedral.htm).

Image 1.2 Christ Church Gate, Canterbury Cathedral (photo Adrian Franklin)

Like many cities of its day, Canterbury was therefore cosmopolitan in its make-up and atmosphere; it had an unusual tempo, it was prone to the excitability of tourists and people away from the everyday, and, owing to its sacred status, it was a liminal space where transformation and ritual change took place. Massive investments were made in accommodating, feeding, watering and selling to the great tides of visitation and many of the remaining large buildings were the accommodation houses and hospitals.

Modern Canterbury

As I look towards the centre of Canterbury today, however, all the signs are that this city is now merely one little cog in a much bigger wheel. When Henry VIII waged war on the monastic order he smashed Canterbury's source of independent wealth and prestige. Although the cathedral continued to convey great status to the city, it went into a slow decline and could aspire to nothing more than to be a market and administrative hub for Kent. Its historic role as a regional hub bequeathed to it the meeting of many roads, and these roads now ensure that it is a retail and service centre and that its traffic is mostly at a standstill. Like most other cities today, it is one of the institutional means of ordering *national*-level social relations. Few of its shops are owned by, and very little of its trade is organised among, its residents. Instead, the somewhat reduced buzz of its centre is only that of well-known national and international retail chains, reproduced across countless other towns in a national and international grid. Its residents enjoy no privileges not extended towards visitor-shoppers and, indeed, there is very little to bind its residents to any kind of socially distinctive institutional life. Instead, Canterbury is but one place among many where *nationally* and *internationally* orientated lifestyles might be located. The symbols of traffic and movement all indicate that the true social centre is elsewhere: the key signages in Canterbury are directions to the major motorways to London, the West, the North, south to Dover and the Continent. The ancient route west along the Stour valley now terminates at the EuroStar terminal at Ashford and the M20 motorway connecting the airports with the Channel sea ports. At best it services traffic between London and Paris.

Its one great ritual symbol, the cathedral, which was once the hub of its monastic and pilgrimage economy, is not the heart of *its* communal life but the seat of the dominant *national* religion, the Church of England. Critically, its principal, the Archbishop of Canterbury resides not in Canterbury, but in Lambeth Palace, London.

As I walk from the wall into the centre of the city, through the opulent Dane Jon gardens, I can see some of the remaining dwellings of the medieval merchant families (though I have to imagine how they once stood in their own substantial grounds). At the hub of medieval Canterbury, on the bridge over the River Stour on St Peter's Street, close to the Eastbridge Hospital, the Old Weaver's House still occupies its water frontage and is now a major tourist attraction. The streets around it are conspicuously well endowed with late medieval buildings, often four storeys high. However, at a relatively short distance away one begins to see the homes built in the eighteenth and nineteenth centuries as Canterbury began to grow from the nation's industrial expansion. There are a few large homes here and there but it is clear that something profound had happened: the social elite were no longer based in such towns, or at least present as a dominating force of the social formation. They had moved to the national capital or to the centres and headquarters of nationally orientated organisations elsewhere. Apart from the cathedral, Canterbury has no such institutions and thus is significant mainly as a market for goods and services produced elsewhere. It is now a retail and service centre, literally a distributing point for larger flows of things and for a much larger entity.

The town's residents are now predominantly working class and lower middle class, commensurate with the downgrading of the city's standing as a social organisation, or rather its lack of it. The University of Kent, that has been built since 1968, went a long way towards restoring Canterbury as a seat of learning and has made it a desirable location, for its rather sedate 'cathedral city' life, a status that gained considerably from the revival in history and heritage after the 1960s. This form of city life is very different from that normally referred to in urban sociologies. Instead of a culturally creative and change-oriented pulse of the new, cathedral cities and small towns with similar social tones have recreated themselves in the latter half of the twentieth century, but in their case by drawing on their more significant role in the past. They have hitched a ride on the heritage bonanza; the valorisation of national pasts, traditions and history and the ending of a modernity that simply rejected its past and tradition. It is precisely in such towns that a large proportion of buildings are original, and even though they had often experienced modernisations in the 1950s, 1960s and 1970s, from the late 1970s onwards they enjoyed a strong period of renovation and conservation, exposing and highlighting rather than hiding and eliminating the past.

The city life of Canterbury has fed off its historic past with regular 'recreations' of the medieval past, the pilgrimage period and historic re-enactments (there are re-enactments of local battles, local armour and military uniform, jousting and falconry). Places like Canterbury have also reinvented their own carnivalesque pasts, especially through reviving old May Day festivals and bonfire societies. These are places where neo-tribal activities find strongholds, where paganism has been revived as a cult (and its revival is a relatively important shift in religious behaviour) and where the old habit of Christian pilgrimage has come back into fashion. Occasionally there is an air of unreality about such places and this of course comes from the compression of time in the spaces of heritage, the theatricality and street-orientations of city life as well as the incongruity between participation and belonging.

Is it all just a show for the tourists, a means of keeping the tourist flow flowing or, does it do something for the participants and their collective experience of the city? Arguably it does change city life and is no different really to any other episode in the invention and performance of 'tradition'. It indicates a new-found drive to find collective expression and coordinates of belonging. It is the willing into being, rather than the objects and narratives, that sociologists should keep their eye on, for the latter are merely props for the former, essential though they are. And indeed we might go so far as to say that their availability and their distribution in places like Canterbury enable them to act in the becoming of tradition. There is not room here to illustrate or analyse the agency and activity of tourist objects in Canterbury, but it is important to flag the role they play here, as elsewhere (see for example Lury, 1997; MacDonald, 1995).

The efflorescence of these activities gave residents a performative and political habitus in the city that was missing until quite recently. They still elected their own council and organised a great deal of social and cultural activity, but this was mere housekeeping compared to the economic, ritual and even military independence that was once organised here and which constituted a strong sense of belonging and identity. One can become excited by the traffic ordinances and petty misdemeanours that seem to dominate the local newspapers, but by and large the town's population were mainly orientated towards national and international events and media for the information that really mattered. Since the 1970s and the arrival of a more refined and extended form of heritage sensibility, it is possible to live in Canterbury and appreciate its own specific past and how that past can be drawn more into the present. Having at least a creditable shopping centre, Canterbury's consumer-residents are also prototypical of what Bauman has described as liquid modernity. They have very few solid elements that bind them together (they are unlikely to organise warfare, trade or religion, for example), they have few if any stable social bonds based on marriage, kinship, locality, ethnicity or industry. Instead, they engage in serial rounds of self-making, finding new selves among the proliferation of possible elements to historical and cultural identities, many of them now local, even if they are today only temporary and highly provisional forms of commitment. One of the most interesting and widely distributed is that loose form of belonging to a local pub. Pubs in Canterbury, as elsewhere, develop their own character, often from their own sense of the past; they typically used old artefacts, photos of pub outings from the early part of the twentieth century, and expose older layers of their past to galvanise a present day community of imbibers. To drink at the City Arms, the Old City, the White Hart, the Seven Stars or the Dolphin is a sociologically meaningful and distinctive experience and an important part of Canterbury's city life. But this is also the capital of 'the Garden of England' (the County of Kent) and this too provides performative as well as symbolic capital on which new identities are made. This tie with the countryside and nature generally is celebrated far more, through farmers' markets, bird watching (the Stour Valley has a concentration of wetland sites and rare birds), fishing, rambling (often along the old Pilgrim's Way) and open garden schemes. Visitors from other cities around the world cannot quite believe that healthy populations of trout, dace and chub can be seen from King's Bridge at the heart of the city, and their astonishment is a feature of the crowds of tourists who assemble to see the Old Weavers and St Thomas's Hospital on Eastbridge. But it is no accident. Rather it is an expression of the importance of the river to the city (stone for the cathedral was brought up the River Stour from France and it has a legendary run of White (sea) Trout).

City life lost?

In the high modern period, around the middle of the twentieth century, places like Canterbury were declining economically, politically and culturally. As Don Martindale argued in the 'Prefatory Remarks: Theory of the City' for Max Weber's *The City* in 1958: 'The modern city is losing its external and formal structure. Internally it is in a state of decay while the new community represented by the nation everywhere grows at its expense. The age of the city seems to be at an end' (Martindale, 1958: 62).

After reading Weber's sociological treatise on the historic emergence of the city, Martindale had every right to pen such pessimistic lines. In 1958, with post-war reconstruction under way, modern welfare states emerging everywhere, a new socio-technical order organised under the auspices of the nation state and a state of cold war between the two modernities dominating world affairs, the ordinary and even the larger cities must have looked redundant by comparison. This was also a modernity that looked forward and buried rather than celebrated or tolerated the past.

Is this how we find contemporary cities today, as a linear extension of this mid-twentieth century position? I think not. First, as we have seen in the case of Canterbury, the generalised relaxing of a futuristic modern imperative and a reconsideration of the relevance of the past has recreated new forms of life there. As we will see in future chapters, the emergence of this new, more tolerant sensibility owes its origins to the expansion of countercultural influences from the 1970s onwards. Crudely, this culture rejected many of the mantras of high modernism and instead tried to be more culturally sensitive, experimental and tolerant. It rejected monolithic standardisations and modernisation drives in favour of a more heterogenous set of influences for the creation of a new form of life; for *lifestyles* in fact. These were then able to draw on culturally specific places, their pasts and their presents within a more sensitive appreciation of the multiplicity of cultures and places.

Second, it is also clear, for example, that the pre-eminence of the nation-state has not lasted even if it is still important. Rivalling the great nations now are the 'great companies', international corporations that emerged in the 1960s and 1970s and the smaller, leaner, mobile but equally significant firms of the 1980s. The critical thing is that they have to operate in space somewhere, but where? What sort of city would they prefer to locate to?

The locus of power and influence tends to follow *their* location decisions, for many others follow in their wake, but their location decisions have tended to shift and change in the past 40 years. At first they concentrated and then they decentralised but now they are merely mobile or, as Bauman (2000) put it, *liquid*: free to choose wherever to locate but having no ties to any particular space for any length of time. Nonetheless, there is logic to their decisions and at least one aspect of this is how *attractive* different cities are to them, and as Richard Florida (2003a) has argued, to their key employees.

With concentration now producing congestion and aesthetically unpleasing living and working conditions, decentralisation and even more mobile means of transport and communication mean that companies competing for key workers have to think about locations that will attract and retain the best in the labour force, especially among what Richard Florida (2003a) calls the creative class. Somehow or other, and this is something this book will investigate, cities had not all experienced a common decline relative to the nation and its various hubs. Some had indeed become dull and repetitive places, others mere backwaters. But others seem to have seen an alternative trajectory for themselves or at least alternative cities emerged somehow through the agency of new groups with fresh ideas, and these were based on a menu of great variety, great social excitement and change, on cultural efflorescence and cultural growth, on lifestyle and lifestyle choices, on social tolerance and diversity. Somehow, in the late twentieth century, a growing number of cities had become distinctive and proactive once more, to the extent that one could begin to talk of distinctive and even opulent and independent civic cultures. It was by no means a return to the independent and self-enclosed cities of the medieval period but perhaps it was a rebirth, a relaunch into something that had at least, in cultural terms, emanated from within the city and enlivened the city with a new lease of life and energy.

Some but not all re-merged in the past thirty years as different types of city where 'city life' became distinctive, attractive and economically significant if not imperative. They had somehow managed to transform themselves from the standardised, planned modern city; made themselves *more* than merely machinic cities for making things and housing people, and returned to a state where the city existed by and for itself, where its citizens managed their fortunes and their risks and saw themselves in competition once again, with other 'player' cities. I see the recent research on places such as Manchester, Baltimore, Seattle and Bristol emphasising these features and others trying to emulate them, for obvious reasons (Brown et al., 2000; Hannigan, 1998; Ley, 1996).

In order to achieve this new and exciting state they had traversed an extremely difficult and enduring idea: that cities were first and foremost inert, passive, machinic effigies to the modern order. Built against nature and designed to contain and control humanity they were places where humanity lost its agency and became insulated and alienated from nature. Beyond work and residence it was difficult to see what other purposes cities were to serve *or become*. As always, change was not ushered in by those who controlled the levers but those on the margins whose interests had become alienated and who practised different values. But in any case the tightly controlled planned city did not sit well with growing demands for freedom and liquidity and the new creative cities manifested a freer, more tolerant, consumerist and entertaining ethos. But before we can appreciate this efflorescence of city life it is important to remind ourselves how the city was transformed by modernity. This is largely a story of the building of new cities and the various makeovers of older cities after their likeness.

2 The Machinic City

The transformation of the city at the end of the eighteenth century and the first half of the nineteenth century remains one of the most significant shifts in human social and cultural life in the entire history of the human species (and, many of its symbiotes). But it is more than the transformation of cities, since the cities of medieval Europe were more or less swept away. They lost their purpose, independence, poise, exclusivity and distinction as pinnacles of human civilisation. Along with the members of the ancient regime who lived in them they were more or less liquefied. But the new kids on the block did not seek a new permanent state of revolutionary change but sought instead to replace one solid form of order (tradition) with another (modern). The city and social life generally became somewhat experimental as the new, proper, just and technically efficient order came into being through the work of theorists and visionaries.

In order to see this we must move on from Canterbury, which lost its power and independence as a focus of medieval city life, and relocate ourselves in the new industrial epicentres of the early nineteenth centuries, a world captured well by Charles Dickens. Charles Dickens spent a lot of his time in Kent and must have known Canterbury well, for at least some of his establishments and more than a few scenes (e.g. in *David Copperfield*) were set there. But places like the newly expanding London and Bristol must have seemed all the more shocking to a man who still glimpsed and romanced the older order of things. In Canterbury, with its weight of history and its small city life dominated by its cathedral, the new industrial order was less evident, but it was pulling both capital and people away from places such as Canterbury into its orbit.

In Bristol, which grew much more and was always dominated by venture capital and profiteering, the city descended quickly into an example of 'Coketown', a term coined by Dickens as the archetypal industrial city for his book *Hard Times* (1854) and refined into a quasi-sociological entity by Lewis Mumford (1961). The nineteenth century 'Coketowns' which sprang up all over the industrialising world were, in these writers' view, the low point in city life. Shocking in the extreme and unsustainable, they did provide the stimulus for the sorts of reforms and designs for the new experimental cities of the twentieth century. Since Karl Marx referred to Bristol, UK, as the hub of capitalism at this time, it offers a very good idea of city life as 'Coketown' (Lovering, 1983).

Bristol

The first stage in the industrialisation of cities took the old city order completely by surprise and their transformation was largely ad hoc, disorganised, momentous and tragic. Bristol had been a thriving port town, and, largely thanks to the slave triangle which its Society of Merchant Venturers dominated, the eighteenth century brought with it unprecedented wealth. In the Georgian districts around Clifton luxurious estates, mansions and grand terraces rivalled the opulence of the nearby princely resort of Bath Spa. The wealth created at the port favoured the proliferation of small manufacturing firms, all based on the resources of the slave triangle, apart from the slaves themselves: tobacco, sugar, cocoa and cotton. Importers and purveyors of these goods then expanded into others: tea, coffee, wines and fine sherries. Bristol was also served well by the discovery of seams of steam coal within its own boundaries, by underground hot springs, the major Western railway route and its position on the gateway to the River Severn, South Wales and the Americas.

It was really no wonder then that when the enclosure movement combined with the promise of better wages in such places, the population of Bristol grew as never before, increasing by 20% between 1801 and 1811, by 15% between 1811 and 1821 and 18% between 1821 and 1831. In working-class quarters such as Bedminster the population growth was staggering: it grew by 39% between 1801 and 1811 and by 74% between 1811 and 1821 (Franklin, 1989: 166–7).

Elements of the traditional, medieval city were still manifest in the cultural life of Bristol. They were there amidst the hustle and bustle of newly crowded industrial districts in Bedminster and even among the shock of unprecedented new wealth in the suburbs to the north of the Avon. However, the old order was not to be tolerated and was gradually eliminated. Up to the nineteenth century religion, art and play were important and central to Bristol's city life, but after 1800 there was a tendency to concentrate on and privilege economic activities and to regard anything else as a waste of time and, worse, dangerous (Mumford, 1961: 508). This is nowhere better illustrated than by the demise of the Bedminster Revels in 1831 (described in more detail in Chapter 8).

According to Mumford (1961: 508), the generating agents of the new Coketowns were the mine, the factory and the railway – and Bristol had all three, eventually. The mine was significant for Mumford because it was the 'slavish routine' that had been originally established as a punishment for criminals that was used as a model for the normalisation of an environment for the industrial worker. This environment, famously described by Mumford as 'dark hives, busily puffing, clanking, screeching, smoking for 12 to 14 hours a day', rested on the supremacy of *the individual.* The guilds had gone and states of work insecurity were extended to all; free competition for labour was normalised and workers were increasingly mobile and on the move. Miners in mid-nineteenth century Bristol came in from almost every mining county of England (Franklin, 1989).

Between 1840 and 1880 there were 21 collieries active in the southernmost Bristol suburb of Bedminster. Coal mining had been part of the rural economy in this area, but as Bristol expanded across the River Avon into Bedminster and became a receiving locality for migrants, new labour supplies created the possibility for new industries. Steel and ironworks sprang up to supply the new iron shipbuilding industry and the building of new super-factories, and from 1860 two mechanised brick and tile works pumped out the raw materials for house building. Bedminster had become a smelly, polluted industrial zone, with other industries taking advantage of local supplies of energy and water: brewing and tanning.

At Ashton Gate, Baynton's brewery complex typified the industrial compound structure of Coketown. Workers row cottages were built around the main brewery at first and then in two court-like structures around new malting facilities. There was no distinction here between work and home and on the campus-like structure there were communal facilities for water supplies, toilets and a washhouse. In 1801 the census enumerator's comments betrayed a certain reticence to enter one of the courts at Baynton's Buildings. He remarked on its 'clannish' atmosphere and reports of a recent outbreak of cholera there. While water remained the key ingredient for making beer, evidently not so much care had been taken with the human supply. Nor, indeed, with drainage, sewerage or air (Franklin, 1989). In every possible way Bedminster corresponded to 'Coketown':

> A blasted, denatured man-heap adapted not to the needs of life, but to the mythic 'struggles for existence'; an environment whose very deterioration bore witness to the ruthlessness and integrity of that struggle. There was no room for planning in the layout of these towns. Chaos does not have to be planned. (Mumford, 1961: 515)

Bedminster, Bristol

Bedminster was one of a few districts that attracted the attention of the Bristol Statistical Society, one of a handful of such societies that were concerned at the parlous state of the English working classes in cities. These early studies provide a very rare snapshot of life in Coketowns. In 1835 they sampled 166 houses in the worst area of Bedminster and found 275 families living in them, of which only 31 were single-person households. The agent carrying out the survey judged that the accommodation of 54% of families was 'close and confined' (we would say overcrowded). The majority (66%) were found to be 'clean and healthy' with only 4% 'dirty and unhealthy'. However, the degree of poverty was significant, with about one-third of the families 'in distress, great want of food, bedding or furniture'. Two hundred and eighty children over the age of seven were sleeping in the same room as their parents or with both sexes in the same room. Thirty-five per cent of houses had no drain or had stopped drains; only 67% had privies and half of the houses did not have a water supply. Aside from the survey, the agent was asked to write some thumbnail sketches of the conditions in a sample of houses. Some had clearly hit rock-bottom:

> E.F. a labourer – widower, with one girl, aged 24 years, who sleeps in the same room, for which he pays a rent of 10d per week. Can read, but the girl cannot. She works as a charwoman; are cleanly but in a state of destitution not easily described; scarcely any furniture in the room. There are two heaps of something in the corner of the room as beds, but not a blanket or any other covering.
>
> K.L. and wife – Lumper's labourer; six children ... all sleeping in the same room, in two beds – one of them on the floor; scarcely any covering to them; family nearly naked and starved.
>
> (Franklin, 1989: 124)

The census schedules of 1841 demonstrate that almost every house in the district, even those doing quite well, sublet spare accommodation to make more money. Very few householders used their upstairs bedrooms themselves, preferring to squeeze themselves in the ground floor rooms and sublet the surplus. In this way both poor, destitute and respectable working class families lived in overcrowded conditions. In the 1970s there was an average of 2.6 persons per dwelling in Bedminster but in the 1840s the figure was 6. Such overcrowding was not simply a matter of poverty, for many of the people in each house had employment. It was also a matter of housing shortage in response to the dramatic and unforeseen influx of migrants from the countryside and Ireland. Twenty-five per cent of the Statistical Society's cases were from Ireland. Such historically unprecedented freedom to move was an artefact of the growing free market for labour.

Machinic culture

But it was not just the new value of individualism finding expression in a newly anarchic state. It was as if the new machinery itself played a part in, was an agent in, and extended a machinic logic and ethic to life in Coketown displacing the humanity of previous city life. Individuals, like engine parts, were free to be attached to or detached from a city life modelled on the machine, but they were recruited into a machinic city where the machine itself provided the new metaphors and relationships for living.

We can say that part of the power of the new machine-driven society was the extent to which it *interpellated and seduced* its first generation of human associates. Paul Johnson wrote of the 'public passion' for machines (Johnson, 1991: 577). The hugely powerful machines driving the pace of life and change, capable of such total transformation, seemed to determine a new aesthetic order, whilst at the same time rendering previous notions of beauty 'traditional' or historic' and thereby discredited. Human value and worth seemed measurable only in machinic terms, in terms of crude labour power; human needs seemed to be newly reduced to maintenance needs, those inputs (crude calorific, liquid needs, shelter and minimal conditions for rest) that would guarantee their short-term engagement with the wider machine order. I am not entirely convinced that the *grimness* that we perceive was necessarily always seen then. We have to recall the excitement of it all, its promise, its mysterious replacement of labour and, critically, what Law (1998) calls *machinic pleasure*. Although Law specifically investigated the machinic pleasure of jet aircraft, he used the relationship between people and steam engines to make his point, and to make the case even stronger for my purposes, here he is writing of a contemporary enthusiasm for steam power, long after its mystique had given way to others:

> The Tern Valley Steam Festival takes places, once a year, in a field outside the small town where I live. It brings together enthusiasts for old machinery ...
>
> Perfect control. The dream of a machine so perfect that it no longer depends on its environment for anything; so perfect, in other words, that it is autonomous; so perfect that it maintains itself. There are so many possible tropes here. Cybernetics; the epistemic

> regimes in high energy physics described by Karin Knorr-Cetina (33); large technical systems, centres of calculation and their translations (34); one thinks, in general, of foundational régimes; régimes, that is, that can defy time, defy entropy, and perform themselves immutably and reliably, for ever.
>
> The pleasures, then, are those of control; control through regulation; through self-regulation; through domestication; inclusion within the system of anything that might previously have disrupted; through the colonising of the Other. (Law, 1998: 35)

In other words the machines that were now literally driving cities were also metaphors for a wondrous new order for city life itself.

I think therefore that old conceptions of the alienation and degradation of workers in Coketown, while important, in many ways missed a vital ingredient, namely that the machinic environment of the early nineteenth century, steam-driven cityscape offered a new order and the promise of perfect regulation in what were clearly unregulated and chaotic times. It was perhaps not a relation of pure domination but of interpellation, of domestication, and of aestheticisations. We, as much as they perhaps, stand in awe of these miraculous machines, transfixed and pleasured. Paul Johnson (1991) captured this often missed aspect of the steam age when he wrote that some of the great engines that still survive from the years 1815–1830 'often have an arresting grandeur of form'; that the hydraulic machines built by Fairburn and Kennedy were 'awesome in their beauty' (Johnson, 1991: 584). 'You only have to look at the *Rocket* in the South Kensington Science Museum to realize that Robert Stephenson loved the creature he designed and built, that it lived, in his eyes' (1991: 585). How much more impressed were the people 'in the thick of things' with these new machines? Or those newly arrived from the provinces?

Some idea can be gauged by the way their development drew crowds, was a *spectacle* in its own right; it became the most central spectacle therefore of 'Coketown' city life. Over 40,000 people waited in Stockton to see the first train arrive in 1825, while in 1829, 10,000 spectators watched the engine trials on the newly built Liverpool–Manchester Railway (Johnson, 1991: 582). And it was not just in England. According to Lissa Roberts (2004), steam engines were popular with tourists in Holland and were considered part of their hydraulic landscape, alongside the older windmills:

> many [tourist] guides featured Zuid Kennemerland, and a stroll past John Hope's estate with its steam engine was often recommended. Guidebooks presented Groenendaal's steam engine not merely as a technological novelty but as an integral part of the landscape, a

> machine to be admired for the 'natural' beauty it sustained. We might regard this constructed continuity as the 'naturalization' of technology. (2004: 254)

A machine aesthetic?

Lewis Mumford's negative characterisation of Coketown 'puffing, clanking, screeching, [and] smoking' can only be seen as negative from the reader's point of view in the future present, yet we are enjoined, wrongly perhaps, to extend our sentiments to those who experienced such conditions first hand. New evidence seems to suggest that such conditions were widely accepted, that they were constitutive of working class culture and aesthetics of the steam age and that they were very quickly normalised and accepted. Certainly, the new steam technology interpellated a new working class of inventor–engineer; perhaps new heroes for a new brighter future for the working classes?

The city machinescape of grime, discharge and noise was inscribed on the bodies of the workers, their skin, their clothes and their homes – but also on their thinking. For the working classes, coal smoke signified the epicentre of successful domesticity. In Stephen Mosley's (2001) history of smoke pollution in one of the worst affected cities, Manchester, his analysis of Victorian novels concludes that a smoky coal fire was firmly established as a symbol of domestic warmth, security and happiness, while the opposite, a fireless house, symbolised ruination and family crisis. The strength of this association, in his view, is one of the reasons why the anti-smoking lobby, warning of respiratory diseases, failed to win the hearts and minds of the working class. Far from being the source of complaint and unhappiness in this Coketown, coal fires and the omnipresent coal smoke were seen as one of 'life's necessities' (2001: 113). But the positive evaluation of coal smoke extended to smoke in general. In 1882, Manchester's Noxious Vapours Abatement Association, a middle class reforming organisation, provoked the ire of a working class crowd who clearly valued 'the smoking chimney' as a sign of a healthy labour market while the smokeless chimney evoked 'misery, layoffs, short time and wage cuts' (Mosley, 2001: 72). Mosley cites a popular (unattributed) poem of 1862 that captures this very well:

> Traveller on the Northern Railway!
> Look and learn, as on you speed;
> See the hundred smokeless chimneys,
> Learn their tale of cheerless need.

Again, we should not allow ourselves to judge these cities as we would our own. Throughout the nineteenth century, trade depressions were one of the greatest dangers to most people. The mechanisation of industry, the investment in large steam-driven factories and their ability to produce high quality goods much cheaper than their rivals was seen as the basis of good fortune and happiness, not the reverse. Smoke and noise constituted the poetics of working class aspirations for stability, comfort and progress. It was no wonder that they had little sympathy with romantic opposition to the dark satanic mills, for they were now home.

Like the collier who does not necessarily dislike being blackened because it identifies who he is etc., I think there was an aesthetic of the machinic expressed outwardly on the body through the patina of soot, grease and industrial grime. It was a look that identified individuals with their role, and relationship with the machine age if not specific machinery, but more than that it marked their *connection* to and *admiration* of the machine; their mechanisation in a new cyborg culture. Just as with the machinic pleasure of the 747 passenger who relinquishes control and establishes a pleasurable dependency on the machine, the early steam industry workers were interpellated into its sudden and dramatic conquest of the hitherto human world.

The extent to which they were recruited into a machinic aesthetic is illustrated by the pattern common to most if not all early industrial precincts whereby the worker's housing and living environment was actually part of the buildings and infrastructure; an indistinguishable part of the machine. There was no spatial or symbolic separation from their life as workers and as householders and their lifeworld was now constituted by the machine. So what if this world was blackened by its effluvia; how was this any different from the stamp of clay, soil and manure that had marked their place in pre-industrial agriculture just a few years previously?

According to Mumford (1961), modern individualism borrowed from the baroque dream of power and luxury, but whereas the latter included sensual outlets such as riding and hunting there was no accompanying sensuality, nor any drive for its realisation in the industrial city. The early industrial culture of Coketown is presented as one-dimensional, drab and soulless yet this is only to judge it by the baroque criteria that preceded it and the romantic aesthetics that emerged as a critique of it. Ideally, however, we should attempt to see it from within its own times, in the thick of things; from its worldview rather than those that were built to replace it.

While so much of the past was ditched, abandoned or destroyed it was not at all clear precisely where things were headed, and they were extremely confusing, unprecedented times. Indeed, as a stereotype Coketown represents an unusually disordered period in which freedom from order, restraints, tradition or culture was expressed as an ideal. With no specific future mapped out the only trajectory in evidence was the creation of wealth and the promise of consumption, riches even. While poverty and degradation was all around, it was conditioned by the potent promise of great expectations. Both extremes feature in the writing of this period. In Dickens there was just as much *excitement* of an expectation realised as there was *condemnation* of the conditions for its creation. While many characters crashed, a great many more, in all stations of life, were sanguine dreamers. New jobs were created continuously, new commodities came on stream from all around the world, new opportunities for migration and enterprise presented themselves and new markets expanded the scope of trade and industry.

Cities were where this energy, excitement and hope found its greatest expression and it is not hard to see why. Cities like Bristol were relatively isolated from the rest of the country in 1800; indeed, its shipping companies were overly committed to the West Indian Interest. In the 1820s the embryonic tobacco company Wills, Ditchet and Co. that would become the giant WD & HO Wills, employed only four men as travelling salesmen and their UK market was at best regional. From around the 1860s this relative isolation changed and the company began to expand in all directions, making connections everywhere. This had a dramatic effect on city life in Bristol. First, the demand for labour grew enormously as a new breed of efficient, integrated steam-powered factories came to replace their grimier forebears. Second, rising profits and the demand for skilled factory work, together with the idealism of Quaker and other non-conformist paternalistic capitalism, resulted in rising wages and more attention to the living conditions of workers – both moral and health conditions. Third, a new mass industry came into being for processed consumables; the demand for the deft handwork of women and girls combined with a much cleaner work environment and profitable products gave rise to a new elite generation of affluent factory workers. These women had money to burn and status to maintain: they paraded their wealth, expressed through fine clothes, on newly built city promenades along the Avon, through new garden parks and along new avenues. These people called into being a massively enlarged retail sector, a more spectacular environment in which to shop and before long an electrically lit showground atmosphere of the city centre. From the 1860s onwards a massive house-building boom accompanied industrial growth but it was no longer unregulated. Indeed, its regulation produced a remarkable transformation that still dominates a large proportion of most Victorian cities in the UK.

Squires Court, 2009

I have just crossed the River Avon in Bristol onto what was the working class, Bedminster side. As I walk I can see on my left an imposing new development of luxury apartments – a spacious penthouse with parking is currently offered for sale there. This development is built over the site of the more squalid Squires Court as described (see above) in the 1841 census. The original court, which came off a dark and narrow lane from the main Bedminster Bridge road, may have been destroyed by the aerial bombardments of Bristol during the Second World War or it may have been demolished before that. In fact I cannot find a single example of these courts standing or, at least, used as dwellings. They were mostly badly built; a hurried response to the first wave of urban growth. But they were built all along this main road and especially among the industrial acreages off to the left where the poisoned River Malago flowed. The higher ground to the right was occupied by dairy farms in 1840 and indeed there was open country ahead for a couple of miles before one came upon the colliery and brewery at Ashton Gate.

Grevilletown

All of the landscape visible from the edge of the industrial heartlands, and for many miles beyond, was built over with an entirely new urban form from 1860 onwards, beginning quite slowly and accelerating particularly between 1875 and 1900. The new built form was the terraced villa, and although it was built in a very wide variety of sizes and qualities and encompassed the respectable working classes and most of the urban middle classes, it gave the impression of a single look or style. This was an orderly look, of straight regimented rows, standardised alignment, fully serviced drains and sewerage but softened and aestheticised, at least in Bristol, by the use of blue penant stone rubble facades and Bath stone lintels and sills. Industrial Bristol was giving birth to a new recomposed amalgamation of the skilled working classes and lower middle classes who worked together in the newly globalised companies such as WD & HO Wills. The new developments were set apart and could never feature in a Dickens novel because here life had become predictable and secure; sober, humdrum and devoid of character perhaps, it was at the same time what everyone wanted.

From the 1880s onwards everyone in such places, even the smallest, had a front garden protected by a stone wall with decorative cast iron railings and many had small but confidently asserted gothic styling. Over the double bay windows the smallest of Welsh slate tiled gothic spires formed a smart almost regal line of architecture: a single design feature that gave the entire development the appearance of a great transformation. However, underlying such developments was not so much a new look to tempt the better classes of renter but new laws. Civic bye-laws setting down minimal standards were required to be enacted by all local councils after the Public Health Act of

1875 and although the style and look (and minimum specification) of these homes varied according to city and region, these laws were largely followed to the letter.

I am now looking at a surviving estate map that belonged to the local landowner Sir Greville Smyth, the incumbent at Ashton Court between 1852 and 1880 and the developer of this area. I can see where former farmland has been redesignated and lines of roads drawn on and named. The entire area that these days is referred to as Southville is named *Grevilletown* on this map. In the estate account books I can see payments made to contractors for the laying of drains and the building of roads, and I can see how each street was divided into plots conforming to the local bye-law specifications, how these were then sold off in small parcels to the twenty or so local builders and then built in a manner that made sure that each house in any given street conformed to standardised alignments (e.g. of height of windows, walls etc.) and design.

Although these homes were not a great distance from the factories and foundries, they *were* a world apart. Unlike Bedminster where the cider- and alehouses occupied every corner, there were no pubs here. Instead, there was the conspicuous presence and the panoptic surveillance of chapels, churches and their halls. Equally, this was decidedly *residential*, a place apart from the commercial and industrial world of the true city. One would only enter this

Image 2.1 Grevilletown order (photo Adrian Franklin)

space in order to return home or visit a home; it was a space of destination rather than transit. In other words these were places of quietude, rest and improvement, places that referenced yet were antithetical to the city they kept at bay. They were not quite suburbs and their economic base was still the factory. Nonetheless, they had made a moral, symbolic and physical break with the machinic city.

Impressive though this was, it was not only the moral, aesthetic and sanitary improvements that disturbed city life at this time. What also changed was the relationship that people had with city space itself and the way that space was subsequently regulated.

Bye-law housing

In the first part of the century the dominant type of domestic space in England was the enclosed court; a small, private cellular arrangement built around semi-communal non-gardened space. With the new bye-law housing, three key changes occurred to what Daunton (1983) calls the house-settlement system:

> First, the private domain of the house moved from a promiscuous sharing of facilities to an encapsulated or self-contained style. Secondly, the public domain of the city lost a cellular quality which had entailed an ambiguous semi-public and semi-private use of space, and took on a more open texture. The dwelling became much more enclosed and private, whilst the external space became waste space or connective tissue which has to be traversed rather than used. The third change is implied in these comments on the development in the private and public domains. The boundary or threshold between the two became less ambiguous and more definite, less penetrable and more impermeable. (Daunton, 1983: 12)

In the cellular city everything was connected to everything else whereas, as we have seen, bye-law housing was a world apart. Daunton may have exaggerated the extent to which new city structures dampened down city life,[1] since one cannot simply read off behaviour from architecture (see Burnett, 1978). Nonetheless, there were other reasons why the nature of street life in English cities changed radically in the mid-nineteenth century.

In addition to significant spatial differences, the nervous governing class of most cities feared the political potential of a poor working class that occupied autonomous and even feared spaces at the heart of the city. Bristol had experienced riots in 1831 that took the city by surprise and which took days of military action to quell. As a result, the Bristol and Bath Constabulary was formed in 1835. The events of 1848 on the Continent sharpened such anxieties, resulting in calls for better order, more surveillance and the presence of law enforcement on the streets. While security may not have been uppermost in the universal preference for row housing and grid plans, it was certainly a sensible move from that perspective. Such places were far easier for police foot patrols, and aside from keeping a general watch for disorder the new police forces were given a wide range of new bye-laws to enforce.

The introduction of new bye-laws targeted what was considered to be levels of street activity that were variously unhealthy, dangerous, a nuisance, illegal, immoral and antisocial. Many cities limited street trading, drinking in public, a variety of 'nuisances', street sports such as racing and gambling, the keeping of livestock, dumping rubbish (even beating carpets), prostitution and so on. The net effect was to greatly reduce the amount of life and colour on the streets. With the introduction of police to enforce the bye-laws, English cities introduced a form of control and surveillance at one and the same time. In Bristol a bye-law even required front doorways to be cleaned before 8.30am.

Daunton asks why the new bye-law villa-styled terraced format proved so popular. After all, the court structures were not outlawed per se, and provided they adhered to new building legislation it seems more obvious that such 'traditional' ways of city life would continue. According to Daunton the legal push factors need to be weighed up against cultural pull factors. Many of those living in overcrowded court structures were migrants from rural England where the housing norm had been the cottage, which was typically occupied by a single nuclear family (Burnett, 1978). Prior to the main building boom of the 1880s and 1890s, builders around the country also noticed that the new villa-styled homes were easier to sell and let, indicating that consumers preferred them but also that many workers could now afford better housing: 'The growth of money wages outstripped higher rents which were charged for a superior product' (Daunton, 1983: 36).

In Birmingham the new bye-law villas were under enormous pressure of demand shortly after they were built while the stock of courts became very nearly abandoned. From the consumer point of view, the provision of more circulating air may have been less attractive as a proposition than the tangible benefits, aesthetic appeal and status potential of a garden. These were consumers who had experienced within living memory the most dire housing conditions combined with hunger and unemployment; bad times. The provision for more space, more privacy and the potential for a leisure space for children's play and gardening was seen as an improvement in a society driven by the notion of improvement and progress. However, in a poor society where there was a finely graded status ranking, there developed a keen sense of a social acceptability in the notion of *respectability*. Thus, the occupation of a house with a well-kept garden could become the outward sign of respectability, containing as it did notions of hard work, orderliness, tidiness and the appreciation of beauty.

There is also some evidence to show that former craft elites used the symbolism of housing and residence to reassert their higher status within the working class (Crossick, 1978), a view endorsed by research on the nineteenth century shoe industry (Rose, 1980). Status hierarchies in England were expressed through physical demarcation and the practice of emulation (see Elias, 1990) and the new housing in Grevilletown was characterised by both. Despite having an overall architectural integrity and look, one soon notices fine but unmistakable lines of difference between the qualities as well as among them. This is spectacularly evident in the size and features of the front gardens that insulate the homes from the street. In Grevilletown they are all quite pinched by national standards, but they vary from the meagrest single line of hedge in a space that would occupy nothing else, up to a small garden of shrubs and small trees, perhaps with a tiled path and terracotta edging. The subject of great care and attention, these frontstage spaces, displayed before the enclosing aspidistras and curtains, became repositories of a household's status and reputation. But these miniaturised natures were also referencing in approving ways, and emulating, the mid-nineteenth century elite fashion for gardening, gardens and nature in general. It suggests that as the grime of the first wave of industrialisation in the first half of the nineteenth century gave way to smarter, cleaner factories sustained by global order books in the second half, that a new form of city life had emerged. It was one also based on the notion of progress and advancement; but it was based on the greater likelihood of a household budget surplus that stretched beyond material necessity and it was based on the emergence of a keener sense of consumption and the spectacle.

In addition to the front gardens that were there to see and to be seen (as opposed to life hidden behind the court), the people who moved into Grevilletown began to take notice of the town's emerging sense of itself as spectacular. Aside from the finer clothes that budget surpluses could afford and sober bodies could model on Sunday promenades, towns like Bristol were growing in an exciting way. Its port had been landing exotic things for over a century, and during the mid-nineteenth century this accelerated. In 1827 Brunel built the Clifton suspension bridge, an event of major scientific and visual significance since this was the beginning of an era of bridge building, rather as the twelfth and thirteenth centuries had been the era of building Europe's great cathedrals. These were showcase developments more than viable economic projects and their impact was disproportionately advantageous: people, the right people, flocked to places like Bristol, where city life was elevated and aestheticised by art, architecture and a planned cityscape.

Two years later and no more than a stone's throw from the bridge, an old snuff mill was converted into a *camera obscura* by the artist William West. The image cast onto the dish for public consumption was a city landscape, now considered something to see. Not only were the new bridge and the Avon Gorge clearly visible (combining nature and artifice in a romantically pleasing manner) but also the newly constructed parklands of Clifton Down, a place of promenading and play. In that they allowed the observer to see but not be seen, such devices were often associated with voyeurism, explicitly so in the case of the one mounted on the cliffs at the Isle of Man, just above a beach renowned for courting couples.

By 1841 Bristol also had a high-speed rail connection to London and three years later it was connected to many points north and west. Its dockyards had also produced the first iron-hulled, steam-driven, transatlantic liner, the SS *Great Britain*, in 1845.

The open-planned nature of this new Bristol meant that the streets and, particularly, its new architectural spectacles brought people together who might previously have been more spatially segregated. Although Clifton Down was in the elite suburb of Clifton, it was given by Act of Parliament to the people of Bristol in 1861 from the Society of Merchant Venturers and has always been a space of social openness. In 1893, with the opening of the Clifton Rocks (funicular) Railway, Grevilletown was connected to Clifton, and the extension of a promenade across the great class divide marked by the River Avon and docks was made possible.

By the turn of the twentieth century British towns had not only acquired a new more orderly look, there was also a very different city life based around the twin ideals of public order and public spectacle. New spaces of public mixing around parks, promenades and architecture were counterbalanced by a residential separation and the observation of social distinction. The association of work and home had more or less disappeared, and indeed a third sphere of leisure was beginning to lay claim to central city areas as well as parklands on the periphery: to the delight of all they built highly ornately tiled, exotically coloured swimming pools. However, it is almost as if the experience of city life cannot be captured in mere descriptions of structural change. The example of Bristol demonstrates that an important element of the changing nature of city life was change itself. In addition to many problems that continued in such places, there was also more hope and excitement, far more transitions that had a positive impact on people's lives.

The home was clearly one of these. Although early nineteenth century model housing built by reformist landowners produced picturesque gothic rural cottages where the emphasis was as much on the garden and its seamless connection to the natural world, it took some time for the idea to be established as a norm in the city. The Victorian bye-law villas were a halfway step towards this. It required yet more shifts in economic, social and political conditions and yet more ways to imagine city life before this was to be realised.

NOTE

1 See Adrian Franklin, *Privatism, the Home and Working Class Culture*. PhD thesis, University of Bristol, 1989, for a discussion of studies of street life in other bye-law housing areas. The conclusion appears to be that social networks and neighbouring were established very quickly.

3 The Solid Modern City: 1

The industrialised or paleotechnic city responds both technically and politically to the question of order in the modern city. In part it responds technically to issues of risk that were new to the enlarging cities of Europe and the USA (new bio-threats such as water contamination; impacts of disease on large populations; new ecologies based on high densities of human settlement; air pollution produced smogs; bacterial opportunists in new industrial complexes and wastes; new threats from mobility of global diseases; imported destructive species that take root in new places etc.), but in part also it responds politically to an outmoded traditional order and seeks to replace it, as Bauman (2000) argues, with a solid modern order, i.e. an enduring one designed to replace it in a more or less permanent, perfected manner.

Capitalism insists on the removal of obstacles to free trade and industrial growth, and given that most industries were city-based in the eighteenth and early nineteenth centuries and also structured by traditional organisations and customs, it is not surprising that cities were one of the first things to be modernised.

The old order of guilds, trade monopolies, municipalities, parishes and privileges, and especially the orderings of rank and birth, had no place in the modern order of things and nor did 'old community supported customs' (Bauman, 1992: 64) and these were slowly but surely swept away in a variety of ways. The challenge occurred first and most abruptly in France, where traditional order was clearly seen as blocking much needed economic reforms and 'progress'. The French Revolution excised a traditional social elite and put in place forms of governance that could experiment with new systems, but it left behind many manifestations of the old order, congealed in memory, everyday cultures and practices, especially in old city quarters and their industries. The old order was based, as we saw in Chapter 1, on the ordering of belonging and assimilation to specific city cultures and space. There was little separation between workplace and residence in the older industrial quarters, and traditional customs regulating home life, work and production were mutually reinforcing and defining of urban cultures. During those decades of massive in-migration to the industrial power cities, newcomers could no longer be assimilated into these localised social structures – they were overwhelmed because 'the numbers of strangers to be familiarised and personalised exceed[ed] human perceptive and retentive powers' (Bauman, 2003a: 8). While this disrupted the homeostatic mechanism of self-reproduction and self-equilibrium of the premodern city, particularly its ability to deal with social uncertainty and thus prevent social change, it did not break powerfully entrenched and longstanding routines immediately.

City life was still based on established interests, belongings and a sense of city corporation, and this could always make its voice heard and assert its will politically. Once the very *raison d'être* and strength of towns, established interests now posed a threat to the external power structures of the nation state that was usurping their power and wealth and to a globalised capitalism that was indifferent to them. The physical structure of the ancient cities that had evolved convoluted pathways and delineations based on these highly complex and relatively fixed social relations could also be seen as obstructions to the free movement of materials and people, especially in respect of much more powerful surges of trade and industry.

It is not surprising therefore that the city itself became the object of *major* reordering, both physically and culturally. Like all other risks and bulwarks, it attracted a new class of socio-technical actant, in this case the architect–planner. And, like most other problems embraced by such specialists, the solution was seen as involving two revolutionary stages. First, sweep away, eradicate, remove and demolish the problem. Then, second, design a blueprint for a better order, one that perfects in a rational way a form compatible with the wider system.

All manifestations of the traditional order could then be eliminated, fragmented, *dispersed*, or in its own terms, *freed* from older responsibilities, rules and obligations, indeed *social bonds*, in whatever form they might have taken. Because the ultimate design brief, the number one principle, was liberation from older shackles and ties. An ancient chapel that was the epicentre of a quarter, the base of a local guild and the focal point of family life – in other words a sacred site to culture there – could be and would be destroyed by the more powerful forces of emerging modern nation-states. In such dark spaces and in the lanes and alleys around them the overlapping social bonds that constituted a sense of belonging and an ethical community could all too easily oppose an unpopular prince or hide an invading army. If the archetypal city for Coketown was Bristol, then the archetype solid modern city has to be Paris, France.

The modernisation and civilisation of Paris

I am sitting in the very congenial Place des Vosges in Paris, having a rather good cup of coffee and a cake at Ma Bourgogne. This is the oldest square in

Image 3.1 At Ma Bourgogne, the best café in Paris (photo Denis Vidal)

Paris and is reckoned by some to be the role model for most squares or public spaces in European cities and beyond. It is also said that this little corner is probably the most beautiful in Paris or possibly in any city anywhere. Either way, it is sublime today. Some most beautifully dressed children are playing (almost) idyllically on the green; the sun is shining, the aroma from the cafés and restaurants is fragrant; there is a couple in the first throes of love laughing attentively at each other; I can see some serious art galleries and an interested crowd of onlookers in each one. I am eternally grateful to Denis Vidal, who first sent me here. There are Internet chat rooms full of people who also stumbled on the Place des Vosges ('PdV') and became as intoxicated with it as I am. There is something serious to learn here about the modernisation of city life but also, I think, about city life itself.

The thing is, unlike most traditional city spaces it was built to be beautiful, but more than that, it was built to be lived in and, specifically, enjoyed. After all, it was inspired by a seventeenth century French king who wished to create a city space that was after the style of a royal palace, and in these leisure and pleasure are the orders of the day. This may be the first example of the very modern idea that cities can borrow from the civilised, affluent and pleasure-driven cultures of the court and [re]embed an amiable, aestheticised and ritual lifestyle in the urban quotidian.

Unlike the haphazard developments of the traditional city with its vernacular architecture and odd alignments and lines, this square of 39 perfectly aligned houses was made in red brick with stone facings and dormer windows and perched over medieval-styled arcades. With the gardens in the centre as a place of quiet rest or play, this space was designed to gather life around it; a place for life to be enjoyed. It was astonishing when it was first

Image 3.2 Meeting, resting and being social in the Place des Vosges, Paris (photo Denis Vidal)

built and it is astonishing still. All around me as I sit here there is one plain fact at work. This is a place of *meetings*.

Today it is not only a place where you might expect to find the shop of a top fashion designer, the former apartments of prime ministers and prominent writers, or the place where you might stumble on a world class art gallery – this is where Issey Miyake has his store, this is where Cardinal Richelieu lived, this is where Victor Hugo wrote and this is where Gallery Vivendi sells art to Parisian collectors. But it is not because it is steeped in history, the habitat of celebrity or the purveyor of fine things that people find it attractive. No. Compared to most city spaces that try to attract (with plaques, footprints etc.) its rather star-studied list of past inhabitants is kept discrete, understated. Rather, what attracts is the social atmosphere and *tone* it generates, its possibility of social transition, recreation and ritual. In other words, it is also 'charming'.

The first ingredient for all human ritual is a defined space that is in some way special in its own right. While right in the middle of things, squares are also, ironically, a closed-off space permitting intimacy, character and integrity that other more open city spaces cannot. They offer, literally, a 'place' *in which* something or things can happen, where people can go, where an atmosphere can be created (and made to linger and be 'soaked-up'). It is all too easy to miss the fact that squares *act* to bring people *together* – in ways city dwellers might not otherwise do. They are places for meetings of people in which both existing ties can be reaffirmed and where new relationships and arrangements might be enacted.

The second ingredient is that the activities are life-changing or affirming. Unlike the quotidian activities of busy streets, which are principally concerned with social reproduction, squares such as the Place des Vosges offer similar activities but which are socially elevated, even if only slightly. So, the cafés, bars and restaurants are not just to provide food, but the space of social meals, where meeting and social transformations can take place. They might be the chosen spot for securing a business deal, a secret assignation, an anniversary, catching up with a friend, a lunch with guests or just for an individual to have some quiet time for thought (literally, re-creation). Individuals and groups may choose to identify strongly with such spaces, making them special or sacred to their identity and culture. In which case they will become 'regulars' and create in such places what Bauman calls *desire* (Bauman, 2000).

Unlike the amorphous nature of pedestrian *traffic* on a street, where people appear and then disappear from view, the social life of a square is more circumscribed, defined and slowed down. Squares offer the experience of *flânerie* to a greater degree: seeing and sensing that there is all sorts of life going on in the city; that it has shape and order, colour and sound. A chance, in other words, to recognise and attend to the anthropology of the city. People talk and gesticulate once ensconced in a square, whether lying on the grass, sitting on a park bench or dining in a café. While walking along a street, people, even when in groups, are less demonstrative, as if their being in a street does not constitute a social event worthy of their performance. But in a square, once stopped and defined by a stronger social field, the architecture, crowd, congregation, movement, drama and sensual information, the individual is interpellated, drawn into something that requires their attention, performance and expression.

The third ingredient is that squares are public rather than private spaces, where one's activities are witnessed and where one witnesses the activities of others. The significance of the presence of others cannot be overstated. Social rituals all around the world take place in public before a congregation, and although the social composition varies – and in the case of modern cities they are not even specifiable beyond such aggregations as *the crowd* – it is still important that some types of activity are conducted before the public gaze, before one's community, before witnesses and alongside those who are party to the occasion. When towns became larger than face-to-face communities and the stranger became the most significant face of the street, social life did not shrink away and die but rather the opposite: it developed forms of social engagement among resident strangers. These took the form of public displays or performances before a crowd of on-lookers. The weekend promenades, for example, were a chance to show off in a public way one's finest clothes, one's relatives and friends *to* the crowd in general, to impress upon a public one's standing and position. Certain places, the purpose-built promenades themselves, but also markets, arcades, cafés, bars and parks, demarcated space in such a way that social aggregations did not lose their definition but were at the same time in the public eye. Such spaces also possess the ritually important capability of generating and even encouraging communitas, a form of social levelling and group-forming sociability between people who are simply fellow travellers. This is seen commonly among those on holiday, revellers in festivals, in sporting crowds, on trains, planes and ships and in resort locations. The phenomenon was associated with the places, first of all, by writers and anthropologists interested in rituals of pilgrimage. But it is a defining quality of the modern city and particularly of those that 'work'.

We can say that, taken together, such places generate what Shields (1991) calls 'aliveness', a form of *social effervescence* that Durkheim also associated with ritual and religious experience. This aliveness is an artefact of the excitement generated when spontaneous social gathering takes place in which the possibility of social transformations and recreation becomes apparent or is anticipated. The significance of architecture and design of urban space to its creation in modern cities seems to be critically important, although it is probably very complex. At the very least, architecture has to create these special places, delineations or urban space. In its design it has also to allow for or encourage social gathering around public performance, whether markets, eateries or bars, parks etc. (see the empirical work conducted by William White in his book *The Social Life of Small Spaces*, 2001).

However, it is also probably true that in order to make these elements work, the architecture has to interpellate people by embodying a spectacle in its own right. Seemingly it has to pull off the impossible: it has to persuade people that they want to be in its space and take part in its social life in advance of really knowing anything about it. It has to hail them and relate to them in ways or using codes that already exist.

Although the Place des Vosges was never a royal residence per se, it was explicitly built in that style, the style of courtly society. As Norbert Elias (1990) argued, this was a style attractive to, much sought after and emulated by the middle classes below it. In other words, the Place des Vosges as a transformation of the codes of royalty and social elite into the city landscape offered the experience of *social elevation* and this, of course, is central to *rites de passage*. At a more immediate, sensual level, the architecture of royal palaces was explicitly lavish, impressive, spectacular and beautiful. It was simply exciting to be inside its walls, to be thrilled by its height, finish and trim. The social miracle that the Place des Vosges performed was in enabling those who did not belong to such exalted places to live some of their life there, to make the extraordinary into the everyday; the profane into the sacred. It is not surprising that the Place des Vosges was built by Henry IV, the Protestant king who restored the renaissance project, begun by Francis I, to the city of Paris. Clearly, Henry was doing something entirely *new* with this development. This new design of conjoined homes around a square rendered obsolete the inward-looking old detached hotels of the nobility, which had maintained huge walls and gates against the volatile public domain of Paris. This is very clear from the nearby

Hôtel Carnavalet, the last remaining example of this form. The King and Queen both kept a residence in the square, but their neighbours were not exactly a court but an embryonic fashionable quarter that was carefully connected to the arteries of Parisian city life, not removed from it.

Place des Vosges inspires London?

Prior to the modernisation of Paris under Louis Napoleon and Baron Georges Haussmann in the latter half of the nineteenth century, the Place des Vosges had inspired as a prototype the building of the principal squares in other European cities. London particularly had a love affair with them, building some 600 by 1850. In London, these squares, with their gardened centres, provided a more-or-less continuous green link with its much larger parks and gardens. By the nineteenth century, when cities such as Paris were becoming choked by urban growth and traffic, London stood out as a city of open spaces, fresh air and respite from its industrial base. And it was while in exile from France in the 1840s that Louis Napoleon admired, while walking in Hyde Park, the *designed* nature of London's inner development. It was impossible not to compare this with the decrepit but 'traditional' nature of most of central Paris.

In many respects the Paris of 1848 was nothing much more than an enlarged medieval capital city. Its street layout had grown according to largely traditional rules and norms of small-scale private development; it was still mostly controlled by a group of influential landowners whose power was independent of the state and it had few of the technical urban services and quality of life measures that were available in most Roman cities. It was clannish in terms of social structure and cellular in terms of its physical structure/architecture, and city life in most neighbourhoods had been insular and unseen. It inspired Balzac to compare it to the dark jungles of Africa and Eugene Sue to describe it as 'The Mysteries of Paris' (Berman, 1988: 153). Mid-nineteenth century suffering in these places was described by the Paris historian Louis Chevalier as horrific with poor health, epidemics, long-term unemployment and overcrowding compounding their plight. It was impossible to view such places as anything but problematic.

On the other hand, Paris was at the centre of one of the industrialising nations and had seen implemented many social reforms during the Revolution and post-revolutionary years. Paris had thus a certain modern outlook and had experienced the same rapid growth in territory and population as London and Bristol. It had also experienced alarming consequences of its growth and technical backwardness. The quality of its water was appalling (cholera killed 20,000 of its 165,000 population in 1832); it had no sewerage system; in some areas overcrowding had become a scandal even by Parisian standards and the unremitting stench never failed to worry a society convinced of the dangers of foul air. Finally, by the late 1840s Paris had reached a point where traffic congestion was seriously dysfunctional. After the social and political upheavals of 1848 France once again settled for a strong ruler and order rather than further experimentations with revolutionary change. Exploiting these conditions, Louis Napoleon returned to France and manoeuvred himself into the position of Emperor Napoleon III by December 1852, with almost unlimited powers to act. Although he was by nature a very conservative man, his determination to transform Paris into a modern city was nothing short of breathtaking.

His admiration of London combined with his interest in a long history of attempts to modernise Paris, from the Revolution onwards. He was particularly inspired by the previous ambitions of the Paris prefect Rambuteau, who tried but failed to establish the policy of demolishing the congested older quarters and narrow streets, replacing them with very wide, straight boulevards that would open the city to light and air as well as free up city traffic. What clearly energised Louis Napoleon was not only addressing particular problems of a growing city with new scientific principles but the very idea that the city can be rethought, restructured and changed for the better. For many commentators this was a turning point and one of the origins of town planning and modern city design. Many, including Walter Benjamin, have read this as an intervention to remove the working class as a political force in the city, or at least to make it less easy for residents to take control of city space through barricades and superior knowledge of traditional living spaces. It is also seen as an inevitable artefact of the new centralised, totalitarian state of Napoleon III which, blinded by the Emperor's faith in Saint-Simonism, ground down the city of differences and autonomy in favour of a singular order and a singular aesthetic of a nation whose salvation would be achieved by the unifying powers of technology (Buck-Morss, 2002: 222). There is of course some truth in all this, but at the same time, in many respects what the new Emperor and his Prefect of the Seine, Baron Georges-Eugène Haussmann (appointed 1853), were able to realise had been anticipated and longed for before the coming of Napoleon III and was every bit as much an artefact of revolution, detraditionalisation and modernisation. Such a major restructuring was only socially, economically and politically possible under those post-crisis conditions when an exceptionally powerful government and a largely unopposed order was restored – leading to what Agamben (2005) called a 'State of Exception'. The State of Exception of Napoleon III only lasted from 1852 to 1870, but in that time Paris was changed for ever and most other cities were to be later influenced by what has come to be called 'Haussmannism'.

It is difficult not to conclude that the Place des Vosges influenced their scheme, as the new design incorporated a lot of features that first appeared there. For example, Haussmann introduced a standardisation of detail throughout the rebuild that few developments other than the Place des

Vosges had ever sought. Along the new network of boulevards snaking their way out of Paris, all building had to comply to strict façade design standards, use of a standardised quarry stone, numbers and alignment of floors, and roof design. Also, like the Place des Vosges, the construction was lavish and stately, giving the impression that this was not a city but a colossal palace. In one stroke the old city of Paris lost its historic heterogeneity of local cultures as expressed by centuries of vernacular architectural styles and status hierarchies and was replaced by a singular, unifying power, in this case a nation state housed within a modern scheme.

Walter Benjamin emphasised the breaking up of working-class Paris and its removal to equally poor conditions on the city periphery but it was as much the revolutionary and modern rejection of tradition and the sweeping in of modern progress through the sorts of technological improvements that only the state could deliver or at least lead and encourage. According to Louis Chevalier, the working classes of Paris, who had fought so hard on many fronts in the nineteenth century, put up no resistance to the destruction of their crumbling homes and may even have been very willing to receive this world (Berman, 1988: 151). Benjamin saw the new railway stations in the heart of the city as the new city gates, demonstrating for the first time that the central areas were now primary sites fulfilling a new symbolic and performative function as well as a location for major commercial communities. Whereas previously the outer edges of the city, its walls and defences, were critical to its fortunes and hence of enhanced symbolic value (cities were often painted from this perspective), henceforth their spatial and temporal marginality would usher in their decline. Cities that had been primarily largely disorganised manufacturing centres were now to become differentiated spaces; political power, commerce and consumption would soon trump production and work in the competition for prime, central city space (the spectacle of which became a new source of inspiration for artists and writers, and through them to their public).

The beat and pulse of the city shifted with Haussmannism to the new city centre, which was specifically built to become a showcase and a playground. The notion that it was a space of pleasure rather than manufacture bothered Benjamin, who felt it was merely a veneer of social equality. If it was beautification it was also merely 'strategic beautification', a sop to secure 'the city against civil war' (Buck-Morss, 2002: 222). But clearly it was much more ambitious than this: it envisaged a new way of living in the city, a new city life, *la vie parisienne*. As Berman put it, 'The Napoleon–Haussmann boulevards created new bases – economic, social, aesthetic – for bringing enormous numbers of people together' (1988: 151).

The making of the boulevards and all of the other planned improvements – water supply, sewerage system, markets, bridges, the Opera and other centres for the arts, centres for local government, parks and gardens and lavish national monuments – created unprecedented levels of business and employment, which, combined with its enhanced commercial and retail activity, powered the financing of the scheme. 'At the street level they were lined with small businesses and shops of all kinds, with every street corner zoned for restaurants and terraced sidewalk cafés. These cafés, like the one Baudelaire's lovers and his family in rags would come to, soon came to be seen all over the world as symbols of la vie parisienne, (Berman, 1988: 151).

But it was more than just a winning economic re-vision for a city. Part of its success depended on people feeling a great desire to be there and for that to occur there had to be an enduring link between its economic and its cultural life. This was expressed in terms of a strong aesthetic base of the sort that had characterised the social success of the Place des Vosges.

If the pre-Haussmann Paris was largely cellular in structure with self-contained quarters and neighbourhoods, then the new design was open and encouraging of a promiscuous public mixing. From a city of neighbours and kin to a city of strangers, the anthropology of Paris shifted from one based on the taken-for-granted world of familiarity to a world in which difference and change became normalised. It encouraged a completely new performative embodied engagement with the city: from the normative predictable and routinised to the racy, unpredictable and transformative. Being cast into the open, before strangers and subject to the promiscuously shared leisure and symbolic spaces of the city placed everyone in the public gaze, for long spells of time in front-stage roles and therefore subject to critical appraisal and new influences. Such a potentially socially transformative state encourages ritualised forms of engagement that are characterised by both excitement and a feeling of communitas. The elevated levels of social engagement that result from being interpellated by this new city (utilising more of the conscious part of the brain) produce that rather remarkable effect of feeling socially closer to perfect strangers. As with pilgrims and tourists on a similarly transformative path, the effect of being fellow travellers erodes the reticence and reserve normally expressed to strangers and even if it is not directly acknowledged or expressed it remains a *potentiality* or *dream*, which contributes to and compounds the overall sense of transformative excitement. This is best expressed in something that was observed very early in Paris and which lies at the root of its success: people feel free to see others and be seen by them. This is a form of intimacy that is probably unique to modern cities and it is their specific qualities that generate it.

Haussmann's new Paris was a city of long, wide, tree-lined avenues that favoured the pedestrian, the walker. In most places the walker was confronted by several highly aestheticised perspectives. First, the new high quality retail shops compressed a world of global goods into a line of visually enhanced, forever changing displays. It was seductive and interpellated or hailed the pedestrian consumer; it created what Bauman (2005) called 'desire' (established foci of aesthetic appeal) as well as setting traps for what he calls 'wish' – hitherto unknown desires that lure the passer-by with signs for new enticements.

Then, there are the other pedestrians, a continuous flow, this time of people both like and unlike each other; both mirrors and reflections and windows into other worlds. Berman asked 'What did the boulevards do to the people who came to fill them?' and we should note here that although not explicit, he appears to be conceding some kind of agency to the boulevards. His answer, drawing on Baudelaire, is expressed through the subjectivity of lovers:

> For lovers like the ones in 'The Eyes of the Poor,' the boulevards created a new primal scene: a space where they could be private in public, intimately together without being physically alone. Moving along the boulevard, caught up in its immense and endless flux, they could feel their love more vividly than ever as the still point of a turning world. They could display their love before the boulevard's endless parade of strangers – indeed, within a generation Paris would be world famous for this sort of amorous display – and draw different forms of joy from it. They could weave veils of fantasy around the multitude of passers-by: who were these people, where did they come from and where were they going, what did they want, whom did they love? The more they saw of others and showed themselves to others – the more they participated in the extended 'family of eyes' – the richer became their vision of themselves. (1988: 152)

Third, the visually distracted pedestrian could look up and out of this immediate space of the shops and the other pedestrians and see into the distance, along lines of trees towards one of the many monuments that crown and complete each of the many segments of any sojourn. These were no mere landmarks, objects that merely happen to break up an otherwise uniform journey. These were also ritual objects, the sacred centres and pilgrimage points of an emerging nation state. Places where heroes and leaders were celebrated; where the great battles, the letting of blood and the giving of life for the nation were recognised and solemnly remembered; where moments in the formation of the political state are removed from the history book and placed in an eternal present in a central public space.

Spaces of public performance

Left merely to flow, most people would simply melt into oblivion, the difference Paris made was that flows were forced to slow and idle, to stop and rest, to enjoy moments of being in the city. As with the squares of London and the Place des Vosges, couples, friends, the lonely and individuals enjoying a moment by themselves found a variety of spaces to inhabit the public domain of Paris. At the great intersections of the boulevards the social spaces of squares were quite deliberately created for their social effect. Thus much of Haussmann's most important designs were for the great squares at Place de l'Étoile, Place Léon-Blum, Place de l'Opéra, Place de la République and Place de l'Alma. In addition, every district of Paris was given its own, more intimate squares. Squares were meeting or resting places where the commercial fast time of the city slowed or stopped.

Large numbers of cafés, bars and restaurants adjacent to or on the streets also offered both social reference points and places of solitude, though it was never a solitude that was disengaged from the hum and throb of the city. The archetype of Parisian occupying this new Paris, engaging in a new form of public participation, was what Baudelaire called the *flâneur,* or stroller. While the speed of strolling indicates that he has slowed his pace down to one that allows a careful scrutiny or study of one's surroundings, the *flâneur,* whether walking the streets and arcades or installed in a café, is an observer par excellence of the pure spectacle of an emergent consumerist culture.

Paris offered an entirely novel experience in Baudelaire's view, the possibility of joyful self-absorption in the material culture and anthropology of a modern city, as if it had never been seen before, as if each moment demanded to be recognised and assessed. For Baudelaire, the streets were where intellectuals and artists must, through *flânerie* as a technique of participant observation, develop new ways of portraying modern life as essentially *city life*. They must, as he said, 'botanise the asphalt'. The idea of the *flâneur* was taken up by Walter Benjamin in his Arcades Project (Benjamin et al., 2002), but he was influenced by the sociological work on it by Georg Simmel. Simmel felt that an entirely new set of modern and urban circumstances, particularly those initiated in Haussmann's Paris, had shaped a new modern urban sensibility and culture. Far from being cast adrift in an anonymous and indifferent city, Paris reconfigured the new individual, combining newly felt freedoms, individualism and rights with a heightened sense of new forms of connection and dependency. Blasé attitudes coexisted with an intensity of mutual fascination and empathy.

It is perhaps a mistake to place too much emphasis on Paris as a city of strangers because even though the crowds included far too many people to assimilate into personal social networks, and even though a large number of people were visitors, travellers and tourists, a large number were simply Parisians who lived there. The Haussmann apartment blocks of five and later eight storeys ensured that Paris was not only inhabited both day and night, a pattern that was to disappear from cities that developed a different modern blueprint, but it was comprised of 'living' neighbourhoods: people could eat, shop, meet, court, idle and work in their own immediate environment. Paris did not develop a particularly different city life so much as actually live a lot of life in a transparent, physical and public way. American and English visitors to cities that share this characteristic, such as Edinburgh, are struck by the same dynamic warmth.

For the same reason it is a mistake to assume that the demolition of the old quarters did away with a localised sense of city life. Large numbers of people would dine and drink, shop and idle in those spaces that were close, familiar and convenient to them, and in so doing build up a sense of locale that others may not see.

Sensual spaces

There is often the assumption that these shifts in urban sensibility in relation to urban redesign all took place in the *visual* register or sense; that it was a largely visual relation and communication. This is what Graham MacPhee (2002) seems to suggest when he describes urban planning as a new visual technology of the nineteenth century. He argues, with Baudelaire, that the old city streets and buildings had formed a repository of cultural memory and meaning, a means of locating oneself in time and space. The new Paris, by stripping this away, detached people from their past and cast them adrift in a permanent *present*, 'where appearances no longer mesh so easily with their framing by the subject, that the frame itself becomes manifest, although it does so as disorientation, distortion, and loss' (2002: 34–5). The excitement and pleasure that was described by the participant observers of this transition is not quite captured by this analysis and one wonders whether reliance on the visual sense is sufficient to describe their experience. While being visually rich and expressed in a new and bewilderingly complex semiotics, was it not also a world of new textures, sounds and smells?

Certainly, the new spatial and sanitary arrangements were designed to create a sweeter olfactory signature for the city and one must assume that the aromas of cafés, perfumiers, bakeries and restaurants were now more discernible. But surely a new sensual dimension was added by the building of so many parks and gardens that broke up the city as a purely human space? Apart from the massive planting of trees along the avenues and squares, Paris had large green spaces for the first time, and when they opened they were a new sensation. The famed 'Paris in the springtime' as a romantic notion could simply not have arisen before Napoleon III commissioned the engineer Jean-Charles Alphand to lay out the Bois de Boulogne and the Bois Vincennes, the Parc des Buttes-Chaumont, the Parc Monceau and the Parc Montsouris. These spaces were not only where nature itself could be sensed and experienced, they were also *quieter* places in a city famed for its unremitting street noise.

The new Paris was clearly also experienced in a more embodied way, since walking became such a dominant and pleasurable means of accessing it, but again the pedestrian experience was intimately bound up with a range of other embodied public performances in shops, cafés, arcades, bars and restaurants.

The impetus for so much of the new Paris came not from envisaging or innovating an entirely new city life but adding more life to the prosecution of work, commerce and social reproduction. The hidden model for so much of Haussmannism was *the resort* (see Franklin, 2003). The possibility of a more touristic, leisure and pleasure-rich way of life in the quotidian had been explored before as coastal resorts became popular places to live permanently and as some cities, such as Bath Spa, regularised and extended their economic base from resort to successful commercial cities. As the famed choreographer and impresario of Bath Spa, and the man responsible for transforming it from a seedy medieval town to a courtly centre in the eighteenth century, Richard 'Beau' Nash must have been known across Europe, if only because so few other inland cities had been recreated in such a complete way. Nash's influence had certainly made an impact in many British cities such as Bristol, Harrogate and parts of London, and, as we have seen, it was the direct experience of London that prompted the specific course of Haussmannism in Paris.

One of the secrets of the specifically excited response of people to the new Paris was recognising that it had been elevated to a place of pleasure, after the style of the tourist resort, but with the difference that from henceforth the mood of pleasure as an end in itself was to be on tap all year around as a part of what it was to live in or visit Paris. This is surely why the improvements that were ostensibly urban, technological and modernising included the building of new theatres and the Opera Garnier, in addition to natural and architectural playgrounds, monuments and dramatic new railway stations the size of cathedrals.

Critics of Haussmann argued that Paris had become merely a playground for the bourgeoisie, but that was never quite true since Paris was before all else an open, public and *national* space. If it was built on the idea of the spectacle, and after the Expositions of 1855 and 1889 and the building of the Eiffel Tower it certainly gained that reputation, then it was a spectacle that people came to see in ever-increasing numbers. Thomas Cook even brought English tourists into the heart of Paris for the 1855 Exposition in some of the first-ever international tourist excursions. Had the organiser decided to run with the suggested plan for a 300m high guillotine rather than a tower, Paris's fortunes may not have fared in quite the same romantic-touristic way, but as it turned out the tower, which had been very unpopular as it was built, was kept rather than dismantled after the event.

Critics also pointed out that in pre-Haussmann Paris, each house was a microcosm of the balanced demography of Paris. The bourgeoisie had lived on the second floor above street level, civil servants and employees had lived on the third and fourth floors, the low-paid on the fifth and students and servants on the sixth. The new Haussmann-styled buildings, and central Paris generally, had a wealthier demographic, even if it was stratified. In the typical five-floor buildings, the socially elevated apartments with balconies were always on the second and fifth floors. The second floor was, of course, traditionally associated with the elite, who wanted reduced noise combined with the smallest climb. The fifth floor was no longer considered fit only for the low paid since from this height one had the best views over the city, particularly after lifts were installed (parisnotes, 2007). After the improvements and improved rental values in the areas that had been rebuilt, central and western Paris became a commercial and wealthy residential zone while industry and poorer Parisians dominated the east-central zone out to the edge of the city.

However, even though Haussmann was sacked in 1870, his style now known as 'Second Empire', continued to prevail until the second decade of the twentieth century, and much of Paris adhered to the look even when the system broke down and was replaced by new legislation. Its only major challenge occurred after 1945 with the arrival of modern architects such as Le Corbusier who took buildings away from the street level and broke up the street-wall look. Nonetheless, most of Paris still retains this look, other French cities have adopted it widely, subsequently, and it has now become adopted as the dominant French 'heritage' style. Style and practicality is one thing, the politics of urban planning is quite another, and the major strength of Haussmannism was also its weakness: it relied on the more or less absolute power of a ruler, and in this respect it shared much with what Mumford calls the baroque city. Here, town planning is associated with arbitrary power and it was for this reason that it came to be distrusted wherever democratic government asserted itself in the nineteenth century (1966: 442).

Haussmann's influence extended way beyond France in fact, and can be seen in many if not most modernising nineteenth century cities. However, it is a central and capital city style that did not dominate the look of the modern Western world. Indeed, it was not influential in those nations and cultures that had not built towns and cities into the air. In the USA and Canada, Britain and Australia cities were to be dominated by a different style: notably, the garden suburb, or if you were less lucky, just the suburb.

4 The Solid Modern City: 2

I am in Penrith, Sydney, Australia on a balmy November evening in 2007. It is heavenly. And yet to all intents and purposes this is part of the greater Sydney sprawl, this is brain-dead suburban repetition, and this is 'middle' Australia's copy of Middle America. Not far away there is a fairly ugly multiplex hotel, casino, golf driving range, nightclub and sports stadium (for the Penrith Tigers rugby club). This is in fact the sort of place that most people these days tend to live or aspire to live at some stage of their life. I am having a stroll around a gently curving road, the houses of which have long sweeping unfenced gardens coming right down to the roadside. She-oaks and feathery wattle trees provide see-through, semiprivate screens for the inner garden areas, and I can see a group of adults, eight or so, sitting around a table having drinks, waiting for a barbecue. The sound is convivial and light-hearted; the smell of something roasting is beginning to vie with the otherwise fragrant, flower-scented zephyr. A glimmering reflective light is hitting the party from a substantial pool just to their left. I pass on, noticing that none of the houses are the same, though they are all spacious, comfortable, well designed and, well, the word liveable just insists on being used. And yet, this is not a particularly affluent suburb; this is 'affordable Australian living' that many people opt for when they decide to have children and buy a bit of space, quietude, safety and respite from the city. Most of the people here either work in, or close to, Sydney, even though there have been garden city-like light industrial developments out here for some time. Either way, these people are not cut off from Sydney life but are very much a part of it. Sydney forms a gravity that pulls them in to work, educational activities, leisure, sport, shopping, courtship and major spectacles. This city life is not opting out of the big city experience; it is merely one of the options. But it is having your cake and eating it, and this was very much in the minds of a small bunch of innovators in the early part of the twentieth century who came up with the garden city and suburban living idea – reviving what had always been an ideal compromise between nature and culture.

Beyond the rebuilding of Paris

The demolition–rebuild strategies that were inspired by Haussmann and taken up in many emerging world cities, including New York and Philadelphia, cross-fertilised with another strategy that would eventually result in the *decentralisation* of city life. The idea that cities would simply continue to expand suggested to many that humanity could be somehow swamped, drowned out or suffocated by them; that even though *some cities* such as Paris could be beautiful, inspiring and life-affirming, most were not and were unlikely to be for most people. Socialists have never seen the rebuilding of central Paris as a model for ordinary working-class cities and living spaces. Clearly *workers* were not going to be offered a palace-like city or a citadel. So, what solid modern blueprint could be devised for them?

Such a view formed in the minds of many of those whose main experience was of the grim industrial cities and who had witnessed a succession of social, political, economic and health problems associated with combining industrial and residential life on a large scale. Even after the heroic mid-nineteenth century 'Victorian age' when Bazalgette designed and built the first metropolis-wide water supply, drainage and sewerage system for London, its vast industrial landscape combined with residential coal burning for heat meant that air was going to be a problem. Dickens did not mix his words when it came to the city's famous polluted fogs (later called smogs). Here he is writing in *Our Mutual Friend*:

> It was a foggy day in London, and the fog was heavy and dark. Animate London, with smarting eyes and irritated lungs, was blinking, wheezing, and choking; inanimate London was a sooty spectre, divided in purpose between being visible and invisible, and so being wholly neither. Gas-lights flared in the shops with a haggard and unblest air, as knowing themselves to be night-creatures that had no business under the sun; while the sun itself, when it was for a few moments dimly indicated through circling eddies of fog, showed as if it had gone out, and were collapsing flat and cold. Even in the surrounding country it was a foggy day, but there the fog was grey, whereas in London it was, at about the boundary line, dark yellow, and a little within it brown, and then browner, and then browner, until at the heart of the City—which call Saint Mary Axe—it was rusty-black. From any point of the high ridge of land northward, it might have been discerned that the loftiest buildings made an occasional struggle to get their heads above the foggy sea, and especially that the great dome of Saint Paul's seemed to die hard; but that was not perceivable at their feet, where the whole metropolis was a heap

> of vapour charged with the muffled sound of wheels and enfolding a gigantic catarrh. (Dickens, 1993: 3)

While *Bleak House* opens with an unforgettable comment on London's inhuman condition:

> Smoke lowering down from chimney pots, making a soft black drizzle, with flakes of soot in it as big as full-grown snowflakes—gone into mourning, one might imagine, for the death of a sun. (Dickens, 1993: 1).

Dickens uses the trope of fog in order to make a moral judgement on London, as much as describing its environment, and arguably it was both the dubious morality as well as its unsavoury condition that produced a generalised desire to leave it and early live elsewhere. A recurrent theme to emerge in the late nineteenth and early twentieth centuries was that to experience and *live* modernity as an essentially urban experience had to be avoided if at all possible. Again, however, it was the wealthier classes who could afford the preferred environment (or at the very least the West Ends, upwind of the great stenches). Disgust at cities, factory towns and capitalism generally fuelled the Romantic Movement's love affair with nature and places on the margin of the human world. Rather than build dwellings higher into the flawed air, the solution that found increasing favour in Britain was to build out, onto greenfield and fresh-air sites.

Here the city planner or architect had a free hand and could dream up an entirely new blueprint for a modern city, a city of the future that could seek to be anything it wanted. This god-like creature followed in the wake of industrial gods, men like William Owen who had meddled and experimented with model industrial communities.

Although this future-orientated city might have sought to avoid the pitfalls of replacing the solid structures of tradition with equally solid and inflexible modern structures, there were very good reasons why they did just this. In the first place, they had only just begun to deploy science and technology in the realisation of industrial dreams and had no idea whatsoever of its unlimited nature. In the view of its architects and legislators, society might be *perfected* rather like the flushing toilet or steam engine had been perfected – and sooner rather than later. The principles of mechanics and systems that were revolutionising industry were being applied to problems stemming from cities and there was no reason to hold back on ideas that promised complete and lasting overhauls. Whatever was needed would be a very large project, therefore the idea to get it right for once and for all seemed elementary. Such was Bazalgette's grand scheme for London's water, drainage and sewerage, for example.

In the second place, the notion of a *constantly* changing society would have been an alien and disturbing idea. Stability and continuity were considered important during this period precisely because there had been so much churning and change. Indeed, one strand of modern thinking (counter-enlightenment thinking) reacted negatively to change and sought a progressive modern future in which key aspects of tradition, such as the family and religion, were not unceremoniously dumped. Many of the first pioneers of suburban housing developments, such as Barry Parker and Raymond Unwin, were inspired by the Arts and Crafts Movement which romanticised the handcrafted, the domestic and the small-scale, in other words, the pre-modern. In some places such as Britain this concern was widespread and shared across the political spectrum. Changes resulting from new modern blueprints were always presented with the gloss of traditional solidities: model villages espoused community values; garden cities claimed to offer a life in the country; traditional materials such as tiles, wood, slate and brick were assembled with a nostalgia for the Middle Ages; they avoided the anonymity of standardisation.

Third, while capitalism seemed to require unfettered freedoms in order to work most efficiently it also required political legitimation, and this came in the form of the modern democratic welfare state which upheld the modern principles of equality and human progress. Political competition tended to favour the production of solid programmes of reform of one variety or another which then resulted in policies and, when it came to the building and modernisation of cities, the drawing up of blueprints and master plans. Indeed, if it was ever felt that a new order had not been achieved, the thought that an efficient, decent, equitable and progressive order *could not be achieved* was barely entertained.

A new solid modern ordering

Although capitalist logic might have asserted complete freedom as its organising (or disorganising) first principle, a point Marx did not miss in his observation that 'all that is solid melts into air' (see Berman, 1988), this era of modernity was heroic rather than sensible, idealistic rather than realistic. More than anything this was an era that believed in the benefits of the application of science as one of its tradition-busting tools. After all, science was there to provide true knowledge as a replacement for the mumbo-jumbo of religion and spirituality and the slavishness of traditional vernaculars. Therefore, the social sciences grew in modernising societies in order to deliver the knowledge necessary to produce a perfected, stable, rational and efficient modern social and economic order. Other new sciences were deployed to this end too: architecture, town planning, environmental science, human geography, economics, transport science and so on. Just as production and distribution might be perfected given enough time and research, so too could the provision of social services, health, housing, urban infrastructures and national infrastructures. The welfare national states of the West sought a brand new type of society based on full employment, modern provision of services, foods and products, progressive improvements in medicine and technologies, more refined systems of education and delivery of well-being, health and longevity. While business had swept away much of its traditional impediments it also required a political framework to legitimise its role and practices and decide exactly which way the new blueprint for a solid modernity was to be drawn (Bauman, 2003b).

This solid modernity also derived, in part, from beliefs in the aims of the social demographic, progressive, welfare state. The political character of modernity and its search for an antidote to the hierarchical, unequal, and unchanging social structures of tradition resulted in those variations on the French revolutionary mantra: '*égalité, fraternité et liberté*'. While sweeping tradition away, clearly enough, what exactly would come in its place was disturbingly theoretical. How these utopian values might be operationalised was not at all clear and, any attempt to operationalise them was likely to be experimental and introduce new abstract measures both for their design and evaluation. It was a subject of great debate and the principal means of deciding upon avenues to try to endorse was the domain of modern politics. In this way, the design and nature of modern cities was neither technical nor political/social but both. Modern cities are always hybrids of socio-technical orderings.

What determined the form cities took in this experimental era had nothing whatsoever to do with how people had preferred to live with one another, the delicate relations, customs and forces responsible for the premodern city; and one is constantly reminded of the slightly bemused looks on the faces of all those moving into the brave new cities of the future.

Progress, change and equality were difficult ideas to operationalise and they all required measures, standards and targets before the task of design could take place. Cities were the most obvious way in which the political realisation of solid modern blueprints could be achieved but because they were predicated on not reproducing the known characters of tradition and were expected to usher in entirely new ways and means of achieving political goals they required a particularly new figure: the visionary designer. This small group of luminaries were responsible for the critical task of imagining or dreaming how a new society might be arranged in space if not in thought. Over the course of the twentieth century their designs would figure among the key icons and shapers of solid modern blueprints.

How well people were housed, fed, employed and serviced by medicine became important to discover and improve. Equality, another dominant value, also deployed abstract taxonomic measures and set up league tables, annual returns and progress reports. How many people had access to schooling, a good water supply, their own family toilet etc.; these became the scoreboard for the playing out of modern politics and policies. The values and their evaluation once implemented through new policies were, like the science model they followed, likely to be expressed in numbers. How many per thousand died from an officially adopted list of diseases or risks? How many had access to family doctors, modern equipped hospitals, libraries and schools? How much open space had been set aside and how much of certain prescribed amenities and recreations was available? How much public transport was there and how far did workers have to travel? Such were the questions that preoccupied the newly formed Statistical Societies. In 1837, for example, the Bristol Statistical Society held its first meeting, during which they discussed the finding of their first survey of poverty in the city. Interestingly, they were as interested in lifestyle as much as crude measures of resources. They wished to know the moral nature of people's circumstances (e.g. who shared bedrooms) and their life chances and experiences (how many books a household had and the number of art works on their walls) (Franklin, 1989).

The great thing about progress and equality was that it *could* be measured; the problem was, however, that measurability over-determined what this new solid modernity had on offer. The view that such measures would be proxy measures for a better city life was assumed rather than thought through or cross-checked in an ongoing manner. I should remind you, for example, that during most of this period from the 1920s through to the 1980s, there was not one single social scientific exercise to establish the degree and distribution of happiness in such societies. That did not come, ironically enough, until the 1990s, when deepening 'postmaterialist' concerns arose for life after the welfare state (Inglehart, 1997). A time paradoxically when freedom and choice had never been so dominant.

Even though cities were blasted by the middle and governing classes as spaces of human blight, their thinking at the end of the Victorian period and the beginning of the twentieth century was not particularly modern. The influence of the Arts and Crafts Movement, the generalised critique of the industrial machine age and the worship of the nobler Middle Ages created a polarised counter-aesthetic. If the model of the industrial city is the machine then its antidote will be nature; if the industrial city is based on standardisation and the straight line then the antidote will be variation and the curve; if the habitat of the industrial city is the street and street life then the antidote would be the garden; and if the industrial city is to be avoided the antidote will be to move out.

To the credit of the successful visionaries of the garden suburb they did not recommend for others what they themselves did not aspire to and live. City life was, in their view, perfectly compatible with the hybridisation of space. Factory workers could come home to tea in their garden just as the architect might. The space of the city that inspired change was therefore the garden; it was not only aesthetically opposite to the industrial landscape it also counterbalanced the experience of industrial work. Gardening was a performative exercise in holding up standards and values that were too important to lose sight of and it is the incredible success of this movement that has created a more ecological sensibility for the more contemporary city of the late twentieth century. The question is where did such an overwhelming and popular enthusiasm for gardening and the garden suburb derive from? It was not inevitable because it did not transpire to the same degree in France and continental Europe as it did in Britain and the USA.

Towards cities of gardens

The gardening revolution of the sixteenth to the eighteenth century in England did not merely produce an abstract floricultural aesthetic: it had much wider social implications. Of particular note was its acceptance and approval as a rational, civilising and improving leisure, inculcating a sense of beauty but also of order. Secondly, gardening was particularly appealing to townsfolk, tempering and modifying the break with those ancient connections with the natural world resulting from the urbanisation of British society in the first half of the nineteenth century. Thirdly, gardening became the medium for fashion and style in which the entire nation could, to a lesser or greater extent, participate. Rural life and that semi-rural life of the multitudinous small English towns held an almost unique aesthetic appeal among modernised nations. From the landscape wildernesses of Capability Brown to the miniaturised lawns and borders of the worker's villa, the national passion for gardening and gardens and accompanying human–nature hybridity transcended class cultures and status groups. Although gardens were often the means by which the English created a sense of privacy around the domestic space, there was also a sense in which the garden was a public space, largely open to the public gaze, if not for public visiting. The public face of an English household was first and foremost its garden and it was through the garden far more than the interior that the different classes became familiar with each other, and that social emulation via recruitment to a gardening aesthetic became possible.

The association of gardening with respectability and moral decorum was established very early on. Nothing could recommend it more strongly than John Lawrence's *The Clergy-man's Recreation* of 1714. Far from inculcating a sense of guilt for so much time given over to leisure gardening, Lawrence was

> 'not in the least ashamed to say and own, that most of the time I can spare from the necessary care and business of a large Parish, and from my other studies, is spent in my garden and making observations

> towards the further improvement thereof. For I thank God this sort of diversion has tended very much to the ease and quiet of my own mind; and the retirement I find therein, by walking and meditation, has help'd to set forward many useful thoughts upon more divine subjects'. (Sinclair et al., 1939: 254)

Although the passion for gardening as a leisure was new to early modern England, the idea of the garden as a holy or sacred place has ancient roots, not least in the idea of the Garden of Eden as a place of original perfection. The association of gardening as a leisure activity with moral and spiritual improvement was suggested at least by the late seventeenth century. William Hughes, for example, suggests that although 'we few'll from Grace and lost the perfect garden given to us as a dwelling by God, yet doubtless by industry and pains taking in that lovely, honest, and delightful Recreation of Planting, we may gain some little glimmering of that lost Splendour, although', he adds for good measure, 'with much difficulty' (Sinclair et al., 1939: 233).

According to Thomas (1983):

> by the eighteenth century flower gardening had emerged as a means by which humble men could prove their respectability. Gardening it was believed had a civilising effect on the labouring poor. It attached a man to his home and it spread a taste for neatness and elegance. Hence, the landlords' practice of building model cottages which had the whole of their garden in front of the house so that they could be inspected by the passer-by. (1983: 234)

Reformers such as Chadwick, Howard and Booth extolled the virtues of gardening as an alternative to the pub, and by the turn of the twentieth century providing gardens and allotments was considered the sign of a good employer for the same reasons that a good gardener was considered a good employee (Williamson, 1982: 104).

William Morris inspired the first garden suburb in England, Bedford Park, in West London, which was started in 1875. 'Its leafy streets of cosy, red-brick houses with their gables and tile-hanging are the epitome of the Old English style ... Bedford Park was a place where [according to an opinion of the time] "Men may lead a chaste correct Aesthetical existence"' (Quiney, 1986: 132). Paternalistic capitalists and progressive landowners were leaders in the housing reform of the English working classes, and it was they who produced the first miniaturised model villas. Of these, Blaise Hamlet in Bristol, which was started in 1811, remains the model model.

Early nineteenth century model housing built by reformist landowners produced picturesque gothic rural cottages where the emphasis was as much on the garden and its seamless connection to the natural world as the house itself, but it took some time for the idea to be established as a norm in the city. These were paralleled by the middle class townhouse, which in the 1820s (e.g. Bloomsbury, London) had no private garden but shared instead a semi-public communal gardened space in the squares between them. Their lavish planting and generous proportions served only to emphasise their quality as a getaway, a romantic urban oasis – a point exploited by the makers of the film *Notting Hill* and the novel (and film) *Line of Beauty* (Hollinghurst, 2004). Daunton (1983) traces a transition from the Bloomsbury townhouse to homes on the Ladbroke Estate in the 1840s, which combined private gardens with a communal garden, to the first villas (detached or semi-detached) and their encapsulated private gardens that became increasingly the norm after 1850.

For more substantial building projects for workers, London and its local governments took the lead:

> When the LCC's Housing Branch architects started to design suburban estates they remembered Bedford Park and how Morris had written in *Art and Beauty of the Earth* of the necessity of changing England 'from the grimy back yard of a workshop into a garden'. In the 1890s the design of the LCC's few small cottage estates progressively moved away from the plain uniformity of the unadorned terrace towards a more varied group of houses in short rows. (Quiney, 1986: 132–3)

Gardens became an even-greater feature of the state-built homes following the Great War. The 'homes fit for heroes' policy addressed an acute housing shortage in the 1920s, but rather than build cheap accommodation to lower standards, the standards were jacked up even higher than the bye-law homes:

> By building the new houses to a standard previously reserved for the middle classes, the government would demonstrate to the people just how different their lives were going to be in the future ... the housing programme would persuade the people that their aspirations would be met under the existing order, and thereby wean them from any ideas of revolution. The new houses built by the state – each with its own garden, surrounded by trees and hedges and equipped internally with the amenities of a middle class home – would provide visible proof of the irrelevance of revolution. (Swenerton, *Homes, Fit for Heroes*, 1981: 81, cited in Daunton, 1982: 293–4)

Such homes were explicitly better and modelled on the new garden-city ideals. Paternalists such as Edward Cadbury and his Bourneville garden city aimed to create a more happy and contented and thereby more loyal and productive labour force. The garden was in a sense a key element of this scheme, both in terms of an open, curving, spacious and leafy country village-like layout as a context for all homes, and in terms of the extent of the gardens provided for each home, which in plots, shape, structure and extent resembled more the rambling grounds of a middle-class country residence. The austere, regimented and gloomy nature of the bye-law homes was soon superseded and surrounded by the open, light and leafy nature of the garden-city-inspired development. Trees, lawns and shrubs were planted all over the development rather than in tightly delineated public parks; the extent of the plantings in each home softened and broke up the lines of the building as opposed to the humble and cowed planting of the bye-law front garden (frequently reduced to the small space occupied by a narrow hedge); the occupants of the garden suburb were less surrounded by the cold public space of Victorian England and more by a semi-communal, semi-rural natural space in which the occupants were themselves naturalised, a social space that looked back to a rural arcadia.

It is tempting to explain the emergence of the modern English-built environment, consisting largely of cottage style houses, as the result of sanitary and political reforms and interests, in combination with critical economic factors such as land prices and rents. In this way, urban gardens might be considered as an epiphenomenon of the urban reform movement. However, these factors cannot adequately explain why the European and Scottish tenement (apartment blocks) did not prevail in the newly rationalised modern English city. After all, apartments offered a better return on land rents and offered all sorts of building economies of scale over the cottage unit. As Daunton (1982: 58) argues, the English style was *unusual* and remains an unsolved puzzle. Could it be, for example, that it was the central (and relatively unusual) position of the garden and garden life in English urban cultures that influenced the shape of modernising cities?

Daunton's analysis of the emergence of bye-law housing and garden city styles following the breakdown of the older cellular court pattern considered and found wanting all explanations based solely on rents, incomes and the pattern of land ownership. He argues instead that bye-laws were used in some cases to prevent certain housing forms, especially the cellular form of courts and back-to-back housing, and in others to 'freeze the form of development and make subsequent change more difficult. The byelaws might take a given house type for granted and seek to remove the worst abuses, rather than to require its disappearance' (Daunton, 1983: 84). Both sorts of strategy, prevention of cellular/court forms and maintenance of cottage styles, are consistent with a view that there were cultural and aesthetic factors involved in the emergence of the English built environment. As Daunton argues, 'Any physical environment will create a particular lifestyle, a cultural definition of housing form. Cultural variables must therefore be reinserted into the argument ...'

(Daunton, 1983: 88). Accordingly, he investigates the housing cultures of the English working class, mapping kinship, family and community factors onto the uses and preferences for rooms and spaces. Unfortunately, this investigation was restricted to a consideration of interior spaces and public spaces. Those semi-public, semi-private spaces of the small working class gardens were left unexplored. However, since it was the garden more than anything that distinguished the bye-law and subsequent English urban houses from those that came before *and* from those built in other modern nations, it would seem, on the face of it, to be significant. What cultural factors might have promoted the garden as a central design feature?

First, it must be supposed that the councils who shaped the housing bye-laws included precisely the sorts of people – paternalists, religious leaders, and reformers – who had underpinned gardening and gardens as an appropriate rational recreation for the working classes. The passion for gardening among the English middle classes and its imputed benefits were keenly recommended to all. In their capacity as councillors no less as paternalistic capitalists, they were in a position to provide more gardens as a desirable component of city life. Gardens orientated people to the home rather than the street, to home-based hobbies and self-provisioning rather than the pub and sports.

Secondly, as we have seen from the period prior to the nineteenth century, the gardening revolution had established a gardening aesthetic at all levels of society, and although the migration trajectories and housing careers of the nineteenth century working classes were complex, it is certainly the case that urbanisation in the early part of the century could not have eradicated that desire for natural beauty to be an element of lifestyle. It was this desire that provided part of the demand for the new housing forms, and it was the healthy demand that maintained and elaborated the garden as a feature of English urban life. It has to be remembered that almost all of these homes were privately rented and, from what we know, renters were fickle and would move in order to gain improved living conditions. The provision of desirable features such as a garden could result in high demand, a feature that was of prime concern to builders and investors.

Thirdly, although both the bye-law and the garden city cottage were new housing forms, they were both nostalgic (but improved) simulations of traditional rural working-class homes or cottages. In this way rurality and a rural life in close proximity to nature was imported into the town. Historically, English towns were trading as administrative centres and were characterised by a mainly wealthy and high status population. Town and city homes emphasised their difference from the country; elaborate and multi-storeyed terraces developed along the street frontages in the strictly limited spaces of walled cities; the former gardens of the medieval period tended to be absorbed by building extensions and new buildings. The working-class courts of the early nineteenth century were the result of a similar process: an original set of terraced houses would have been extended around three sides of their former garden area, leaving a court area in the middle and a passage back out to the street. In other words, the new bye-law and garden city cottages were entirely novel to the Victorian city but were based on a housing culture that predated the nineteenth century. But importantly, the Victorian period and its aftermath broke down the distinction between town and country. The variation in their style across the country can be accounted for in terms of the vernacular architecture of rural cottages in their hinterlands that became favoured by the bye-law creators precisely because they were local people. What they had in common was their increasingly suburban openness, a city phenomenon that would become greener and leafier the older it got, and the presence of gardening, gardeners and gardening culture: 'its most committed form, membership of the Royal Horticultural Society, rose from 2500 in 1894 to 14,500 in 1914,' (Lowerson, 1995: 13).

Garden cities and beyond

There can be no greater legacy of the gardening revolution perhaps than the 'garden city' itself. A revolution in natural aesthetics and the embedding of this close relation with nature in popular culture and lifestyle became so significant that it shaped the modern city and modern urban lifestyles to the end of the twentieth century. Garden cities were eccentric in their early, experimental Bourneville days but as we have seen they grew to dominate the English and American architectural and planning movement. The first UK state housing building period between 1918 and 1939 was almost completely rendered in that style; private estate developments or garden suburbs followed fashion and street names changed from the regimented street, row and roads of the Victorian bye-law development to avenues, closes, crescents, drives – even gardens – and other organic or rural references (Granges, Meads, Glebes, Walks, Greens); New Towns appeared in the garden city format both before the Second World War and afterwards. If the bye-law villas and cottages moved the country into town, the larger garden cities went a step further and moved the city back to the country, producing a hybrid of nature and culture. An advert for the garden city of Milton Keynes, UK, shows an Arcadian picture of a man fishing in a pool with trees forming an arbour through which may be glimpsed the only building, an old windmill. Underneath, the caption reads 'In Milton Keynes we are outnumbered by trees 15-1' (Finnegan, 1998: 37).

Ebenezer Howard was the founding father of the garden city concept. In his *Tomorrow: A Peaceful Path to Real Reform* (republished in 1902 as

Image 4.1 Garden suburb Hampstead, London (photo Adrian Franklin)

Garden Cities of To-Morrow). Howard established his core ideas – largely for urban reform. He is remembered for his advocacy of planned living spaces and communitarianism, but his professional contribution as a planner, architect and urban theorist conceals the extent to which the gardening revolution was carried through and extended in his work. In documents relating to his plans and ideas, no less than in descriptions of the garden city concept in urban sociologies, the origins of the idea are masked: it seems as though the desire for garden spaces, proximity to nature and the hybridisation of nature and city derives from the brilliant visionary, Howard, when in fact such a desire already existed. Howard's contribution was to fuse the gardening aesthetic with the social utopia. Although he is considered a revolutionary for advocating not only the *planned* city but also a *different city*, it is clearly the case that his ideas were formed as much from the negative experiences of dramatic city growth as from the *positive* aspects of the bye-law housing movement. The greening of the late nineteenth century city and its key new phenomenon, parks and gardens, were simply extended and elaborated by Howard with a socially utopian twist that invokes again the idea of Eden. Grey (1983) sums up the garden city concept very well:

> Garden cities ... would combine all the benefits of both town and country with none of the disadvantages. They would have modern industry and housing, provide secure employment and all the services

> of the modern town or city, and yet enjoy the healthy atmosphere of a country setting. The built-up area would contain a considerable proportion of parks and greenery; the houses would all have gardens, and be within a short distance of woods and open fields. In such an environment, tuberculosis, typhus and other diseases endemic in the pestilential conditions of the big cities would be eradicated. For the first time, the town dwellers would be able to engage in the healthy pursuits of gardening, sports and country walks. At the same time, the garden cities would be of sufficient size to offer all the familiar forms of urban entertainment. (Grey, 1983: 20)

Considerably more people could expect to have their own gardens, a point not missed by the bourgeoning gardening press: 'As modern building proceeds, it becomes more and more evident that some garden space is wanted by nearly every household, and it is very gratifying to notice that the old back-yard, that is, a paved space where washing could be dried but nothing grown, has disappeared from the new towns of this century (James, 1940: ix–x).

Howard's garden cities were utopian to the extent that they were planned to produce a community and commonwealth for their respective residents – an aspiration that never truly developed. Partly this was because they required enormous capital to build and only local or central governments had the means to implement them. Howard's success was underpinned by a passionate belief in his principles by a large and powerful following in Britain, who became formed into the Garden Cities and Town Planning Association and who subsequently built the two model cities at Letchworth before 1914 and Welwyn in the 1920s. The garden city concept also crossed the Atlantic:

> In the United States a group of architects, notably Clarence Stein, popularized Howard's approach. Working with local authorities and developers, they constructed several places across the country including Garden City, New York, outside of Manhattan, and Baldwin Hills, California, which is located in Los Angeles. Ebenezer Howard lived to see the opening of the New York community in 1928. (Gottdiener, 1994: 302)

In Gottdiener's view, Howard sits alongside Le Corbusier and Frank Lloyd Wright in conceptualising new urban environments in the twentieth century, and although North American examples of Howard's influence lack both the utopian and the industrial content, his ideas are still put into practice by developers of large suburban residential projects (Gottdiener, 1994: 303). The lasting residue of Howard's concept, and one that makes it very relevant today, is mixing humanity with nature rather than perfecting humanity through rational planning; removing humanity from nature in fact. It has become such a culturally given, taken-for-granted phenomenon that it is now very hard to see its very specific cultural aetiology.

The same is true in contemporary Britain from the end of the Second World War until the 1980s, but it is not surprising perhaps that the British state used Howard's principles to build hundreds of garden city projects. The garden city idea became the cornerstone of post-war reconstruction via an all-party support for the 1946 New Towns Act. These towns were typically planned to reduce pressure on the larger metropolitan centres and London in particular is ringed by them. By the 1970s, when critics began to appear, iconic garden cities such as Milton Keynes became cast as the opposite: they were bye-words for planning blight, concrete jungles, rootless suburbia and small town anomie. Finnegan (1998) explores this paradox using a narrative approach to the city, teasing out the narrative conventions and cultural implications of its multiple tales. In doing so he gives us a rare glimpse not only of the idealism of Howard's enthusiasts within the Development Corporation but the serial waves of residents who left London to be newcomers in a new town. Their stories provide an important test of the durability of garden-city concepts but also the extent to which the garden and the garden city as a human–nature hybrid has endured as a prominent aesthetic in Britain. It is quite evident from Finnegan's respondents that it has.

Paradise mislaid? Tales from Milton Keynes

Planning for Milton Keynes, a north Buckinghamshire London overspill town, was begun in 1967 and the project was largely completed by 1992. Housing and employing over 150,000 people it was the largest urban development project ever undertaken in Britain. In commemorating Milton Keynes' 25th anniversary, *The Times* newspaper labelled the project 'Paradise Mislaid'. Sensing a consensus view among its readership that it was a project gone wrong – a readership exposed to such critics as John Osborne, who called Milton Keynes a 'gleaming gum-boil plonked in the middle of England' or Dave Rimmer who described it as 'unbearably new and depressingly desolate'– *The Times* summed up Milton Keynes thus:

> Milton Keynes was the last desperate throw of a generation of British planners who were distasteful of the traditional British towns and cities and had the political power and public money to fashion the environment to their will. (24 January 1992)

Such a view is hard to square with the opinion of its developers, whose press briefing paper of 1990 described it as an attractive city:

> set in undulating North Buckinghamshire countryside and blessed with two rivers, a canal, streams and a cluster of small villages brought together by a network of old lanes and historic highways, the Designated Area provided a rich foundation on which to build a city to which people would respond with pleasure. (Finnegan, 1998: 29)

On the face of it, Milton Keynes sounds an ideal compromise between the rural aesthetic running deeply through British culture and the necessity of dealing with the congestion that makes the city impossible. Moreover, it went further than Howard in hybridising town and country, humanity and nature: 'Milton Keynes is a low-density city, dispersed rather than radial, and with the country *in* the city rather than surrounding it' (Finnegan, 1998: 39). As Finnegan unravels the narrative tales, it is clear that Milton Keynes became the butt of jokes and criticism not because it was a horrid place to live – which of the critics had lived there? – but because the idea of planning and modern architecture had produced a vocal and influential circle of critics in the quality press. Milton Keynes was simply the last and the biggest project on which to vent their spleen. The anti-modernism of the mid-1970s to early 1980s produced a stodgy nostalgia for all things medieval and old: crafts replaced design; natural dyed clothes replaced high-tech fashions, even the Mini car was produced with a wooden shooting brake style called the Mini Countryman. Before the birth of the postmodern neo-traditional style that was to dominate British architecture in the 1980s and 1990s therefore, Milton Keynes was conceived in a clatter of derision: it was principled but desperately unfashionable.

Partly, of course, fashions were beginning to change in respect of the aesthetics of nature. The critic of Milton Keynes singled out 'the environment' as a privileged nature under threat from the hybrid garden city. From the early 1970s *environment* emerged as an aesthetic discourse of nature that was, ideally, to be kept separate from humanity. Detested by the chic set of London and the rural elites (who had a traditional claim to living in 'the environment'), Milton Keynes finally began to find supporters – among its residents. The longer they lived there, the more roots they put down, the more exposed to its growing planting of trees and shrubs and flowers they became, the more they liked it. In the face of the barrage of national criticism local residents were equally vocal in their rebuttal. Such views recount how, 'far from soulless concrete, Milton Keynes has now emerged as a notably "green" city ... Local writing about Milton Keynes townscapes celebrates their wildlife, light, the sky or the uniquely pointed beauties of particular localities' (Finnegan, 1998: 50). But how representative were the views of the local literati? Finnegan was surprised by the extent to which her respondents placed emphasis on the natural aesthetic of Milton Keynes; indeed, it was one of two main themes in their accounts. Milton Keynes emerges as a 'green city', 'nature within, rather than opposed to the city' (1998: 164). Finnegan marshals a battery of evidence for this conclusion. Typically, respondents were surprised and delighted by the hybrid city.

By 1986 Milton Keynes could inspire a romantic poem from the local poet Anita Packwood that identifies its hybridity as an aesthetic object. The poem mentions 'the point', which readers might think to be a lighthouse or a promontory, but which Finnegan tells us is a multi-screen cinema and nightclub. In true hybrid style, Packwood has 'Myriads of daffodils, Dancing slightly in the evening breeze' juxtaposed to a new nightclub for humans (1998: 163).

This poem is naive, but touching nonetheless. One can immediately relate to the author's delight in familiar buildings and plantings, set beneath a gloaming sky. One can even understand how such a sugary, miniature landscape is rendered universal through its place beneath sky and stars, and its subjectivity to the greater order of seasons and weather. But it has borrowed a rustic pastorale style for a new, planned city precisely to make the point, presumably, that any creation of buildings and configurations of plantings can be aesthetically pleasing; and, importantly, that all pastoral landscapes are 'man' made. One suspects the 'point' to be a deeply ugly building, part of Osborne's gum-boil, but how stable or inevitable is that view? How contingent is that judgement upon proximity, familiarity and experience? As J.B. Jackson, Heidegger and Ingold all argue, landscaped natures are an artefact of culture, integrally implicated in its design and becoming, not opposed to it.

In a later chapter (Chapter 6, The Ecological City) I will make the argument that sentiments such as these which are both primordial, Victorian and contemporary, give solid foundations and a home for environmentalist concerns and biopolitics and reshape the nature of the city as a particular kind of habitus. For outsiders perhaps, the poem, the poetics of particular cities, cannot always work well; we find it difficult to suspend our disbelief; we can neither create a hindsight that might give places like Milton Keynes the patina of age and heritage, nor conjure up the necessary familiarity to create a rose-tinted image of it as home. We cannot contrast it with its inhabitant places of origin, their long-established tastes or habits and expectations. We cannot see this side of Milton Keynes as nature, it remains for many years as its generic 'new' town or its derogatory blot on the landscape; but after a relatively short period its residents create a nature to be appreciated, they watch it grow, see birds nest in it, pick its blooms and let their children watch sticky buds unfurl.

This poem is useful in pointing up the difficulty in grasping the meaningfulness and beauty of the modern 'ordinary' small city or of entering the aesthetic lifeworlds of ordinary city life. The ordinary setting and lifestyle of people only a hundred years ago is immediately prone to romantic gloss, and although the ordinary house, garden and environs of the small housing estate has yet to be aestheticised by a generation of poets and writers, we cannot infer that its residents remain aesthetically neutral and unmoved. Happily, all the evidence is rather the opposite: that in the miniature landscape of backyards and gardens people have created settings that are centrally important to what it means to have a decent city life.

5 The Dysfunctional City?

One of the most interesting shifts in our thinking about cities and city life occurred during the 1970s and early 1980s when optimism and confidence about finding the means to produce ever-better cities gave way to anxiety and pessimism; the new thought that most, if not all cities were becoming dysfunctional, unsustainable and *inherently* problematic. The dysfunctional city, with its odours of decaying Victorian infrastructure, sprawling suburbs, its hard-to-let housing, difficult-to-police estates and neighbourhoods, its gangs, its drug-ridden streets and citizens cowering behind gated communities was the universal symbol of the collapse of the modernity project (see Atkinson and Helms, 2007). As a human technology whose historic purpose was defence, the contemporary city was more recently specifically targeted and spectacularly vulnerable to enemies (human and non-human) who were impossible to identify, whose ability to penetrate its defences relied on exactly the same freedom and mobility that the city required for its wealth creation and adaptive advantages. As a social formation that was built on proximity, ease of communication and functional interdependence the contemporary city was being stretched by its own scale and at the same time ground to a halt by dependency on gridlocked systems of automobility. Equally, the modern city as the triumphant humanist citadel against the ravages of nature, a place of safety and effective risk management, also became one of the most potent symbols of human environmental dysfunction. Not only were its inhabitants 'at risk' from natures that had breached invisible and unregulated defences, but they experienced all of the new dangers of the risk society in a super-concentrated form: its pollution was unprecedented, its toxic sources were legion, it was vulnerable to germicidal and chemical terrorism, its hospitals and institutions plagued by new types and forms of infection that found perfect, sustainable conditions inside regulated modern architectures (super bugs, golden staph and Legionnaire's disease etc.). And, those risk factors that were related precisely to the locational advantages of successful cities were being amplified and regularised by changing climatic conditions (flood, wildfire, earthquake, tsunami, wildfires in the USA and bushfires in Australia etc.; see Chapter 9 for more details and see also Nigel Clark, 2000).

Today the confidence of those who came up with the new blueprints for the modern city, how cities 'should properly be' in the period before the 1970s, seems breathtaking and dangerously deluded, but equally, the speed with which such schemes were abandoned and criticised seems equally puzzling. Before looking more closely at how the city environments they created became 'dysfunctional', it is important to appreciate the sociological foundations of their confidence and opportunity to make such draconian change. It is only by appreciating the sociological specificity of their urban legacy that we can fully appreciate exactly why they seem to have failed, in the way they did, when they did.

Zygmunt Bauman has offered a valuable means of making sense both of the arrival of their blueprinting for the modern city as well as its demise. From the mid-nineteenth century until the first half of the twentieth century the emerging modern states were dominated by a group of intellectual movers and shakers whom Bauman (1992) calls 'legislators'. They were brokering a relatively novel form of cultural ideology that had formed under new conditions prevailing first in the absolutist, and more spectacularly in modern nation states emerging in the eighteenth and nineteenth centuries. Under such conditions the intellectual class who presided over high culture gained enormous power and influence, and great confidence in their role as leaders of social change and improvement. As Bauman puts it:

> Metaphorically, the kind of authority in which such a vision of the world established men of knowledge could be described as 'legislative'. The authority involved the right to command the rules the social world was to obey; and it was legitimized in terms of a better judgement, a superior knowledge guaranteed by the proper method of its production. With both society and its members found wanting (i.e. shapeable yet heretofore shaped in the wrong way), the new legislative authority of men of knowledge established its own necessity and entitlements. (Bauman, 1992: 11)

Never before in history had such a self-confident new class of legislators been let loose to create new conditions as well as destroy old ones, and the zeal displayed by members of *la république des letteres* or *les sociétés de pensée*, including the urban visionaries Haussmann, Le Corbusier and Ebenezer Howard, seems today to be crass as well as arrogant.

We are used to the idea of culture as necessarily *relative*, but the form of culture informing the legislators was not; it was absolute, perfectible. Finding the perfect cultural form was therefore imperative and incumbent upon this class of men; it was a test of their competency:

> The intellectual ideology of culture was launched as a militant, uncompromising and self confident manifesto on universally

> binding principles of social organisation and individual conduct. It expressed not only the exuberant administrative vigour of the time, but also a resounding certainty as to the direction of anticipated social change. Indeed forms of life conceived as obstacles to change and thus condemned to destruction had been relativized; the form of life that was called to replace them was seen, however, as universal, inscribed in the essence and destination of the human species as a whole. (Bauman, 1992: 21)

It is only now that we can perhaps consider the audacious confidence of the architect Le Corbusier in the 1920s, as well as the veneration he and others like him received:

> The city of today [1922] is a dying thing because it is not geometrical. To build in the open would be to replace our present haphazard arrangements, *which are all we have today* by a *uniform* lay-out. Unless we do this *there is no salvation.* ... The result of true geometrical lay-out is *repetition* ... the result of repetition is a *standard*, the perfect form ... (Le Corbusier, *The City of Tomorrow and Its Planning*, 1929; cited in Bridge and Watson, 2002: 25; emphasis in author's original)

On a smaller scale, in the 1930s, when architects were under the spell of *form follows need* (or function), 'there was a belief, if not in perfection, then at least in perfectibility' (Glendinning and Muthesius, 1994: 308). In relation to the design of the modern flat, the architects Yorke and Gibberd wrote that 'if present day building technique were in itself sufficient, a perfect home could be achieved (1938: 8). Glendinning and Muthesius (1994: 308) remind us that in 1944 a 'scientifically correct' bungalow was erected and exhibited outside the Tate Gallery. None of this was the flexible moulding of form to the fickle and individualised demands of the contemporary consumer, but the search for *universal standards* that would satisfy human needs, universally, on a mass scale.

But designers and architects were not alone. The sociologist Donald Bogue, writing in the 1950s, was no less self-assured of the ability of social scientists to deliver a rational, socially ordered city:

> The urban environment is a setting for a series of social problems, such as crime or delinquency and hostile race relations ... Present physical structures will constitute a small proportion of the cities of 2050. Planning for this building and rebuilding and long-range social work based on scientific research should be able to reduce present inadequacies of the urban environment. Renewed social research

> upon the urban community, from an objective point of view, using representative samples of data and modern research techniques, should produce much of the knowledge that social engineers will need in order to handle social problems which, in the nature of the case will be largely urban problems. (Bogue, 1955: 101)

Although planners have never achieved the legitimacy of the more established intelligentsia their emergence as 'change professionals' had a profound impact on the form cities eventually took, and they too began to demand more universal application. It is not surprising therefore that in 1951 the National Resources Committee in the USA argued for more powers and *wider* influence for planners:

> In general, local planning agencies need stronger and wider authority in order to exercise jurisdiction over all matters relating to community development, and, where a county or regional planning agency does not exist, not only within the municipal boundaries but over the entire area now urbanised or likely to become so and as much of the region beyond as bears relation to the proper development of the urban community itself. (Cited in Hatt and Reiss, 1957)

In his *Patterns of Urban Life*, Ray Pahl (1970) made the point that those like Lewis Mumford and the National Resources Committee who found themselves in powerful positions to influence the ways cities were to develop in the post-1945 period often rested their firmly held theoretical views on very flimsy evidence. It was a period in which, as Pahl says, 'the good life [was] directly related to physical surroundings' (1970: 118). In relation to the segregation of motor traffic from pedestrian movement in Radburn, Mumford wrote that the newly created walkways facilitated social interaction 'along a spinal green that formed the inner core of the town, and by its very constitution furthered face-to-face acquaintance'. Pahl rightly argued that this and other social effects (political cohesion, formation of 'neighbouring', community mixing, community identity) 'are asserted rather than demonstrated' and he points up what he called the fallacy of 'architectural determinism' (1970: 106, 119). This was epitomised by the influential study by Festinger, Schachter and Back in 1950. They wrote:

> the architect who builds a house or who designs a site plane, who decides where the roads will and will not go, and who decides which direction the houses will face and how close together they will be, also is, to a large extent, deciding the pattern of social life among the people who live in those houses. (Cited in Pahl, 1970: 105).[1]

Pahl saw the widespread application of this idea as nothing more than 'slavish adherence to fashion' (1970: 118). And there is an undisputable fashion-aesthetic that characterised the implementation of modern design in the city that *undermined* its claim to be expert. As a preface to the causes of the rejection of modern design in British cities in the early 1970s, Glendinning and Muthesius (1994) suggest that one core problem was the appearance of fads and experimentation rather than the delivery of scientifically assured replacement living spaces: 'If there is one basic and simple characteristic of architects' research and preferences, it is the fact that they keep changing, quickly and radically' (1994: 123). Worse, by asserting conviction and preference over knowledge, the architects and town planners were short-circuiting the way in which the social scientific research should properly inform the design and building of cities. Indeed over this period it is not only true that sociologists did not routinely work with planners and architects, it was also true that they dismissed each other's claim to expertise. Between them they created not confidence in 'legislators' but the opposite, opening up the possibility for a new breed of 'public opinion' makers such as Alice Coleman, Christopher Brooker and Oscar Newman to destabilise the modern city project. It was clear to the sociologist Ray Pahl, for example, that the received and preferred view of building village-like structures in order to engineer 'traditional' village-like social solidarities was based on nothing more than belief and golden age fantasies. This was particularly true for the belief that reducing physical distance between people (different classes for example) brings people together socially. As early as 1948 Ruth Glass had warned against such reductions.

> It is not clear why the resuscitation of village life within urban communities should be regarded as being so delightful and so progressive nor how it is to be accomplished ... The mere shortening of the physical distance between different social groups can hardly bring them together unless, at the same time, the social distance between them is also reduced. (Glass, 1948: 18, 190; cited in Pahl, 1970: 119)

For Pahl, urban planning and city building was becoming dysfunctional because, following Glass's doubts, evidence from studies in the 1950s was beginning to refute key elements of architectural determinism/theory. Kuper (1953) found that reducing social distance is as likely to increase antagonism as social solidarity; Mitchel (1954) failed to discover any relationship between the physical positioning of homes and the development of friendship; while for Mann (1965) trying to discern and engineer appropriate physical neighbourhood entities was less important than considering the social relationships themselves (Pahl, 1970: 119).

Regardless of such debates and disputes and interdisciplinary rivalries where there ought to have been the mobilisation of interdisciplinary cooperation, the key problem emerging from this was a crisis of confidence in the legislators themselves. They had been given wide-ranging and extensive opportunities to demonstrate the truth of their claims and even though their original plans were often compromised severely by penny-pinching councils, it was becoming clear that much of the theoretical underpinning of their intervention was found wanting, and particularly their method of arriving at it. As Bauman argues, the following of correct methodologies was critical to the legitimation and demonstration of Legislators' superior knowledge. If there was a crisis of confidence in this knowledge, the days of their ascendency and hegemony might be numbered. Pahl's *Patterns of Urban Life* was published in 1970 but it is an early hint of a growing critique of, and discontent with, the blueprinted modern city; how in fact it was developing dysfunction and *legitimation crises* from its very inception. Of course the realisation of urban dysfunction rested on far more than that, as we shall see, but it is possible to identify such a rift as opening up the possibility of further scrutiny, doubts and anxieties.

Community studies

The discipline of social anthropology that had been so effective in studying the social structure and social relations of small-scale face-to-face communities became a principal means by which those concerned by the churning nature of modern cities attempted to resolve these debates. Often, as in the case of Young and Willmott's (1957) classic study of the transition of working-class culture from 'traditional' inner city neighbourhoods out to new-built outer city modern estates, a mix of methods, including extensive social surveys, was used. Indeed, some 16 years later Young and Willmott deployed the same methods to study the impact on family and community life in London more generally.

Far from upholding the view of influential architects Alice and Peter Smithson (see Glendinning and Muthesius, 1994: 122 for a discussion of their world and influential following) that community was no longer a desirable, feasible and valuable object for city planning and life, these studies showed precisely that the starting point of urban renewal and modernisation was in most cases a rich and densely knit community where work, leisure and kinship overlapped to provide valuable social support, cooperation, life chances and perhaps most important of all, a sense of belonging and worth. Even in less traditional towns, such as the car-building town of Dagenham, UK, it was surprising how quickly new community structures emerged from within the cultural repertoires of their inhabitants (Willmott, 1963).

In the USA sociologists and anthropologists achieved similar results in major metropolises such as Los Angeles as well as the industrial city (Berger,

1960; Keller, 1968; Seeley et al., 1956). Additionally, however, general concerns about suburbia also proved to be somewhat exaggerated. As a result of many social elements of design (cul-de-sacs, play areas, community infrastructures etc., many did become village-like and even, in the case of the new town Milton Keynes, achieved, in the minds of the inhabitants, a pleasant cross between rural village and city neighbourhood (Finnegan, 1998).

There were other studies that mapped the new emotions of the modern city from new and exuberant youth cultures emerging within the context of unprecedented affluence and mobility on the one hand (see Cohen, 2002) to the emotion of loneliness and exclusion among the poorer, less mobile elderly (see Townsend, 1973). Indeed, the first serious study of social isolation in cities emerged within the community studies literature, establishing the need for further state intervention in social care and the need for community development work (Seabrooke, 1973; Sheldon, 1948; Tunstall, 1963; Weiss, 1973).

But these sociologists did more than provide an empirical corrective for overly hasty policy initiatives and change. They also created the space in which to pause and think about a process of change that belonged to the so-called 'enlightenment' trajectory of human history in which 'the individual' was to be set free from the constraints of tradition and achieve their true potential. While they had clear affiliations with the political left, these sociologists adopted the counter-enlightenment role that sociology had often played in the past. They pointed out that modernity does not have to de-traditionalise urban *culture* in order modernise *society*; that tradition offers many people precisely what they need to support them in new circumstances and that many so-called traditional cultures (such as working class culture in the USA and Britain) were actually adapted to, if not predicated on, change itself.

Nonetheless, as some of these studies pointed out, things in cities can never be left to chance and tradition alone. Cities were places where institutions, cultures and neighbourhoods could spin out of shape and were often heading into unknown territory. Many still sensed a foreboding about the modern city, often from new, hidden dangers.

Dysfunctional modern cities

Urban dysfunction can be identified in almost all of the expanded post-1945 cities in the world but particularly those that became the massive hub cities and regional capitals. Dysfunction was identified with, first, the methods used to build and manage greater population densities in the central city areas, particularly those associated with modernising the housing and everyday spaces of lower-income neighbourhoods, and second, with

Image 5.1 Erno Goldfinger's House, Hampstead, London (photo Adrian Franklin)

the more laissez-faire strategy of permitting unregulated growth of suburbs for the more mobile, affluent, home-owning middle classes. Both of these strategies were built on the backs of successful prior experiments in which the built and planned form per se was heralded, as we have already seen, as the longer-term solution. The development of Corbusian cities in the sky seemed at least a potentially luxurious and exciting thing to extend from the wealthy elites of American state capital cities to the slum-dwelling poor of British industrial cities.

Equally, the highly successful garden suburb, home to architects such as Erno Goldfinger in Hampstead, London, seemed a perfectly reasonable idea to extend to skilled workers wishing to leave crowded central city locations for a model industrial village, or middle-class professionals looking to create leafy commuter-communities in the country.

Cities in the sky

Cities in the sky and cities in the country went badly wrong in many cases, though for very different reasons. One created a sense of social malaise and unease right in the heart of the city while the other blighted the very environment it was intended to dissolve into. In the 1970s and beyond the modern city attracted a louder and more vociferous band of critics.

Image 5.2 66 Frognal, Hampstead, London (1938) by Connell, Ward and Lucas (photo Adrian Franklin)

> We have seen one of the great fantasies of our time burgeon forth from the minds of a few visionaries to make a hell on earth for millions of people. And now it is over, leaving only what remains of our wrecked, blighted, hideously disfigured cities behind. (Christopher Booker, *Spectator*, 2 April 1977)

> Remember the incoherence – congested streets, choking with exhaust, freeways splitting neighbourhoods open like broken dolls' houses, tower blocks out of all proportion with human scale and sensibility, the deserts of concrete and asphalt where vandals cut down the trees as soon as they are replanted, the 'open space' quite empty, full of blowing rubbish, the areas waiting for demolition with half a sordid block gutted and wretched elderly remnants of humanity clinging to what is left of their once habitable homes. It is not the whole picture. But it is part of it, and it can surely leave one with a sort of horrified wonder that societies of such wealth should leave themselves with so many marks of squalor and decay. (Ward, 1976: 52)

While Haussmann planned the new central Paris to be a bourgeois citadel and a national showpiece, most other city centres retained their port and industrial functions, as well as their working populations and cultures. Their attractiveness to migrants meant that in addition to their own low-skilled poor, big cities also had large communities of migrants attempting to get a foothold on the ladder of social mobility. By the end of the Second World War the modern city faced not only rebuilding in many areas but also a housing crisis: absolute housing shortages and large areas of substandard slum dwellings. Such was this crisis that it became a dominant political issue and in places such as the UK moved an agenda forward very rapidly. Everyone, including the legislators of the post-1945 housing crisis in Britain, believed in the beginning that the sordid, nasty, unhealthy conditions of the slums and worn-out Victorian terraces were responsible for the condition, culture and disapproved-of behaviour of their inhabitants. If such people, desperate to be rehoused, were removed from the overcrowding, filth and immoral influences of the slum and given smart, new accommodation with all mod-cons, then they would be transformed into ideal citizens and admitted fully into the bosom of modern city life. Tower blocks in groups or as part of mixed development schemes could deliver them to the promised city quickly, efficiently and luxuriously.

Between 1945 and 1969 some 4 million publicly built and owned homes were built throughout Britain, and at 60% of all new homes they dominated the landscape, particularly the inner city which was the subject of so many government redevelopment and slum clearance schemes. No East European state built such a high proportion of the new stock during this period. Although only around 40% of the new homes were in blocks of flats (they were normally part of large developments with other forms, notably the row and semi-detached cottage), it was their dominating place in these developments that set them and their inhabitants apart.

Unlike Augustine's 'City of God', which was a utopian city designed to reorient urban sinners back to perform their spiritual side and aptitude for creativity and moral worth, in the city envisaged by Le Corbusier, Geddes and Mumford the key performers and performance itself was technical: 'The answer was to be found in techniques and they coined a quasi-evolutionist vocabulary for technology ... "ecotechnic", "paleotechnic", "neotechnic". Individual love and reason had failed the city so they resorted to a home-made stew of science, sociology and bureaucratic administration' (Raban, 1974: 16). At the end of the 1970s, when all but a few of the high-rise schemes had been judged a disaster, the buildings, architecture and all the other ingredients of the stew were blamed for the failure. Raban is right to describe the British experiment as a home-made stew, an assemblage of a number of things, material, social, bureaucratic, theoretical, spatial, because we know from the plaintive tones of Glendinning and Muthesius's apology for the tower block, that elsewhere the architecture itself could work very well. But it was not because it was an arbitrary hotchpotch that it failed. It failed because ultimately it was not sympathetic to the city people it was designed to help; what looked like an heroic, communitarian vision was in fact (another) demand that they, the city, must be moved, changed and improved. Such schemes demonstrated an antipathy to the messiness of cities that will always throw up areas of poverty and transition, and to the freedoms so characteristic of the city to permit and encourage wide-ranging behaviours and cultural difference.

According to Raban we misread the legislators motives: 'As happens so often in the manifestos of modernism what looks, at first sight, a brave energetic release from slavery of old habits of thought, reveals itself to be a shrilly puritanical backlash' (1974: 20). Raban argues that many utopian new cities are driven by rejection and despair. Campanella's seventeenth century utopia, *Civitas Solis (Sun City)* also began with the architecture: 'The Sun City and [Corbusier's] Radiant City – really the same place – are both expressions of apprehension, disgust and despair, and we should not fall for the assumption that utopias are usually the work of optimists. Far more often they are thinly-veiled cries of rage and disappointment' (1974: 22).

The essential heterogeneity and mixedness of the traditional city was being purified by such schemes; the insistence on standards and standardised

Image 5.3 Highpoint I, Highgate, London. By Berthold Luberkin 1935 (photo Adrian Franklin)

living was as much the advance of intolerance as it was of equality. Many other aspects of city life were purified from the new living spaces: the street (whose role in social life, the life cycle and surveillance was profound), the pub (another, equally profound network), close kin networks, the garden, the association with companion animals and even domestic animal production in back yards, the proximity to busy markets, communication networks, shops and city institutions and so on. The demolition of such areas was one violation and the rebuilding of the new schemes, often a long distance away on greenfield sites, was another. As much as it was giving material benefits it was rejecting and destroying culture, tradition and city life. The fact that the new lifeworld was to all intents and purposes the cultural opposite of what it replaced demonstrates its underlying backlash. There was little room left for people to perform, create, recreate and ritually transform in these city spaces. Their performativity had been determined in advance; life here was not to be performed but preformed. Rather like its concrete structure.

At Lege and Pessac, France

Exactly this process occurred in Lege and Pessac, near Bordeaux, when Henry Fruges, a factory owner, commissioned a young and largely unheard of Le Corbusier to build a complex of manual workers' housing. In justifying his design for these workers' dwellings, he railed against sentimental traditionalism (the 'folkloric brigade' as he called them) and complained of French resistance to the modernising world. He built simple, concrete boxes with long, plain, bare walls, long rectangular windows, and flat roofs in rectilinear terraces. They were brilliant expositions of Modernism and as Alain de Botton notes, they expressed aesthetically the architect's admiration for industry and technology and his vision for cities and city life itself to be realised in its likeness. Again, no room for individual performance on the production line or, symmetrically, expression in a performative home world. So far from building homes that the workers would like, the architect *explicitly* rejected their culture, their taste and their way of life and attempted to use his architecture to change them. Architects of the Modernist movement 'wanted their houses to speak. Only not of the nineteenth century. Or of privilege and aristocratic life. Or of the Middle Ages or ancient Rome. They wanted their houses to speak of the future, with its promise of speed and technology, democracy and science' (de Botton, 2006: 62). De Botton is astonished at Le Corbusier's arrogance but the fact was that in the 1920s architects were clearly *legislators* in Bauman's sense of the term, experts whose better opinion should hold sway. In the case of the workers' houses at Pessac and Lege, it was the factory owner rather than the workers who were swayed. The workers were simply not able to share the same dream.

> But the new tenants had a very different idea of beauty. It was not they who had their fill of tradition and luxury, of gentleness and refinement, nor were they bored by the regional idiom or the detailed carvings of older buildings. In concrete hangars, dressed in regulation blue overalls, they spent their day assembling pine packing cases for the sugar business. The hours were long and the holidays few. Many had been dragooned from outlying villages to work in Monsieur Fruges's factories, and they were nostalgic for their former homes and parcels of land. At the end of the shift in the plant, to be further reminded of the dynamism of modern industry was not a pressing psychological priority. (de Botton, 2006: 164)

Over time, the tenants only recourse was the dangerous path of subversion – a path so often called vandalism, sabotage, defacement or graffiti. They softened and traditionalised Le Corbusier's masterpiece. They added a pitched roof, textured by tiles to spoil the clean line of the flat roof. They placed shutters on the windows and picket fences around garden plots to make them rustic, and they placed gnomes and fountains in their gardens to ruin its pure *form*. Sadly, not everyone could do this, particularly when the buildings and developments were on a grander scale and bureaucratically managed.

Attempts to purify the city often began with the creation of new sites, typically either away from where the new inhabitants had lived or altered in such a way that it was unrecognisable. Mostly they were spaces set apart from the city proper, either at a distance or in network voids. Wherever they did join with the existing city, their special look and their placement in a park rather than on the street set them aside in a way that non-everyday institutions – hospitals, asylums, prisons and barracks – often are.

At Hartcliffe, Bristol, UK

The Hartcliffe Estate in Bristol was built five miles to the south of the city centre on the site of several former farms acquired by the council using compulsory purchase orders. Taking advantage of central government subsidies for slum clearance schemes, Bristol City Council began to rehouse people from central and eastern working class areas in 1951, often before roads, pavements and services were complete. Most of the rehoused people came from nineteenth-century-built terraced homes where the density of kinship networks and neighbouring was very high (Madge Dresser, 1983). The scale of the slum clearance and use of high tower blocks as a cheap replacement was in reality not the carefully deliberated, planned decision of the city but the artefact of a central government subsidy system.

Typical of such developments, Hartcliffe sits in its own parkland cut off from the rest of the city by service roads. Although only a third of the homes

Image 5.4 Not exactly on top of the world: High rise towers, Hartcliffe Estate, Bristol (photo Paul Burton)

were in high rise towers, they dominated the landscape, but they were also, paradoxically, isolated from each other by senseless expanses of grass. Today burned out debris from cars and household appliances have created a surreal-looking sculpture park out of the nothingness. The designers always thought that open spaces would encourage mixing and relaxing leisure, after the manner of the Victorian park, but these were not busy planted parks with private areas, pathways and features that encourage walks, meetings and parties. These are minimalist, featureless voids that simply created, as architectural models, the greatest visual impact for the towers as they made their bid to impress potential clients. But equally, from the contractor's and municipal landlord's perspective, such developments were subsidised homes for the poor and costs, including maintenance costs, were to be minimised. On such a windswept, now denuded hill site, such open spaces were also oppressive for much of the year.

Hartcliffe has a dismal track record. One of its local high schools has closed and two others have serious problems (*Education Guardian*, 25 October 2005); it experienced riots in 1992, which flared very badly for three days, and it has a serious drugs, crime and anti-social behaviour record. Many of its shops remain closed after years of battering and break-ins.

The spatial anomaly of the site was compounded by its spatial isolation from the city. Ten thousand dwellings were built with only minimal bus services at a time when hardly any of the tenants could afford a car. However,

Bristol's design for its rehoused people is most evident in its original plans to make Hartcliffe self-contained. In order to do this, municipal facilities sufficient for a small town were originally proposed, but when the scheme ran out of money the build went ahead and was completed without them. The end result was a major settlement too far from the city to avail itself of the facilities and to maintain its prior social contacts and lacking most of the social institutions that typically contribute to social order in any neighbourhood. As John Mortimer (1982: 90) dryly observed: 'The entry into the promised land was indefinitely postponed and "The Just City", we were told with increasing irritation, would prove far too expensive to build.' Hartcliffe was and still is an incomprehensible and 'heartless' scheme.

As with many of these developments, the initial tenants were extremely pleased to be rehoused in brand new, modern homes. Almost all of the first generation of tenants were from respectable working class and lower middle class backgrounds and were earning average wages for the city. Indeed, the rents were relatively high in such areas and the inference could not be made that they were socially marginalised, even if they were spatially marginalised and cast adrift in a malformed urban place. Similar stories of good beginnings are typical. Glendinning and Muthesius (1994) argue that the experience of Andrew Balderstone, a sheet metal worker from Edinburgh, 'epitomises' most of the stories they heard while researching *Tower Block*. Andrew moved into a twenty-storey point-block, John Russell Court, in 1964:

> 'For the first five or twenty years things were really great, everybody kept the block spotless ... you were really proud. The problems started when they started moving a different type of tenant in ... really rough people from the worst slums.' Night after night this couple four floors above them fought each other violently, came in drunk from the pub, turned loud music on, throwing things out of the window. Soon there were four or five families just like them. 'They had this crazy idea that by spreading the bad ones out among the normal tenants, you'd bring them up to your level, but what happened ... they brought us down. It was like a cancer.' (Glendinning and Muthesius, 1994: 323)

At Millbrook, Southampton, UK

Raban had his tower block story too, this time from his home town of Southampton. He described Millbrook, built between the 1950s and 1960s, as 'a vast, cheap storage unit for nearly 20,000 people'. Millbrook had a similar anthropological biography to John Russell Court. In the late 1960s Raban interviewed fifty of its residents: most complained of theft and vandalism and the complete disappearance of neighbourhood goodwill and trust and of its replacement with 'incipient paranoia about the malevolent habits of the people across the corridor ... Here social worlds were shrinking' (Raban, 1974: 21).

Like Hartcliffe, the impression one is left with is not so much the failure of theory and modernism but a failure even to bother to implement fully its more enlightened and socially progressive intentions. Hartcliffe was neither a modern city nor the extension of the old; it fell half way between, with none of the advantages of either. Because this was not a city or a part of it, it was, as Raban would call it, an anti-city. It had no city life.

And the point I want to make here is that there was actually an intolerance of city life among the theorists and innovators and perhaps also a more specific intolerance of specific groups of people on the part of city legislators. The theorists wanted to wish away one lifeworld and replace it with something better; the city legislators could not quite bring themselves to let the people at the bottom of *their* hierarchy have it, in full.

> Were one to read [Millbrook] as a novel, one might say that the author had read and copied all the fashionable books without understanding them, and had produced a typical minor work in which all the passions and prejudices of the current masterpieces were unconsciously and artlessly reflected. It is full of heartless innocence, a terrible place to live precisely because none of its effects are truly willed. (Raban, 1974: 22)

Glendinning and Muthesius argue that the true blight of high rise developments came in the late 1960s, ironically, after the housing crisis had been largely solved. By then Britain had produced something of a housing surplus and those on the waiting list grew more choosy where they went, and, what sort of house they went to. Hardly surprisingly, cottage-style houses were far more popular than high rise. Then again, as an artefact of their success in rehousing so many poor and slum-dwelling people, council housing lost its appeal as 'new and modern' and gained instead the association with poverty. This was not an illusion: by 1970 there was a much higher proportion of unskilled and 'households with no earner' in council housing than there had been in 1955 or 1960. Combined, these two effects undermined the social viability of the tower blocks, and as it became harder to let them to respectable working class households with a good housing record, so a higher proportion were let to problem families and individuals. So, the downward spiral began.

Ultimately many of them became hard-to-let, hard to police and hard to justify to local electorates and from the 1980s onwards the dire material and social conditions in the tower blocks rivalled anything ever recorded in the pre-war slums. In addition to the Ronan Point collapse in 1968, the towers were often plagued by condensation and damp problems as well as equipment malfunction. By the 1980s they had reached their nadir and many were condemned for demolition or 'blowdown' as it was euphemistically known, which was often turned into a spectacle rather like a public execution.[2] According to the figures in Church and Gale's 2000 report *Streets in the Sky*, something like 40% of the tower blocks were demolished between 1980 and 2000.[3] Glendinning and Muthesius talk of 'the frenzied destruction of thousands of *allegedly* "unlettable" high blocks' while Rochester in Kent 'took the scarcely creditable decision to blow up its entire multi-storey stock for purely aesthetic reasons – to rid the skyline of high flats[!]' (Glendinning and Muthesius, 1994: 322).

Rochester aside (and Rochester was, after all, making a bid for heritage tourism trail fame as part of 'Charles Dickens country'[4]), the indignation from their supporters was not always fully justified. While it is clear that they can be good homes, that a lot of their problems were exaggerated by a hostile media, that a lot of their problems can be remedied and that they were, historically speaking, victims of circumstance, it is also true that a lot of the suffering they caused never really surfaced because unless it found expression as a problem they were seldom researched.

Raban, for example, points to the *tyranny* of the tenants' spatial segregation from city life. Even when the tower blocks were still appreciated as new this was a novel form of suffering; a privatism that did not have a vocabulary, could not be expressed or performed and was therefore experienced quietly and unheard. When problems began in a block and were amplified by such close proximity they did so in the absence of normative social controls of the sort that Robert Roberts described in his *Classic Slum* – a rare ethnography of the culture of precisely those places that were removed into streets in the sky. Written from the vantage of the social hub of his mother's corner store in a Salford slum, Roberts recalls how the matriarchs of the neighbourhood 'stood guardians ... over our community'. Critically, they had everyday, extra-domestic spaces in which the work of social order might be enacted/performed and the little corner shop was clearly important:

> In and out they trailed from early morning to an hour before midnight, little groups that formed and faded, trading with goodwill, candour or cattishness the details of a closed society. (Roberts, 1974: 42)

Roberts was at pains to point out the moral and social messiness of the slum, how both good and bad were thrown together, rather like the tower blocks. However, the tower blocks lacked the social vitality and authority of the slum's matriarchs. The scope of their combined surveillance and the reach of their collective social control can only be marvelled at:

> Over a period the health, honesty, conduct, history and connections of everyone in the neighbourhood would be examined. Each would be criticised, praised censured openly or by hint and finally allotted by tacit consent a position on the social scale. Misdeeds of mean, cruel or dissolute neighbours were mulled over and penalties unconsciously fixed. These could range from the matronly snub to the smashing of the guilty party's window, or even a public beating. (1974: 42)

This was by no means uncommon, as Elizabeth Roberts found in her oral history of working class Barrow, Lancaster and Preston between 1890 and 1940. The wife-beating husband that moved into Andrew Balderstone's Edinburgh tower block would not have been tolerated there and may have been 'dealt with' by other local men, no doubt on the advice of their wives (Roberts, 1984: 194).

According to Raban, the intensity of social encounters of Robert Roberts' slum were reduced in post-war Southampton 'to the weekly visit to or from a mother and father in the city centre'. But the other, hidden, side of the sociologist's measures of social interaction is the new experience of aloneness, with its own form of intensity (Franklin, 2009). I know of very few sociological works from the 1960s and 1970s that attempted to penetrate the way people coped with the new times, spaces and routines of everyday life in tower blocks. Clearly, however, Raban's brief foray disturbed him: 'The stay-at-home mother in a tower block flat can be as alone as an astronaut marooned in space: indeed the sociological space in which she moves is almost as uncharted' (Raban, 1974: 21).

In the early 1960s Young and Willmott's work on the East End of London as well as Jane Jacobs's influential book attacking modern design in housing established the view that there was an absolute gulf between the experience of old and modern city life (Jacobs, 1961; Young and Willmott, 1957). However, it would be a mistake to think that the architects were even *intending* to recreate or improve on the city life of the slums and older working class quarters. It is instructive to remember that influential architects working in the formative years of the 1950s, often under the spell of Le Corbusier, not only rejected the built form they were seeking to replace, they also rejected its promiscuous self-contained sociability as outdated. Explicitly rejecting the backward-looking and romantic work of sociologists, influential architects Alison and Peter Smithson, for example, wrote that 'the concept of a balanced, self contained community is both theoretically untenable and practically wasteful' and 'in modern urban society there are no natural groupings above the level of the family'. Instead they believed their architecture could initiate new creative associations of new, more mobile modern cultures and their architectural sketches often included illustrations of 'a number of collaged-in groups of people, engaged in intense, though unspecified, kind of communication' (Glendinning and Muthesius, 1994: 122).

Hartcliffe was a broken estate and lifeworld by the time riots broke out between youths and the police in the summer of 1992 over the incident of a stolen police bike being brought back as a trophy. Hartcliffe was not an isolated incident that summer and similar riots broke out on the Stoops and Hargher Clough estates in Burnley, the Bracknenhall estate in Huddersfield, the Ordsall estate in Salford, the Wood End estate in Coventry, the Ragworth estate in Stockton-on-Tees and the Marsh Farm estate in Luton.

In Hartcliffe, few if any of the shops in its central Symes Road were trading following years of break-ins, vandalism and robbery. In 2003/4 the local police recorded 1704 incidents of anti-social behaviour, which included 886 criminal damage incidents, 156 noise incidents and 363 abandoned vehicles. On one day such actions took up 40% of local police time (Safer Bristol Partnership Executive, 2006).

Suburban dysfunction

The original idea of the suburb was a little utopia, a pleasant space not too inconveniently out into the sticks or too up-close to the pace and grime of the inner city but half-way between; a compromise yes, but one that delivered the goods. Such is the image projected by London Transport's 1908 posters, produced to sell the idea of London's northward expansion into the villages of Golders Green, Edgeware, Hendon and Finchley. Today, Hendon is a wasteland of mediocre to low-end suburban development and in-fill, a traffic nightmare at the crossroads where the former northern ring road meets the M1 and mired in suburban sprawl for miles in every direction.

In those cities that did not regulate it, especially those in the New World where very different economic and social conditions prevailed, suburban sprawl on a massive scale has become their defining characteristic. Mark Peel (2005) calls them 'Frontier Cities' and it was these that created a maelstrom of anti-urban sentiments both in relation to their own specific futures as well as cities around the world in general. Los Angeles, Auckland, Christchurch and Melbourne, for example, sprawled in the nineteenth century to densities of a mere 5 persons per acre while in Britain and the Eastern USA cities contained nothing less than between 8 and 93. The densest suburb of Melbourne, Fitzroy, managed 37 to the acre compared to London's 363, Chicago's 273 and Boston's 184. By 1900 the relative newcomer Perth, in Western Australia, had spread as far across a SW–NE axis as London had on its N–S axis. According to Peel, the reasons for this staggering growth was not because they were culturally more attuned to suburban life or because land was necessarily cheaper, but because while in Europe the suburban movement was something only middle class people could afford, in the Frontier Cities, owing to their own growth dynamics and higher working class wages, moving to the suburbs was something everyone could and did do, as soon as they could.

Much of this dynamic was fuelled by the arrival in Australia and New Zealand of wealthy immigrants flush with cash for new house building and these cities developed powerful services highly tuned to city-building. The original elites abandoned their central city areas and moved out to graceful suburbs in the hills while inner city space was occupied by waves of poorer occupants first from Europe and later Asia. In the USA similar ethno-spatial patterns prevailed, except that the strong residential segregation as between white and black populations has always been described as 'white flight'.

It is unlikely that the anti-suburban-sprawl movement would have gained such a global grip as an issue without the behemoth, Los Angeles. According to Mike Davis, such social anxiety is often attributed to maladjustment to change, but he asks 'who has anticipated or adjusted to the scale of change in Southern California over the last fifteen years?', and we could just as well say the same thing about the previous period of its expansion in the twentieth century (1998: 6). Los Angeles now occupies an entire region, with an area almost twice the size of Ireland but a GNP on a par with India. It has a population of 15 million focused on two 'super-cores' and is expected to grow by up to 8 million in the next generation (1998: 6).

We can organise the case against the sprawling suburb into three related problems:

1 environmental and ecological problems;
2 the destruction of central city life and the cost of sprawl; and
3 health consequences.

Environmental problems

During the period of twentieth century suburban growth, environmental sensibilities switched from 'wise use', something that was consistent with economic growth, to 'sustainability', something that was concerned with the *consequences* of economic growth. Many accounts of suburbia relate how the very impulse to move out of the city to the rural fringe, and the experience of childhood and family life being tied to specific landscapes, natures and settlement structures does not prepare people for the wave of building that will render them 'further in' and their own private Eden destroyed. In Adam Rome's *The Bulldozer in the Countryside* (2001), he argues that the great battalions behind the defence of wilderness were predominantly drawn from the affluent suburbs, that the very experience of living in the suburb sensitises its inhabitants to the leading edge of the loss of farm and natural environments:

> The residents of post-war suburbs lived in the midst of one of the most profound environmental transformations in the nation's history. Every year, a territory roughly the size of Rhode Island was bulldozed for urban development. Forests, marshes, creeks, hills, cornfields, and orchards all were destroyed in order to create subdivisions. Though some of the environmental consequences of suburban development were invisible to untrained observers, others were obvious. Again, and again, the destruction of nearby open spaces robbed children of beloved places to play and the losses hit home more vitally than the threats to far off sites like Echo Point ever could. (2001: 8)

According to Bruegmann (2004) and Davison (2003), suburban Australians and Americans were especially receptive to such books as Barry Commoner's *The Closing Circle* of 1971, and by 1976 Barbara Ward was making powerful connections between suburban sprawl, pollution, destruction of natural areas, water and air problems as well as reporting the initial waves of community action to curb sprawl in American cities. The citizens of Pataluma, 40 miles north of San Francisco, voted four to one for a 1972 ordinance that would restrict growth of the city to no more than 500 units per year for the next five years (Ward, 1976: 95). The sense one has from re-reading these 1970s books is that human development, particularly the gathering forces of suburbanisation and the creation of ever-larger cities, was one of mankind swinging out of control and that a major wave of regulation, navel gazing and community action was required to restore some kind of order. As I will argue below, a lot of this order was now based on the newly perceived need of a balance between humanity and nature and not merely the unswerving march of unfettered human progress.

Destruction of the city centre

By the early 1970s, in the USA one of the first dysfunctions of suburban growth to reach epic proportions was the negative effect it had on the city centres:

> By the end of the post-war boom years the inner cities of Newark, Detroit, Saint Louis and others reached a crisis stage. As jobs and residents disappeared, many owners simply walked away from buildings. Some of the buildings were demolished; others were destroyed by deliberate arson ... It became common to compare American city centres with 'Dresden after the war' and to marvel

> that a country rich enough to put a man on the moon could let such a thing happen. (Bruegmann, 2004: 47)

This was when Mitchell Gordon published *Sick City* (1963), when Jeanne Low published *Cities in a Race with Time* (1967) and Charles Jones and Layne Hoppe's *The Urban Crisis in America* (1969) set the tone for a generalised panic about city dysfunction. Urban renewal projects were often built on the large spaces cleared during this period, but since they continued to house a largely poor, disadvantaged black and migrant community they seldom achieved anything like a renaissance. Simply, investors could not see investment potential, only the quick profit for building dormitories. This also sparked a major wave of gentrifying opportunism, although that was also met with a mixed reception by urban critics; and as Bruegmann points out, it had the effect of reducing population densities in such areas. In *City of Quartz* Mike Davis (1998) writes at length on how the outward movement of the affluent middle classes and their vociferous defence of their rights to pay low taxes and uphold/augment property prices sucks the life out of poorer suburbs closer to the centre while at the same time setting up major symbolic and territorially driven fears and paranoia.

The argument has always been made that suburban sprawl is far more expensive than denser, more compact city forms since the cost of all of the services necessary to plug extra homes into the city system increases with distance from the existing networks. This in turn takes funding away from the centre to the ever-distant periphery. In 1974, a federally funded report, *Costs of Sprawl*, concluded along these lines. According to Bruegmann (2004: 123), its review of the literature was dominated by anti-sprawl opinion and research reports emanating from the US academy. The report sought to model the relative costs of planned, denser development versus unplanned low-density development and of course found that in development costs alone, the latter is more expensive. Although the cost–benefit analysis of suburban sprawl is far more complex than that, 'the conclusion of this report, no matter how shaky ... served as a statistical rock on which the anti-sprawl lobby has erected the ever-growing edifice of an argument that sprawl is inherently inefficient and therefore must be curbed' (Bruegmann, 2004: 125). Today, the sprawl debate is more nuanced and the financial and ecological costs are more finely calculated and distributed. Some, and this includes Bruegmann, argue that in fact the cost of not sprawling is greater – which is why in fact sprawl continues apace, albeit in a modified form with more medium rise and more expanded core service areas for new suburbs.

Health consequences

One of the principal reasons for modernising cities was to engineer the possibility of healthy habitats for humans at unprecedented population densities. Part of that was to inject more fresh air into city life, with greater spaces between buildings, open spaces and parks. Suburbs were, of course, logical next steps that were conceived as muscular experiences; gardening, walking and sporting possibilities were all conjured by suburban life. Serial, leap-frogging developments that produce sprawl and its necessary technology, automobility, were blamed for the decline of health, particularly in large American cities.

Howard Frumkin et al. (2004) describe suburban life as automobile-orientated, with young families having no sidewalks or walkable destinations from their homes. In the space of one generation, between 1960 and 2000, the annual mileage of the average American driver has gone from 4000 to 10,000 miles. Equally, over the past twenty years the average rush-hour has grown from 4.5 hours per day to 7 hours per day. Consequently the average number of hours that drivers are stuck in traffic has grown from 6 hours to 36 hours per year. The average mother spends one hour per day in her car transporting children or shopping. In 2000 only 26.2% of adults met the recommended levels of physical activity while 61% of children aged 9–13 do no exercise when not in school. According to Frumkin and colleagues, many people think that in the sprawling suburbs 'Things don't feel right' (2004: 90). They argue that obesity and type 2 diabetes are clearly related to this lifestyle but the health concerns are wider than physiological well-being. In a recent study, Russ Lopez concluded that 'higher levels of urban sprawl were associated with an increased risk for being overweight or obese among adults' (2004: 157).

Traffic fatalities in the USA are averaging around 40,000 per annum and traffic accidents are the leading cause of death in the 1-24 years age band (Ewing et al., 2003). Frumkin argues that the increase in traffic accidents can be related to city sprawling, particularly on the most dangerous stretches of road that were built in the style that sprawl typifies: 'multiple lanes, high speeds, no sidewalks, long distances between crossroads or crosswalks, and roadways lined with large commercial establishments and apartment blocks' (Frumkin, 2002: 204). Ewing et al. measured the relationship between urban sprawl and traffic risks and concluded that 'sprawl is a significant risk factor for traffic fatalities, especially for pedestrians' (2003: 1543).

Well-being is also adversely affected by sprawl according to Frumkin and colleagues. City life lacks diversity, boredom is common (most young people without a car or a licence live in subdivisions without shops, community centres, public transport) and is increasingly incommensurate with an aging society. Water quality and adequate supplies of water are also affected by suburban sprawl since less water and snow melt is returned to underwater aquifers and more merely runs off into stormwater flows. Large suburban developments can also contaminate nearby surface water and thus enter the water supply.

Inner city dysfunction

Until relatively recently, with massive urban regeneration projects emerging across the globe, inner cities had been in social and cultural flux, largely, as Lawless (1989) argues, as a result of demographic and labour market changes in the 1970s and 1980s. In Britain, as elsewhere, they became the focus for very sustained governmental attention, not least because they were very significant places of poverty and multi-ethnic communities. A sequence of Partnerships, enterprise zones, urban development corporations and Task Forces have been aimed at their amelioration, with mixed results. Not much has happened despite the 'Sustainable Communities' and 'Respect' agenda pursued by the Blair government in the recent past. As Raco (2007) argues, much of the resources as well as new policies addressed symptoms rather than underlying causes of crime. Rusted-on poverty, compounded disadvantage and complex social and psychological problems have created what Bauman (1998) calls a new form of 'vagabond' in the inner city. No longer insulated or defined by the institutional cultures of unionism that had maintained the spirits, status and well-being of the unemployed in the interwar years, the contemporary unemployed are socially isolated and present less as laid-off workers than failed consumers. Critically for Bauman, the inner city poor are mired in space, while the rest of the population are characterised by their mobility, their flexible and multiple potentiality in global markets and places. This confers the lowest possible status on vagabond culture and has created new emotional intensities in the city. As Raban (1974: 148) wrote:

> Today, the overwhelming fact of life in New York, if not in London, is the violence brewing in the streets. Indeed poverty and violence are clearly related: both are primarily dependent on the attitudes people hold toward strangers. The indifference that generates the one, and the hatred that animates the other, stem from the same root feeling. If a city can estrange you from yourself, how much more powerfully can it detach you from the lives of other people, and how deeply immersed you may become in the inaccessibly private community of your own head … in the city we have made hatred a dreadfully easy emotion.

To be mired in postcodes that fail you for employment, credit or even the delivery of post is to be structurally locked out of liquid modernity and it is no wonder that neo-tribalisms of the sort that are characterised by violent gangs, drug trafficking and the trafficking of sex slaves has filled the vacuum.

NOTES

1 It is interesting that despite Pahl's criticism of architectural determinism, 'the one practical suggestion' in his book concerns the benefits of building sheds for local (presumably council) tenants to use informally and change according to life-cycle and demand by different groups. The provision of 'some extra communal space' might, he argued 'benefit considerably' small clusters of 8–12 households (Pahl, 1970: 119–20). Although more cautious of the inevitability of such benefits, Pahl's suggestion was locked into or constrained by debates of the time.

2 See Glendinning and Stefan Muthesius 1994: 327. They include an image of a Media Pass to the 'Viewing Platform' for the blowdown of Queen Elizabeth Square, Gorbals, Glasgow, 12 September 1993, in which one person died and four more were injured by falling debris.

3 According to Chris Church and Toby Gale (2000) there was a total of 6544 built and around 4000 remain; thus 2544 or 39% have disappeared.

4 One tourist information site describes Rochester in the following terms, none of which would be enhanced by a high rise tower skyline:

> *I peeped about its old corners with interest and wonder when I was a very little child.*
> Charles Dickens
>
> Lying some 50 km from London, Rochester overlooks the River Medway. It is a historic town which gained importance from its strategic position on the London to Dover road. A short wander around the town immediately makes apparent why Dickens was so fond of the place. It's a lively and friendly town with old, lop-sided, half-timbered buildings. Most date to the 18th century while others are some 600 years old. The long high street with its medieval city walls is lined by Victorian lamps and flower baskets which hang outside the little boutiques, cafés and interesting souvenir shops, all leading to the main tourist attractions; Rochester Cathedral and the Norman Rochester Castle. http://www.itraveluk.co.uk/content/162.html (accessed 12 August 2007).

Part Two

MAKING CITY LIFE

Introduction: The liquid modern city

In its various manifestations, the dysfunctional city was a gathering together of doubts and misgivings about the modern city, doubts about humanist strivings to create a perfected way of living using the application of science – and social science – and the application of 'correct' design principles. I want to set the scene here for the multiple ways in which this humanist vision was softened, challenged, transformed and reversed. After the great age of blueprinted futures, Bauman's 'solid modernity', there were no singular urban projects that can be discerned to take their place. Rather, the city became the subject of multiple and heterogenous orderings, a more eclectic and confused modernity at all levels; politics, design, architecture, habitus, culture, economics and style. In the absence of yet more master re-orderings after the 1970s, the modern city became more tolerant of existing and other forms, became more inclined to weave others into its growing and much expanded cultural community and devise more ways of living harmoniously with other cultures, its own pasts and non-human city life. City life became more heterogenous, open-ended and other-orientated. Critically, it stopped thinking that 'a modernity' could be simply imposed by expert human will and began to see city life as a multiplicity of relationships, cultures, objects and natures which required thinking about their connections, values and their well-being and the quality of life. Thinking about the city therefore stopped being utopian and began to build an ecological mentality. Nothing was perfect, and in many ways it was a time of flux and mess, of political awakenings and experimentation, but a new orientation or stance, or project perhaps, was palpable. My argument is not merely that a new ecological sentimentality came into being in relation to the non-human world; I want to argue that this ecological line of thinking came to influence the way we approached most elements of our city world, taking the form of an ecological ethic. The origins of this ethic are complex and multi-stranded but it will be seen that it was in the city especially where this was nurtured, where it developed a stronghold and from where it was replicated and repeated onto more and more relations of a globalising modernity.

Whereas the solid modernities we looked at in Chapters 3 and 4 tried to impose humanity onto the landscape and the world, largely through its city command centres (the city almost became a model for the ordering of the rest of a human-dominated world), it has been increasingly clear that a different political modernity has emerged in which the raw imposition of power and structure has been challenged by a new impulse: the interlinking of an accommodating reflexive modernity, one that recognises the naivety and unworkability of singular, machine-like solutions and instead strives to forge workable links with a great variety of the entities that make up our cities. These include ethnicities and cultures, natures and environments of the city and its wider footprint, historic spaces and their residency, enterprises and bureaucracy, tourists and hosts, consumer-power and the creative classes, the dependent and the needy, non-humans in the form of machines, viruses, animals and texts that act and have effects. The recent study of automobility (Miller, 2001; Sheller and Urry, 2000) shows how the car figures among all of these entities and that the new modernity is constituted in conditions of great complexity (see Law and Mol, 2002; Urry, 2003a).

Anything other than the grand projects of modernity was bound to be messier but, if it is based on a more ethical, flexible and tolerant regime of politics and the distribution of power the possibility for a more sustainable, agreeable and what some might call 'livable' city life becomes more possible; not guaranteed, not evenly or fairly distributed always, subject to far too many externalities and conflicts in places, but, distinctly possible – especially if some solutions and practices that do work form the basis of change elsewhere.

If cities could be considered to be powerfully independent islands by the great modernisers of the twentieth century, it is certainly no longer the case, and so even cities have to be imagined into much wider and complex figurations of global magnitude (see Amin and Thrift, 2002). Greater mobilities and velocities have virtually cancelled space as a barrier, which means that cities are in more effective competition with one another, have become more substitutable one for another and with this has arrived the notion that cities and their citizens lead both civic and globally based lives and thus operate on a wider field of vision and remit.

From the 1970s on, the residents of cities became the cultural and political vanguard of the environment movement and ecological thinking (Tranter, 1996). Ecological thinking is not merely the application of sound scientific thinking, a movement whose metaphors are the scientific ones of system, community and membership. Critically, the ecological stance to the world, trying to create a fit and accommodation is consistent with, and derives from, the ethical politics of postmaterial cultures, cultures that depend upon and work routinely with the diversity of different entities that combined constitute the world and each other. The ecological sensibility derived from science as well as the ecological politics of post-1970s cities converged and informed each other, but at the centre of these lines of thought lie the ethics of tolerance, the aesthetics of diversity, the extension of rights, the pragmatics of sustainability, the possibility and the realisation of a networked world, and the ascendency of consumer power (Castells, 1996; Serres, 1992; Touraine, 2000). But also, core notions of the modernity project: justice, equality, progress (modified to be progress per se, and not merely *human* progress). As Alain Touraine argued in the aptly titled *Can We Live Together?* (2000: 296–7):

> It reminds us that human beings are no longer the conquerors of a nature where there were almost no clearings. Having acquired the ability to transform or even destroy their planet, they have become responsible for it. Their actions can no longer be inspired by a faith in boundless progress; they must be inspired by an awareness of the threats to humanity's survival, and particularly of the need to preserve a diversity of species and cultures. We are now aware that our survival is bound up with that of all elements that make up our environment, and with the need to defend cultural diversity rather than replace it with the unity of a globalized economy.

In Chapter 6 I will first sketch, and it can be no more than a sketch, some outlines of this transformation from the humanist city to what can be called a post-humanist ecological city (a city that tries to recognise and then model itself on the mutual accommodation of difference between the heterogenous entities that comprise and co-constitute it). I will sketch in the arrival of new values to guide such a transformation and in doing so I will home in on the last quarter of the twentieth century as a period and space of change – that continues into the present era.

It is banal to reckon history in decades or even see decades as having a unique shape and character but we always need objects and texts to make sense of the world and a decade is nothing more than a device (in my hands anyway). In any case I am going to be difficult by extending the 1970s to include the late 1960s as well as the early 1980s because this was a period in which we can see particular types of things happening, small projects being pursued by a lot of people in a lot of places that were successful and, in being so, constituted something of a major transformation. What was this transformation and how can we characterise it? We need to consider how people started to create their own city outside of the authorities that had up until then determined its look, its life and its possibilities. Beginning with housing, a new social movement comprised of many cultural elements began to rework the city in new ways. I will sketch some of these now but they will form the main content of Chapter 7, 'City Lifestyle'. We also start to see the beginnings of a consumer movement and consumer power that will eventually become a major constituting power of the new era. The innovative impulse of this age also created a new form of entrepreneur like Anita Roddick and Richard Branson, and new entrepreneurial spaces in the city, often taking over cheap rental space vacated by industry. These spaces were often less formal and market-like, combining production (often fashion and craft) with retail with services for food and drink, frequently attracting in-crowds and becoming a spectacle. As we will see, they were often the launch-pad of enterprise and initiatives that rippled out across the city, creating theatre as well as commerce.

A spontaneous efflorescence of arts and crafts developed a more *creative* dimension to city life. Informal, formal, commercial and free forms of creative entertainment extended existing forms of entertainment industries often in clusters and interspersed with retail, bars, food, new markets and cafés.

These spaces become more theatrical and 'performative', interpellating shoppers with new challenges and activities; normal conventions of city retail and entertainment industries become transformed, hybridised and blurred giving greater performative potential to the new crowds who came to respond to the new city vibes. New street markets appeared everywhere and gradually became recognised and formalised: at Camden Lock, London; the Valley in Brisbane; Melbourne Lanes and Chapel Street; at Rochester and in the heart of Bath and Bristol (see Gregson and Crewe, 1997a, 1997b, 1997c and 2003 for the proliferation of new 'transformative' markets that formed around the theatrical circulation of second-hand goods). The proliferation of these culminated in 'car boots' and other specialised markets.

I will then turn more specifically to one of the nubs of change, the challenge to humanism. If humanism is an expression of human triumphalism, supremacism and so on, then it is of course not only arrogant it also blinds us to the possibility of a different, more accommodating way of living in the world. From relatively slow beginnings, in recent years posthumanism has become a dominant intellectual project in its own right which will in turn have a major effect on the way in which humans can be challenged and changed. The specifically new characteristics of a posthumanist world or ontology can then be sketched in: the cyborg city, city wild life, animal cities.

This sketch is developed into three more detailed chapters which follow. Chapter 7, 'City Lifestyle', will explore in more detail the manner in which living spaces, particularly the home, neighbourhood and day-to-day life, shifted in line with global currents, consumerism, and the new creative culture of cities. Looking at how the inner city areas were transformed through so-called gentrification we can see how these various influences impacted on how people lived their lives. They were more creative; homes became the focus of self-expression and connoisseurship (see Colin Painter's *Contemporary Art and the Home,* 2002); people frequently restored the historical and cultural integrity of place consistent with a generalised sensitivity to cultural and ethnic traditions, home entertainment and sociability.

Chapter 8, 'Cities of Spectacle and Carnival', extends this trend in lifestyle into the more central and public spaces of the city, in order to analyse the new centrality of spectacle to city life. Markets, public art space, festivals, eating out and the new night time economy. Why did this emerge and why is it now so central to the very life of contemporary cities? Why did the social space of tourism become imported into the so-called regeneration of contemporary cities? It will be argued that this is not merely the extension of consumerism and commoditisation into more areas of the city but a critical way in which people have renegotiated a sense of belonging and connection to *particular* cities through particular forms of performance and ritual. Rather than look to neighbourhoods and streets for this performative connection (a performance that belonged to the reproductive nature of producerist cities) city spectacles enrol its residents into the creative energy and impulse of the city with its emphasis on culture, diversity and consumption. This is partly because everyone worked and a large number worked in the service class CBDs, focusing energy and disposable income into tighter special zones. City centres provide gateways into global creative and consumer cultures in ways that most neighbourhoods cannot, although those neighbourhoods that focused in those areas of spectacle are always the most desirable. We have to find out why cafés emerge as a new space and form of sociability in the spectacular city.

Chapter 9, 'City Natures', examines the dramatic shift in relationships between human city dwellers and their non-human neighbours in the city as well as those outside. The ecological cities stopped viewing cities as islands and began to open themselves to their broader ecological connections. Sociologists and geographers particularly began to develop an urbanism that was co-constituted by humans and non-human life forms; an urbanism of *post-materialist* sentiments that was based on anxieties and a putative responsibility for its own ecological footprint (Inglehart, 1997). Science and natural history changed under these circumstances too. No longer required to present nature as 'other' and separate, and therefore purified as a representation, film makers and dramatists as well as scientists were then able to explore the promiscuous interminglings of nature and humanity as well as their co-constitutions (Franklin, 2003; Thrift, 2001). The 2000s have been an exciting period of new urban research therefore, with some ground-breaking new perspectives and findings. These include, for example, Hinchliffe et al.'s paper on urban wild things and cosmopolitanism (2006), Gandy's 'cyborg urbanisation' (2005), Smith's 'world city actor-networks' (2003), Whatmore and Hinchliffe's 'living cities' (2003) and Franklin's 'burning cities' (2006).

6 The Ecological City

Towards an ecological city

Up until the 1970s, the various eras of modernity and the cities that were built during them carry the stamp of their great architects, planners and designers: the city became synonymous with their vision and their names. Hence we have distinctive eras and cities dominated by Haussmann, Mies van der Rohe, Lloyd Wright, Howard and Le Corbusier and Seidler. Since the 1970s there have been many important architects but none of them have become or even sought to become the leading edge of a future-orientated, technologically driven project let alone become a synonym for their own times. This is very significant. None of them have seen their work, individually or collectively, as the production of a blueprint for life, one that supersedes previous outdated versions and therefore justifies the makeover of cities or substantial parts of cities in their likeness. During the 1970s the International Style of Le Corbusier and his followers gave way to what was ineptly called Postmodernism. Instead of superseding International Style, Postmodernism simply mocked it for its pretentious, cold, dispassionate and inhuman nature and then embarked on a radical project of stylistic eclecticism, upholding, re-using, and mixing styles from modernism and every preceding type of Western architecture to create not a correct, perfect or scientific life world but a very different objective: to make cultural and historic connections, synchronicity with the environment and the past, building to engender happiness, joy and aesthetic pleasure and buildings that were spectacular or amusing (de Botton, 2006; Harvey, 1989). This is not to say that the very reverse was often produced, as the successful publication *Crap Towns: The 50 Worst Places to live in the UK* (Jordison and Kieran, 2003) attests. While this book is clearly not a scholarly source, the very *identification* and interest in the aesthetics and lifestyle values that adhere to towns and cities and an awareness of *city differences*, and especially the idea that so many fall short of being desirable to those who live in them, is proof of sorts that this new sensibility, or what Wolfgang Welsch (1997) calls an 'aestheticisation process' has taken place. That the book has become a bestseller demonstrates that it has struck a chord and will no doubt feed into the more generalised competition between cities for key or creative workers as an important element in attracting (what used to be called merely) 'capital' (Florida, 2003a, 2003b, 2008; Landry, 2001).

Postmodernism was an inept epithet because there was nothing particularly unmodern in these values; all of them expressed democracy, progress towards well-being, the applications of science and technology (the industrial arts flourished in this time) and so on in some form. But there was a palpable shift in consciousness. The view over London or Paris or Melbourne began to show signs of 'continuity-in-change', of relations between elements and entities rather than segregations (i.e. de-differentiations), more eclecticism and mixture and a more robust sense of curiosity to relate to 'the other' (Lash, 1990: 173). A city of separable 'elements' held together by 'systems' seemed to be giving way to a more promiscuous, messy set of relatings between more rhizomic heterogenous assemblages (to use the language of Deleuze and Guattari, 1999). It had not been blueprinted but was nonetheless on a trajectory or line of flight. It was less obviously a system of humans among themselves and increasingly an ecology of machines, natures, environmental elements, hinterlands, texts and humans.

The new sensibility was about being open and receptive to the agency and cultures of others, and seeing what might happen if they were combined, allowed to cross-fertilise, inform one another, rather than be kept apart.

An ecological metaphor for city life?

In *Sociology Beyond Societies* John Urry (2003b) makes the case that metaphors are necessary to sociologists and others in order to capture an understanding of society and social life. Metaphors can tell us what complex social entities such as cities *are like*, what they resemble and on what terms they are ordered. The anti-modernist narratives behind changes in the city from the 1970s onwards while not complete in any sense can be fairly clear in metaphorical terms. This was the ebbing of the machinic, command society (which David Harvey (1989) sees as an epiphenomenon of the modern organisation of civil society during wartimes) and the rise of an ecological society in which authority is more *distributed*, where events tend to be underdetermined and where outcomes derive from a new multiplicity of autonomously acting but interlinked authorities and entities. As Bauman (1992) put it in *Intimations of Postmodernity*, 'the centre of gravity shifts decisively from heterogenous control to self-determination and autonomy', but in the absence of central control there had to be a generalised *ecology of relatings* (Haraway, 2008), between entities that had been formally directed from above and a corresponding shift in the way individuals act *vis-à-vis* others. The paradox of neoliberalism and the extension of freedom carry with them the irksome, heavy weight of responsibility and decision making, things that had hitherto been taken care of by those in authority (Crook, 1999). The *ecological* linkages that replaced former lines of command were constituted, in part, through a spontaneous efflorescence of new postmaterialist values and ethical debate.

> In the absence of a universal model for self-improvement, or of a clear cut hierarchy of models, the most excruciating choices facing individuals are between life purposes and values, not between the means serving the already set, uncontrollable ends. Supra-individual criteria of propriety in the form of technical precepts of instrumental rationality do not suffice. This circumstance, again, is potentially propitious to the sharpening of moral self-awareness: only ethical principles may offer such criteria of value assessment and value choice as are at the same time supra-individual (carry an authority admittedly superior to that of individual self preservation), and fit to be used without surrendering the agent's autonomy. (Bauman, 1992: 65)

And, as he concludes in his passage on postmodern ethics, 'the limits of the agent whose autonomy is to be observed and preserved turn into a most hotly contested frontier. Along this borderline new issues arise which can only be settled through an ethical debate' (Bauman, 1992: 66). So not only are individuals and entities forced to engage with others but they do so in a newly emerging atmosphere of ethical evaluation and expectation.

It is in the larger cities where difference, variety and conflict are intensified that ethical debate became a part of governance itself; something that would shape most of the outcomes in one way or another. One can appreciate also how autonomous agents became at the same time increasingly reflexive as they retuned themselves to and attended to the clatter and clamour of 'relationships with others', necessary technologies, objects and the quantum of things that seem to Thomas Hylland Eriksen to fill our lives and create a sense of *fast time* (Hylland Eriksen, 2001). By others I do not just mean relations between human neighbours, human communities, interest groups, lifestyle groups, age groups and so on but relationships with the past, with history and tradition, with culture, with health (food, alcohol, drugs, weight and fitness) and identity, with machines and information and with territory and place – all of which have a multiplicity of objects and spaces that demand that ethical decisions be made about them to do with respect, preservation, use, interpretation and connection to the city. But the ecological metaphor works well because in the absence of supra-local city and national authorities managing risk and our relationships with 'the environment', an absence that emerged as an important new post-materialist value, cities became distinguished by their special reflexity in relation to nature. Of course ecological consciousness (in the environmentalist sense) works well in my ecological metaphor but these specific ways of relating to the natural world were in part an *extension* of the way humans were beginning to relate to themselves and with things in general (see also Touraine, 2000). While the modern city might be designed and governed along similar lines anywhere, the ecological city is sensitive to itself as an *environment*, to its hinterlands, its cultures, its natures, its climate and its position in global flows of goods, people, natural phenomena and capital.

All this is a *very* different ecological take on the city from the Urban Ecology associated with the Chicago School of Sociology in the 1920s–40s. Urban Ecology tried to infer something universal about the operation of cities from some of the common patterns that modern cities spontaneously made. In doing this it deployed the ecological metaphor to describe discrete human zones of the cities as if they were different vegetation types or discrete ecologies and they used these blocks of city space and models of human behaviour in them to account for common patterns of change and juxtaposition. In this sense, the metaphor worked to liken the city to an organism or self-referencing ecosystem and to account for its function and evolution in terms of the workings of its parts. It was a very crudely constructed metaphor; it was not very successful and, worse, it was wrong because cities were shown not to work in this way (Pahl, 1970).

The sense in which I would want to apply the ecological metaphor derives not from the mapping of ecology and the isolation of blocks of function and agency but from the way all ecologies involve highly complex relationships between a heterogenous assemblage of constituents in such a way that every part is to a degree co-constituted or becomes constituted through its relatings. This metaphor is very different but it is particularly suited to the way cities began to operate in neo-liberal or postmodern or, as I prefer, liquid modern times (Bauman, 2000).

The 1970s

If the earlier modernity was a technocracy, the modern era from the 1970s onwards was a techno-cultural ecology and its leading thinkers came from very diverse but hybridising backgrounds. Germaine Greer's *The Female Eunuch* (published in 1970) questioned the biological assumptions of gender roles and illuminated their cultural orderings as merely *conventions* that could be challenged or informed from elsewhere. The Centre for Contemporary Cultural Studies in Birmingham became an epicentre of cultural discovery in almost all areas of city life as diverse as soccer, youth, the workplace, the home, and the law (see for example, Clarke, Critcher and Johnstone, 1979). Not only did it identify culture where none had been perceived before, it established sensitivity to culture as an inevitable dimension of city life which then became part of a new reflexivity and around which ethical questions could be framed. From now on people not only sensed culture but they could now ask: what culture do we want? How can cultural difference co-exist?

In 1971 John Mortimer successfully defended the cultural pioneer magazine *Oz* against charges of obscenity thus establishing a climate of entrenched civil liberties, cultural relativism but also tolerance in measures not thinkable, or not so *explicitly* so, before. Mortimer argued that '[the] case stands at the crossroads of our liberty, at the boundaries of our freedom to think and draw and write what we please' (*The Times*, 24 June 1971). 'Writing what we please' was important not because of freedom of expression per se (in the Miltonian sense of religious and political freedoms) but because of the effects of writing: writing was also creating the very lifeworlds they wanted to create and inhabit but not in such a way as it negated the lives of others.

The Beatles broke up in 1970 after having pioneered a form of international musical eclecticism, experimentation and, again, tolerance. Their intervention and continued work in solo careers did much to establish the 'world music' scene, the peace movement and environmentalism. They are mentioned here not merely because they were influential but because they came from relatively humble urban backgrounds and were some of the first to sample the breaking down of former solid barriers to freedom and mobility. Norman Mailer relentlessly pursued civil liberties, rights and cultural efflorescence in the USA, founding along the way such 'alternative' papers as *Dissent* and *Village Voice* – all of them characterised by their focus on ethical content (he was recently quoted by Christopher Hitchens (2007) as saying 'Culture is worth a little risk', and of course ethical debate *is* a risky business); E.F. Schumacher's *Small Is Beautiful* was published in 1973 in response to the humbling effect of the oil crisis and an emergent environmental consciousness (he wrote: 'wisdom demands a new orientation of science and technology towards the organic, the gentle, the non-violent, the elegant and beautiful'). Essentially he was merely asking us to extend an ethics to all our relationships and not just those with humans.

It was largely if not exclusively in the city where these cultural shifts took place and spread. The work of all of these people was political but not expressed through the normal political channels of power. Rather, it was the unleashing of *cultural power* and it was going to be the medium through which the city expressed itself increasingly. This form of power, as Amin and Thrift so elegantly argue, is not to be thought of as underlying structures, 'but rather as *lines of flight*; accumulations of a *passion to construct the world in particular ways*; impulses that constitute how and therefore what things are to be controlled; modes of practice that are also modes of thought' (Amin and Thrift, 2002: 106).

Looking around the world's cities one can see a lot of these idea being expressed in architecture from the 1970s onwards although one of the things you don't see is the wholesale redevelopment and makeover that characterised so many modern eras before it. On closer inspection one sees a lot of the older stock of buildings painstakingly restored or converted into new uses without changing them overtly. Across the deindustrialised Western world, where once cities housed massive industrial developments, a large proportion of its now idle apparatus was retained and reused from the 1970s onwards (rather like charity shop clothes) where before they were demolished without a thought. Many had been transformed, shrine-like into a new heritage manifestation for which some groups would have a special totem-like connection (MacDonald, 1995). The 'look' of the built line and the city skyline thus lacked architectural integrity but was being broken by the intermingling of styles and periods. This is the look that best reflected the 1970s and 1980s sensibility and it was thus very prominent in the work of its architects. One thinks of the broken lines and eclecticism of Robert Venturi, the playful and ironic buildings (and even tea pots) of Michael Graves (the Portland Building in Portland, Oregon looks as if it could be a Beatles album cover), the eclectic improvisations of Helmut Jahn (see his jazzy design for the United Airlines Terminal in Chicago airport) and the modest Sea Ranch Condominium of Charles Moore, which blends seamlessly into the Californian coastline environment. Moore inspired a new generation of architects to consider the ecological fit that their building might and should, where possible, make. It is a move or turn that would extend rather than stop right there.

Cities, especially large metropolitan cities, are the boldest expressions of any historical era and exemplify its values and character more than any other material manifestation. Rural landscapes across the world remain remarkably constant despite profound social (and technical) changes, but cities are not only products of their age, even if they have only reshaped the foundations of previous eras, they seem to be the first to draw fire and criticism when things are perceived to be wrong. Equally, when a new age is dawning it is on the surface of cities that it begins to inscribe itself first. As the centre of political, cultural and administrative power the principal cities attract and retain an ancillary class of engineers, architects, designers and artists who are called upon to realise the material and aestheticised expressions of social and political elites, their values, forms of governance, commerce, often through showcase projects, often in prominent city spaces (Betsky and Adigard, 2000). However, the stirrings of new demands for change may not arise first among this governing class since their fortunes are so often tied to those in power or to rationalised dominant paradigms. As George Bernard Shaw's John Tanner remarked in his *Revolutionist's Handbook*, 'The reasonable man adapts himself to the conditions that surround him ... Therefore, all progress depends on the unreasonable man' (*Man and Superman*, IV), and so it is often therefore *outsiders* – students, the artistic avant-garde, new social movements (political, consumer, sexual, gender, race/ethnic etc.) and the so-called 'hippies', 'creative classes', together an important social strata of any major city – who painted in the first brushstrokes and begin to live life in a new way and will new lifeworlds and circumstances into being.

Portentously, in April 1970 the horse *Gay Trip* won the Grand National steeplechase. The 1970s were the beginnings of an epoch of revolutionary social and cultural transformation and from David Bowie's gender-bending rock through the sexually liberating magazine *Oz* to *Spare Rib* and the *Gay Times* and organic gardening, everything, including received norms of sexuality and gender, had been subjected to the most rigorous criticism and experimentation. The 1970s created a culture, still alive today, that thrives on transformation and change as a permanent state and its role in the creation of new forms of city life cannot be underestimated.

In July 1970 enthusiasts brought Brunel's revolutionary ship the SS *Great Britain* back for restoration in Bristol docks (where it was originally built). It had to be for profoundly important reasons because it was returned from the Falkland Islands at great expense. Such a move signalled that the new modern future was not going to be achieved by rejecting the past but by being inspired by it. Prior to the 1970s the modern impulse was future-orientated and it worked as hard on destroying the past as it did on finding a future. As tourism scholars who specialised in the new heritage phenomenon found (Coleman and Crang, 2002; MacDonald, 1995), one cannot destroy the past without creating a sense of loss and when that loss seemed to be the extensive industrial culture of Britain, it proved too difficult to bear. Personal biography was inscribed on the sorts of everyday objects and spaces that were retained and showcased. Critically, the impulse to preserve the SS *Great Britain* belonged to the gathering *heritage* sensibility that has been much mocked but it was an instance of a very important transformation. The search was no longer on for a singular aesthetic, a new look for a new perfectible age. Instead, aesthetic beauty was being found in new places, in pre-industrial cultures, in the pasts, in textures and surfaces of old buildings, on the fringes and in newly discovered popular cultures from the past and present – in the nooks and crannies of all forms of city life.

The postmodern reaction to a culture of serious-minded functionalism was to blow raspberries using whimsy and absurdity and the adherence to the past provided a form of reversal and quirkiness which became an anti-motif. The

Beatles did not eschew sentimentality but actively sought it in such things as brass bands, old uniforms and transcendental religion. Everyone knew that brass bands were the epicentre of working class collective sentiments and they were not to be simply thrown away or forgotten. Nobody was to be forgotten. It sounded interesting against the jangle of guitars.

New communities of interest were coming forward to be defined and identified by objects, pasts and spaces on the verge of extinction but now to be recoded *heritage*. This is how city life in places like Canterbury came to be changed and set on a new line of flight. There was a lot of recoding going on in city life now. Instead of finding the correct form, 'good taste' transformed into *eclectic* taste, mixtures, hybrids and fusions. Instead of seeking the best way to live and identifying forms of life to reject and reform, a new kind of *empathic curiosity* took its place. If there was a degree of intolerance or rejection it was for modern utopias, futures that left the past and some groups behind, for the technocracy and science found to be working for corporations rather than the common good, for progress rather than diversity and bureaucratic, standardising forms of governance. We developed comedy around the anarchic technology of *Red Dwarf*; we identified with the inmates in *One Flew over the Cuckoo's Nest*; *2001: A Space Odyssey* and *A Clockwork Orange* spoke to us in strange ways, disturbing us out of a dependency on 'psychological care' or belief in psychological health.

Today, Brunel's ship is the centrepiece not only of a maritime heritage museum but of the remodelling of the industrial docklands of Bristol into a new living space and cultural centre for the city. Critically this new living space underwent transformations that were more than merely human. For example, the water in the docks was no longer a poisoned industrial sewer but a restored part of the original ecology of the River Frome that flowed into it, and the huge basin became a viable fishery and with it ducks, swans and cormorants came to live too. Even trout, a native of the Frome, could be seen rising in the dock in the evening. In 1989 one of the most significant companies in the world, Lloyds of London, relocated to a new building opposite the SS *Great Britain*. It seemed to seal an alliance between cultural efflorescence and business, the past and the present, that was being sealed in many other prominent cities. Analysts began to notice a strange new epiphenomenon: the most successful cities and companies were those that associated with and located to places of diversity, tolerance, cultural industrial growth and environmental reflexivity (Florida, 2003a; Landry, 2001).

Questioning humanism

The first stirring of change may be expressed in a number of places, by a number of people in a number of different ways without coordination of any form or self-conscious plan or objective. The new directions that were taken, largely as a reaction to dysfunctional modern cities, came from many congregations and took many forms (some social, some environmental, some technical, some cultural and some from architecture and design) but the forms of city life that resulted were very different, often defining themselves through opposition to those of the modernist city. There are a number of adjectives that have be used to describe and characterise the various forms that succeeded the modernist city and therefore describe the work that these people carried out – postmodern, surmoderne, 'second modern', liquid modern, disorganised, creative and so on – but I am going to suggest that while all of these have their merits and uses, none of them quite captures the trajectory of its development in global terms. Almost all of these options are *humanist* in orientation, being concerned mostly with describing and diagnosing social, economic, cultural and political change – a domain explicitly focused on framing humanity as an entity unto itself, more or less self-contained and self-determining or emancipating. But as we have seen with the simple case of the Bristol docklands, we are talking about more than just changes in the human sphere. What was being sensed, dreamt and strived for was transhuman. Ecological metaphors emphasise a world of differences in connection; different categories of things being assembled into complex webs of life. Cities only *seemed* to be a purification of the human through the ordering that was directed at the elimination or control of nature. But as Bruno Latour emphasises in *We Have Never Been Modern* (1993), we have always been completely entangled in the non-human, but more importantly, one of the artefacts of modernity is the very *proliferation* of human–non-human hybrids, entities that are nothing other than these entangled elements of the human and the non-human. 'The environment' as it presented itself to modern city dwellers in the 1970s and 1980s was clearly one that they could no longer ignore.

Humanism is a form of anthropocentricism which proceeds as if other forms of agency matter little since their agency is inconsequential or they either are, or will be, subsumed under human control. I am going to argue that while it is indeed vital to understand and characterise changing circumstances in terms of their human dimensions, relationships and patterns of behaviour, they are not the only ones that are important or defining of the way contemporary cities came into being nor how they are being shaped for immediate and more distant futures and lines of flight. Arguably, contemporary and future cities are characterised most by their *heterogenous relationships* with both humans and non-human entities, and perhaps increasingly so. The 'new urbanism' that Sudjic and Amin and Thrift are pushing us to explore with new techniques and theoretical tools is inspired by Bruno Latour, Katherine Hayles, J.F. Dosse, John Law, Donna Haraway and Sarah Whatamore.[1] This promises to be a major shake up of what has been known as *urban studies* and interestingly it is now widely felt that a much larger pool of disciplines and knowledges are required to properly reveal the constitution of city life. As Amin and Thrift argue, this work is heading 'towards a different proactive of urban theory based on the transhuman rather than the human, the distantiated rather than the proximate, the displaced rather than the placed, and the intransitive rather than the reflexive' (2002: 5).

There are three very good reasons for moving beyond the (limiting) ontology of humanism. First, as humans attempting to organise life on a global scale in forms of organisation and relations that are increasingly mobile and fluid, and with increasingly diverse and shifting social and natural compositions, it has become only too obvious that the *management of this complexity requires us to relate to more and more elements simultaneously* and that these will be both human and non-human and all manner of hybrid entities besides. If the imperialist industrial capitalism (that characterises the first phase of modernity) could simplify and model exploitative, one-dimensional relationships with the external world and outsiders, pursing largely material goals, that is no longer an option and no longer the only aim. John Urry's examination of *Global Complexity* concludes that inevitably *cosmopolitan* tendencies accompany globalisation:

> Such sensations of other places can create an awareness of cosmopolitan interdependence and a 'pan humanity' (Franklin et al., 2000). The flows of information, knowledge, money, commodities, people and images 'have intensified to the extent that the sense of spatial distance which separated and insulated people from the need to take into account all the other people which make up what has come to be known as humanity has become eroded' (Featherstone, 1993: 169). (Urry, 2003a: 136)

Urry views cosmopolitanism as a specific artefact of globalisation, in a potentially positive way. He asks: 'Is a set of "global values" and dispositions becoming an emergent and irreversible implication of global complexity? Are "societies" increasingly forming themselves *within* such an evolving complex and will they be subject to scandalised disapproval if they do not display cosmopolitanism upon the global screen?' (2003a: 133). The idea that social centres such as the major cities are now forming themselves in relation to a much wider set of still-evolving constituents that form the community they must deal with, invokes an ecological metaphor, or at least an ecological metaphor is more apt here than *social system* or *social structure*.

Moreover, as he argues, such relations are not restricted to human–human relations: 'one paradoxical consequence of global complexity is to provide the context in which universal rights, a pan humanity, relating not only to humans but also animals and environments, comes to constitute a framing for collective action'. (2003a: 136). When Urry posits such ecological relations, it is at the major crossroads of global complexity, the major cities, that it will be most entrenched and normative. The ecological metaphor is fitting here because, like ecologies, cities are not species-specific, are not bounded by space (even though they are, of course, spatialised), involve all entities in relations that are 'always-already-intertwined' (hence it is not possible to bracket off some and exclude others) and because of their complexity and virtualities, cities never hold to blueprints but instead generate and therefore possess *potentialities* (Amin and Thrift, 2002: 4).

Second, partly through the experience of this very different world of complexity and fluidity, and partly because we have continued to enhance our own bodies through all manner of cyborg-creating technologies, it now occurs to us more often that humanist models that pose a world of humans among themselves are no longer quite what we need in order to understand our world and the life that is possible, desirable and 'next'. Bauman makes it perfectly clear in *Liquid Modernity* (2000) that this is what interests most people rather than an unchanging world of solids and settled certainties.

Third, humanism is questioned as a result of continued frustrations with 'The Great Divide' (the separation of, or gulf between, the sciences and the humanities), which can be thought of in the active sense of institutionalised rigidities and the working out of disciplinary interests, that keep natural science and social science, humanity and nature ontologically separable and separated. Ironically there are few who think this is how it should be; most feel that science and social science should ideally 'work together' and some research councils are putting significant funding into new initiatives.[2] More and more intellectuals are now beginning to see assemblages as the object of their investigation rather than entities specific to disciplines. Urban studies should have been the leader of the pack in creating such bridges but because it has tended to get bogged down in policy debates the view from their window has seen only the activity of humans and often only a sub-set at that.

If the city was once single-mindedly about the maintenance and defence of its (human) citizens (against other humans and nature), an entity that was designed especially and solely for this task, and subsequently became a unit that was particularly organised around the demands of production, we can say that this is certainly not so any more. As city dwellers, our concerns now extend into vast global figurations which are dependent upon and are mediated by equally complex socio-technical interfaces and forms of agency that we do not understand, control or predict with any great accuracy. Some of these are forms of agency that we have had some hand in unleashing on the world, in other words they are hybrids of human and non-human agency (GM crops, carbon emissions, the car, BSE or mad cow disease, bird flu etc.), others are forms of agency that form in direct response to our impacts on the non-human world, entities that push against us in ways predictable and unpredictable (for example, fires still rip through Australian cities and some of the most expensive real estate regions of the USA with consummate ease with all the knock-on effects from international cooperation, new strategies to manage risk, elevated real estate insurance and so on); while others are routinely engaged with the human world, creating effects that are typically either discounted or unseen (we are protected by a number of organisms that live unseen on our skin; companion dogs provide protection against ill health and depression) (Franklin et al., 2007).

It can be argued that this was always the case, even in producerist cities; however, as a result of changes in the modern city and the modernist mentality of the mid-twentieth century, human concerns became less tightly focused on an entirely human world, particularly one that focused unswervingly on matters of production and exchange. Much though we might think that the age of neo-liberalism extended forms of rational organisation and control (even more effectively and without distraction) into more and more areas of our life (and it really did), it did not do so without creating an imperative to relate to our cities, their hinterlands and the world in general in more *ecological* ways. And by that I mean developing and extending forms of relating to humans and non-humans that recognize the importance of maintaining that relationship; recognising that there are complex chains of interdependence that are required in order that such a complex world can be maintained.[3] But it would be a mistake to assume that this was merely the active pursuit of self-interests. While the case can be made for mutual interests, it is also the case that increasingly, relationships and relating with others and engendering a life of great diversity, colour and difference is seen as a positive, pleasurable and desirable end in itself. That it has become an important part of the *life* that most people want to have. And this is yet another irony of the consumer/leisure society. It is possible to think of it as wasteful, unnecessary, shallow and frivolous but there is no disputing the seriously engaged way people have desired greater diversity, evaluate variety and difference positively and develop aesthetic appreciation or connoisseurship of its increasing aestheticised surfaces (Welsch, 1997).

The case being made in this book is that this is not only becoming true generally but that it is being realised especially in the major cities – which is why (ironically perhaps) they are enjoying a renaissance (people are returning to many cities after having abandoned them) (Crouch et al., 2007: 16), why the best cities seem to exemplify the new ecological values[4] and why the hunt is on to understand in more precise terms how a city can be tuned in to a more ecological wavelength (Landry, 2001). The opening page to Charles Landry's book *The Creative City* tells us that it 'explores how we can make our cities more liveable and vital', how cities can become a 'vibrant hub of creativity, potential and improving quality of life'. These are all interesting expressions – liveable, vital, vibrant, quality of life – which indicate to me that what people are looking for and what makes a city successful is the fact that a particular kind of *life* can be had there – not simply that wealth can be made, that housing is sound, equitable and affordable and that services are available. People want to reach out beyond material comfort; they seek a more aesthetic life, with more diversity and connectivity, where they are, or can be, performers of that life and where that life is not taken at the expense of others, human and non-human. It is a big demand, a new project that may or may not work out or fold everyone in[5] (there will be winners and losers), but there are important positive elements that distinguish it from previous epochs of modernity: it seems to be deliberately focused on tolerance rather than asserting standardisation (a useful ethic for an increasingly mobile world); it asserts a radical decentring rather than staying unswervingly on the 'main chance'; it is pleasure-seeking, aesthetically charged, hedonistic and fitness-orientated.

Material and military security are no longer the prime interests of an urban culture since these have been taken for granted for a long time by most cities in the West (though of course because cities are still porous new internal and external dangers emerge from time to time) and have been superseded by concerns that could only be pursued under what Ronald Inglehart (1997) has called *postmaterialist* conditions.

Postmaterialism ushered in the possibility of developing additional desires limited not only to maintaining life but *changing* and *improving* life itself: producing new leisure-rich lifestyles (aesthetically orientated, health and fitness orientated, intellectually orientated, spiritually orientated), introducing new expectations from life (cleaner air, healthier food, more diverse beers, cheeses and olive oils, faster cars, more air travel, more self-contained living spaces) and developing new value-driven politics (environmental, sexual, cultural etc.) (Inglehart, 1997). New lifestyle orientations and their organisations connect individuals to networks of people and objects that extend far beyond the workplace and home, and beyond the confines of humanist notions of *progress*. Moving beyond issues of access and exploitation for human needs, postmaterialist orientations involve issues to do with quality, sustainability, ethics, morality, pleasure and aesthetics. They profoundly alter the relation between humans and non-human objects away from a simple modernist model of consumer and consumable to more complex ecological issues about coexistence, interpenetration, sustainability and sensory connection.

Just at a time when Bauman and others can see consumerism as the metaphor for all forms of relating, just when we have indeed become supreme, unsurpassed consumers of the world, this very fact pulls us up and forces us into a different form of relating to the objects we consume. Bauman does concede that consumers and consumption have changed profoundly. When food has become abundant and cheap, our concern shifts from the satisfaction of the hungry body to the desire for an aesthetic, fit body. When luxurious personal transport became available to all we became concerned for the quality of air and the possibility of walking more, cycling or running ... In such a society where consumption had extended beyond material necessity, he concedes that the *manner* in which we consume has become the basis on which we judge ourselves and others. Connoisseurship or the aesthetics of consumption places us in a very different relation to the objects we consume because it can also invoke veneration, respect and admiration. It is not enough that we can eat; the object becomes how to eat *well* and its expression becomes a mark of social distinction. Connoisseurship can also encourage frugality, restraint, collection, preservation rather than gluttony. We expect to consume far less of the objects we most desire for they acquire a semi-sacred aura; the Lamborghini may not be thrashed to death and worn out by its admiring class of millionaires, but paradoxically, used sparingly, kept pristine. Carp and trout accrued sacred status among the growing legions of Western anglers and instead of consuming them more, they avoided consuming them at all.

Despite being a throwaway society (and I would not wish to make the case that we are no longer wasteful), research shows that in fact we are very loathe to throw anything away since by the time we tire of possessing something it is a sure-fire thing that it will have become aestheticised, desired, used or collected by others, thus entering second and many subsequent circuits of exchange. This is the message coming from those who understand the growing significance of second-hand goods markets. Nicky Gregson and Louise Crewe spent six years researching the world of second-hand culture in England and report among other things that attending car boot sales was the single most popular weekend leisure activity (Gregson and Crewe, 2003). According to Neilson/NetRatings (2007) half the population of the UK visits eBay on their own once a month, eBay visits constitute 11% of all Internet time and in 2006 total sales reached $52 billion – over half the size of New Zealand's GDP.[6]

The city is now not only a machine for living, but a machinic, cyborgian way of life. Where we end and machines begin is no longer clear or important because so much of our senses and forms of connection with the world is mediated by seamless connections with machines. Without the millions of computers we are intimately bound up with, our cities (even our homes) would grind to a halt. Cities have been fashioned by the agency of designers and architects, yes, but they have also been fashioned by and will continue to be fashioned by the agency of machines and the co-agency of machine and users who come up with both new uses and new machinic possibilities.

The suburban cities of the USA and Australia were never in the minds of those who designed the motor car but it was the motor car that made suburban living possible to imagine. Car driving was supposed to be a means of transport, of improving the getting from A to B, but cars were made in such a way (again, it was an object that was mantled with aesthetic appeal) that 'the drive' became the object of the car and not only the means of achieving its object (to arrive somewhere else). As cities get bigger new technologies make it even harder to remain unseen and anonymous, not less so. The distinction between zones of work and home have become blurred as more and more people work from home or on the move using new communications technologies. Fast trains and air-links mean that some major cities are closer in real time travel than the small towns on their own outskirts. The comparison between what is possible through technological mediation in an average 1970s home compared with one in 2010 is staggering and in fact in many ways cancels almost all forms of differentiation and connectivity based on space. Thus we can go shopping, take a look out over the Pacific Ocean, have a face to face chat with a mate who is on holiday, place a bet on a Hong Kong horse race or put in a day's bidding at art auction houses around the world and at the same time sell those items we bought the week before. I can even check out the conditions at my favourite Colorado trout stream before deciding to go fishing there.

Second, cities are no longer mostly self-absorbed in a world of humans among themselves. From at least the 1980s people in cities have begun to develop an important sensibility towards and relationships with non-human life. To begin with, the politics of the environment and even of issues that relate to specific environments very far from the city are dominated by city dwellers. The single largest political demonstration in British history focused on the banning of fox hunting and it was delegates from rural Britain who descended on London to protest to urban Britain generally about their biopower over the countryside. Hunting has also come under attack from city dwellers in the USA, Australia, New Zealand and elsewhere (Franklin, 1996, 2002). Cities have also rediscovered, embraced, encouraged and developed themselves as natural habitats and often as refuges for species that have become threatened in their own so-called countryside habitats.

Third, cities have become acutely aware of their own ecological footprint within their own regional hinterland as well as globally. Ever since New Orleans in 2006, the notion that a major city could be abandoned as a result of a tenuous understanding of nature and arrogant human supremacism has become a reality and encouraged a more ecological frame of mind (Pickering, 2008).

Whereas the modernist city sought a planned new order with major central city rebuilding projects forming its principal intervention, the ecological city typically proceeds more cautiously, watchful of its footprint, mired in ethical debates, stakeholder rights and consumer demands and opinion and with far more energy and money being expended on the integrating technologies of lifestyle infrastructure and creative industries. A cool expression of efficiency eludes the ecological city since it wishes to position itself as the effective medium for the co-existence of opposites and entities in tension. This is why it puts so much energy into and supports the development of cultural industries since these are invariably bringing cultural elements onto a performative platform where they enact and encourage others to perform rituals of transition and change. Cities rely on attracting capital and increasingly visitors. In both cases, the mobile tourist class and the creative workers who make it up are seeking the excitement that these spaces of transition offer; catharsis, redemption, tolerance, recreation, intellectual stretch, cosmopolitanism and the development of mastery and connoisseurship, health and sustainability. In the modernist city such things were sought for a matter of a few weeks a year, on holiday – continuing a far longer tradition of pilgrimage and seasons of ritual reversal and renewal. Today material plenty permits more time for such reflection and refinement and supports therefore the building of a very different, open-ended form of city life (see Franklin, 2003 for a complete account of this process).

NOTES

1 Ash Amin and Nigel Thrift, *Cities – Reimagining the Urban* (2002: 3–4). They are also inspired by many others including Deleuze and Guatarri, Walter Benjamin, Margulis and Agamben.

2 The UK Engineering and Physical Research Council, for example, has several initiatives to fund projects across the Great Divide: e.g. Partnerships for Public Engagement, New Dynamics of Aging and Connecting Communities in the Digital Age. One set of advice for applicants reads 'Research Clusters are **not** required to be multi-institution but should aim to be multi-disciplinary'.

3 In this sense the ecological metaphor owes a debt to Norbert Elias's figurational sociology and his civilising thesis. Elias argued that there were moral, cultural and social implications of the expansion of rationalised forms of production and governance and that new forms of manners and sensibility resulted in complex and unintended ways.

4 This is one of the clear results from Richard Florida's study of the contemporary cities, *The Creative Class* (2003a).

5 I take Neil Smith's point about urban rejuvination, gentrification and the new middle classes. They have taken the lead in bringing them about and they have been among the most important winners as a result, but I simply do not see the unfolding of new creative cities as a capitalist plot or logic; that it has only systemic structure, is built merely by interests, or can be reduced to a Marxian economic analysis. This is to ignore precisely what I am trying to describe here, that aside from the commercial and entrepreneurial action, a lot of people have been trying to build better, more tolerant and enjoyable city spaces. This seems to me to be obvious and the fact that the baby boomers who largely carried it out did not come from privileged backgrounds but mostly from lower middle class and working class backgrounds means that it is always half wrong to say that they acted against the working class.

6 According to Wikipedia the GDP of New Zealand was 103,380 in 2006.

7 City Lifestyle

Urban life is strongly mediated by membership and belonging to long-established forms of culture and sociation: social class, ethnicity, religion, nationality and the historical compositions, conflicts and juxtapositions of these structuring taxonomies all continue to undergird the life of any city anywhere. Any analysis of the city that does not understand how these play out in any one place will therefore be deficient but equally those analyses that rest only on these taxonomic variables will miss a critical point: that while city life in most countries still carries the palimpsest of a producerist/industrial society with its relatively rigid and fixed stratifications and distinctions, and is therefore still a background structuring influence, the contemporary city is also the exemplar of its reversal, undoing or liquefaction. If there were such things as 'mainstream' or 'conventional' ways of life, of the sort that 1950s anthropologists of the American and British city were trying to capture in their ethnography, then the arrival of lifestyle might be thought of as a move away from them. For lifestyle is all about the complete realisation of an *achieved* way of life, status and identity and the rejection of ascribed status and stable ways of life.

New forms of identity and belonging have made their presence felt in cities that are based on this switch from industrial manufacturing to cultural and service industries, and from production to consumption as the prime mover of urban ways of life. Urban ways of life are increasingly stylised; fractured along lines of style and choice; heavily influenced by the more central role of the arts, creative industries, the culture industries and the design/fashion/style nexus. City life is now multiple and arranged into lifestyles that correspond to the liquefying times that give rise to them.

Among the most important sources of this liquefaction and recomposition are:

1 The arrival of a consumer society, and consumerism.
2 The deregulation of labour markets, especially in financial sectors, and the greater freedom of more categories of migrant to access urban labour markets.
3 The rise of the creative and cultural industries.
4 The growing significance of an owner-occupying majority of residents and their cultural work in restoring and aestheticising homes and neighbourhoods.

5 Greater levels of social and geographic mobility.
6 The colonisation of inner city areas by countercultural communities, and the establishment of an artistic, creative and avant garde cultural 'atmosphere': Ley's 'structure of feeling' or Shields' 'living on the edge'.
7 Further colonisations by commercial and professional middle class groups who not only promoted new forms of inner city development but their preference for such areas contributed to a revived inner city as a favoured corporate location.
8 Subsequent cultural and developmental transfers to suburbs and suburban centres made after the likeness of the revived inner city, what Ley calls 'retro-fitting the suburbs'.
9 Very significant convergence between economic and cultural development in urban climates where a greater proportion of productive activity is concerned with cultural products and services and where such commodities are characteristically mantled with more aesthetic content.

These changes have not merely affected the anthropology and cultural composition of most cities around the world but they have changed what it is to live in these places, how to live in these places, and are the reason why there has been a renaissance of the city.

This chapter will sketch in the coordinates of these changes, as well as locate key cultural shifts such as the arrival of counter-cultural groups, gentrification and the establishment of gay and lesbian quarters, the arrival and impact of consumerism, the focus on pleasure, pleasurability and self-transformation, and so-called inner city deviance, its surveillance and control. Once these are established, we will be in a position to analyse the specific contents and character of contemporary city *life* and perhaps account for its rising popularity and economic and social significance.

Lifestyle

But first some attention must be given to *lifestyle* as a concept and even as a characterisation of contemporary Western societies. It always runs the risk of becoming a cliché (and spawning many more: empty-nesters, yuppies, 'post-'68' etc.), not least because it has become a template for the identification by marketers and journalists of *lifestyles* themselves, which have been many, varied and cross-referencing; but therefore also confusing, often vacuous or arbitrary. Clichés often arise when a word, often a perfectly good term or concept, simply comes from nowhere and becomes ubiquitous and the butt of jokes. According to Geoffrey Nunberg, 'in the whole of 1967, the word lifestyle appeared in the *Chicago Tribune* exactly seven times. Within five years that figure had jumped to 3300, and the word was on everybody's lips. A newspaper cartoon showed a little boy coming home from school who tells his mom, "today we learned about the unalienable rights – lifestyle, liberty, and the pursuit of happiness"' (Nunberg, 2006: 1).

The butt of the jokes are of course the clichéd enactors of specific lifestyles, not lifestyle itself. Within the cultural political economy of lifestyle there is much competition, criticism, enmity and jealousy. Because lifestyle owes its origin to its counter-cultural antecedents, the notion of cool is very central: which is why 'cool' has become generally synonymous with 'good' or good style. The early jazz clubs, speakeasies, bars and clubs – deep in the heart of the early twentieth century city – were significant in developing a form of individualism commensurate with their counter-culture aspirations. It inspired the personal politics of 'cool' and 'hip', which, as Pountain and Robins (2000) maintain, now dominate contemporary forms of individualism (and we can say lifestyle) everywhere:

> Cool is an oppositional attitude adopted by individuals or small groups to express defiance to authority – whether that of the parent, the teacher, the police, the boss or the prison warden. Put more succinctly, we see Cool as a permanent state of private rebellion. Permanent because Cool is not just some 'phase that you go through', something that you 'grow out of ', but rather something that if once attained remains for life; private because Cool is not a collective political response but a stance of individual defiance, which does not announce itself in strident slogans but conceals its rebellion behind a mask of ironic impassivity. This attitude is in the process of becoming the dominant type of relation between people in Western societies, a new secular virtue. No-one wants to be good any more, they want to be Cool, and this desire is no longer confined to teenagers but is to be found in a sizeable minority even of the over-50s who were permanently affected by the '60s counter-culture. (2000: 142)

Until the advent of the *sociology* of lifestyle, there were few performative, active concepts designed to describe the way people lived their lives, how they orientated themselves through the life course, how they *chose* a particular *kind* of life. In many ways, of course, the terms 'tradition' and 'culture' were used before the advent of 'lifestyle' and these tend, if not absolutely, to circumscribe a life, to describe the pattern and content of a largely unvarying style of life. Tradition of course appeals to a sense of the timeless unquestioned content of a life, a life dictated by past precedent, creed and law, while the cultural turn that accompanied the analysis of modern and more recent times attempted to capture the dimensions of class, youth, regional, national, migrant and ethnic (etc.) cultures as if they produced some degree of fixity and identifiable collective content (literally *a culture*) to the lives and orientations of those who belonged or subscribed to them.[1] We might say that prior to the proliferation of lifestyle in the modern West, sociologists tended to work with the idea of lives that were socially and culturally structured, determined by some enduring notion of particular *ways of life*; that individual lives were synonymous with the values of collective and cultural collectivities. When Young and Willmott wrote *Family and Kinship in East London* (1957), their aim was to capture sociologically the urban way of life of working class people in East London. They knew in advance that this would be very different from the urban ways of life in Levittown, Chicago or indeed from the small town life recorded by social anthropologists, such as John Davis's Pisticci in Italy (Davis, 1973).

The lifestyle turn, by contrast, suggests a radically different society and sociality where both ways of life and knowable and enduring cultural entities have been displaced, fragmented or even liquefied by the rise of individualism and consumerism. Where ways of life were overdetermined by social structure, lifestyle tends to be characteristically underdetermined. Lifestyle largely replaces (but not completely ...) the structuring role of class and other stratifications (which is one reason why sociologists Pakulski and Waters (1995) can talk of *The Death of Class*). They remain palimpsest-like as cultural backgrounds but they no longer hold so much sway over individuals and fewer individuals and institutions have roles that include their inculcation. As Featherstone argued in one of the first attempts to raise lifestyle as a fitting metaphor for social and cultural analysis, it can be defined as 'individuality, self-expression, and stylistic self-consciousness. One's body, clothes, speech, leisure pastimes, eating and drinking preferences, home car, choice of holidays, etc., are to be regarded as indicators of the individuality of taste and sense of style of the owner/consumer' (1987: 55). Summing up the subsequent utilisation of lifestyle by sociologists, Sam Brinkley suggests that they 'have considered lifestyles as accomplishing two things: they affirm as sense of self or identity, but they also differentiate individuals from others, thereby contributing to the further stratification of social groups (2007: 111). As Brinkley affirms, this was a capacity noted by Max Weber as early as 1946 but it had become a *distinguishing* feature of the societies described by Bourdieu in 1984 and even more strongly by Bauman in 2000.

> sociologies of lifestyle bring together two important aspects of social behaviour: the subjective dimensions of human agency, and the objective structures that compel people to behave in the way they do. Moreover, lifestyles are seen as increasingly prominent in modern societies where the domain of uncontrolled

> choice is seen as expanding – a defect partly attributable to erosion of the old culture of 'mass' consumption defined by uniformity and mass production, and the growing influence of a more personalized culture of consumption. As such, patterns of living mediated by consumer markets, what we can call 'consumer lifestyles', render personal identity a project of personal choosing. Identity is an activity of aesthetic self-fashioning or creative improvisation, which we undertake in the many choices that compose our lifestyles – choices in food, clothing, travel destinations and so on. (Brinkley, 2007: 112)

The origins of 'lifestyle' are indeed frequently attributed to the breakdown of Fordist mass production (and its mass cultures) and the restructuring of production and economies in the 1980s following the fiscal crises of the late 1970s, the advent of Reganomics and Thatcherism and the general freeing-up of labour markets, financial controls and state regulation. Such conditions removed the overweening influence of paternalistic capitalism and welfare states, and cast the individual adrift, and, as Bauman notes, forced to make (often difficult) decisions that were hitherto taken by others. Lifestyle can occasionally strike one as relatively superficial as compared with class, tradition and culture, somehow less solid and less consequential. This is because it *is* less solid but it is far from inconsequential because the decisions and choices that individuals must now make are not purely aesthetic; as we have seen, they are also ethical, political and moral, to do with health, risk management, financial security, providence and intergenerational transfers (upwards and downwards).

Those accounts that see these transformations and thus lifestyle as originating in the economic changes in the 1970s and 1980s and a politics that was consistent with making such profound changes are often advanced as sufficient to account for the rise of individualistic consumer culture but there are at least four other stories that need to be told before we can understand the significance of lifestyle in its specific historical manifestation in contemporary cities. Although there are of course rural and semi-rural lifestyles and these have become extremely important in places like the English countryside and the Australian 'sea change' phenomenon (leaving the city for a small coastal community), and although there can be lifestyle in any location (migrant, ex-pat, grey nomad etc.), lifestyle has been *particularly* associated with the city and especially the inner areas of the major cities. This is not because such areas are different in kind or even because people who live there are more individualistic, consumerist, or make different choices but because they have a different intensity, or what Ley calls a 'structure of feeling' (Ley, 1996: 38); but because this reflects their potential for variety but also their creativity, since many of the styles themselves originate there and their originators, what Florida calls the creative class, increasingly chose to live in or nearer them and make new lifestyle the object of their creative impulse. The stories that can be told concern therefore:

1 The inner city and the arrival of consumerism.
2 The historic colonisation of the inner city by the artistic and political avant garde.
3 The centrality of pleasurability, aestheticisation and its city ordering in the likeness of tourism.
4 The consummation of these three in the form of what Gary Bridge (2000) and Tim Butler and Garry Robson (2003) have called the 'habitus of gentrification'.

The inner city and the arrival of consumerism

Like any of the stories that comprise the emergence of lifestyle in the city, the origins of consumerism have social and political as well as economic foundations and the human agency stories are frequently about a relatively small group of politically progressive young middle class people living in the inner city. Although consumption was likely to change during the long economic boom in the aftermath of the Second World War, the arrival of consumerism, consumer power, consumer consciousness as we know it, was far from inevitable. Certainly it did not arise spontaneously in every quarter of the Western world. Neither did it arise when it is often held to have arrived, in the early 1980s following the fiscal crises of the late 1970s, the economic restructuring and flexibilisation of mass industries, the extension of consumer credit and the proliferation of commodities in the new post-Fordist world. All of these factors propelled consumerism along but in a way all of them depended upon the existence of a new kind of consumer and a consumer culture that had made their appearance much earlier, between the late 1950s and the 1970s.

In the mid-1950s the Western world was suddenly inundated with an unprecedented *range* of products, many of them entirely new. The origins of the spectacular department store and the arcades belong to an earlier urban period in the late nineteenth century, but although many people flocked to see the fantastic, lit shop windows at that time, such conspicuous consumption was then the preserve of a minority even if real wages rose among the employed. However, the early decades were dogged by economic depression and then from the late 1930s until the late 1940 war pretty much ruined the pleasurability of shopping.

The new post-war consumer was the result of dramatically rising affluence, the end of rationing (in the UK), the extension of markets in the post-war period and particularly the extension of the US consumer markets and levels of consumption to Europe and Australasia. In Britain, for example, real disposable income per capita rose by 30% in the 1950s and a further 22% in the 1960s (Alexander et al., 2007: 6). Car registrations in Britain rose from 5.5 million in 1960 to 13.5 million in 1973 and the number of supermarkets where a weekly shop could be brought home in one journey rose from 10 in 1947 to 6300 by 1960 and 28,000 by 1970. In the USA new shopping centres began to open at ever-increasing rates: some 5000 opened between 1963 and 1969 (Ley, 1996: 176). Generalising, one can say that many British and European consumers were confronted by a shift from familiar almost unchanging forms of consumption and product choice to the shock of both the new *products* and unprecedented *choice*. *Which? 50 Years, 1957–2007* argues that many of the new products made exaggerated claims, many were dangerous, shoppers had little or no advice on what or how to buy in this new marketplace, and they seemed to have few if any rights (*Which? Magazine*, 2007). Moreover, the producers themselves provided hardly any information about their own products so the making of informed choices, let alone sound, rational choices, was a precarious matter. In many cases individuals heard of the availability of new products but could not find them or other comparable products easily. While this aroused criticism and the call for more regulation (the National Council of Women called for the British Standards Institution to become involved in the regulation of consumer goods as early as 1946), the most significant effect appeared to be the excitement aroused by the opportunities to see and buy goods on a level never imagined before. Gareth Shaw and his team at the University of Exeter are currently conducting a project called 'Reconstructing Consumer Landscapes, 1945–75'. They are particularly interested in shopper reactions to new shopping experiences such as supermarkets:

> Mollie Tarrant, a commentator for the British Market Research Board, noted in 1964 that: 'To an unparalleled extent, the housewife can also shop for food, household goods and other things in the one store. Inside the supermarket she is in a new and exciting, although to some people a confusing, atmosphere. She may shop to music or relayed sales messages: she is confronted with new products, daily bargains, unusual forms and colour combinations in packaging and increasingly sophisticated methods of display.' www.sobe.ex.ac.uk/research/consumer_landscapes/shopping/rise.html
>
> (Accessed 1 December 2007)

The new, exciting and confusing state of shoppers was widely perceived and acted upon. It was one of the key sales lines for the growing market for marketing and radio and television advertising: shoppers needed more information if they were to develop confidence in a product. In 1964, for example, in Australia *The Journal of the Retail Trade Association* ventured that 'The housewife of the 19th century had a limited education and needed the help of a specialist sales person. National and mass marketing nowadays makes for a more informed consumer who can be expected to choose intelligently from the open stock presentation' (Kingston, 1994: 101). However, the claims of advertisers were seen by the early pioneers of consumerism as part of the problem rather than the solution.

It is ironic then that one of the key pioneers of consumerism was not an economist, a marketer, an advertiser or an entrepreneur but a sociologist who had previously written the Manifesto for the Labour Party's successful 1945 election campaign, and by the late 1950s was the Labour Party's Senior Research Director. Aged 34, Michael Young had recently completed the urban sociological classic *Family and Kinship in East London* (with Peter Willmott). He had also pitched the idea of a consumer advisory service for the 1950 Labour Party Election Manifesto to Harold Wilson, then President of the Board of Trade. Wilson rejected the proposal outright, arguing that it was already being done where there was a need for it: in respect of cars by the Automobile Association and in respect of electrical goods by the British Standards Authority.

However, Young had seen the results of an internal Labour party survey which clearly showed that there was a lot of public need and support for it. Moreover, there was such an entity in the USA, in the form of a reputable magazine *Consumer Reports* that offered impartial advice on consumer goods and services and had done so since 1936 (Young, 2007: 6). The main sticking point for a similar venture in the UK was the widespread belief that this sort of magazine would run into its more stringent libel laws; that any damaging information (critical or comparative) on a product could give grounds for legal action. Michael Young tested this proposition with a top lawyer who found no such impediment in British law and when a friend came up with the winning title *Which?* the project got under way.

It was to be a magazine that tested, assessed and compared similar products and therefore offered the consumer informed choice, safeguards and advice. Evidently it was much needed, since some of its earliest findings showed the extent to which manufacturers were prepared to lie in the absence of effective information. *Which?* showed how all aspirin tablets were identical despite their wildly varying prices and claims and the bizarre fact that the law did not require orange juice to actually contain the juice of any oranges or anything from an orange at all (Young, 2007: 7).

Nonetheless, even journalists were wary of British libel laws and nothing was printed about the embryonic magazine after its launch, despite its scandalous findings. It was only through a friend of Young's on *The Times* that a bye-line was published by the women's correspondent. It was enough: at the end of the week it was published they had picked up 7000 subscribers and further coverage by an astonished press. They had sufficient funds to sustain the magazine and it never looked back. In the early years they tested basic products like toasters, prams, radios and fridges. *Which?* became an institution as well as the trusted guide for major and everyday purchasing. However, they expanded into more and more areas of consumption of goods and services. In 1963, the year the contraceptive pill was launched *Which?* published a contraceptive supplement which included a 'Best Buy Condoms' feature. After that, sister *Which?* magazines were launched, starting with *Motoring Which?* in 1965 and *Money Which?* in 1968. *Money Which?* was among the first to demonstrate the arbitrary charging structures and paternalist delivery of banking services, arguing that banks should be like any other service or commodity. More than that, this magazine offered to help subscribers 'invest, borrow, insure and (legally) avoid taxes' (Young, 2007: 14). It was among the first to test the harmful content of cigarettes and publish league tables and the first to show how few toothpastes actually contained anything that fights tooth decay. It also saw its role as fighting to change laws as they related to consumer affairs and rights. So, for example, it successfully fought for the Unsolicited Goods and Services Act of 1971, the Fair Trading Act of 1973, the Consumer Credit Act of 1974 (which required true annual rates of interest be given in adverts and product information) the 1980 Competition Act, the Financial Services Act of 1986, the access to Medical Records Act of 1988, and the 1990 Property Misdescription Act.

By the 1980s, when consumerism is often thought to have been evolving into the defining mentality of the age, it was clear that *Which?* had already affected something of a revolution in consumption and consumption styles. Consumerism is typically considered to be an artefact of what Miles (1997) sees as a monolithic 'consumer capitalism' that creates 'a way of life' that is dependent on the illusion of freedom and choice that consumption offers but cannot deliver. As he says, 'by creating a society dependent upon the exploitation of undifferentiated design – design which is lauded as individualistic when it is patently not – consumer capitalism is able to reproduce itself'. By contrast, Miles argues that in the USA consumerism has been described as 'a movement to protect consumer interests'. The problem with divorcing these two forces or movements is that they are clearly related. *Which? Magazine* was clearly a consumer protection organisation, but to imagine that it had no impact on the development of consumerism is simply wrong. First, consumerism is often thought of as the exercise of individual choice but the techniques and confidence required to make choices are not given but learned through increasingly mediated processes (Bauman, 2000 calls this 'connoisseurship'). Arguably, *Which? Magazine* did not so much protect consumers as produce them in the first place: confused and duped post-war shoppers were given the facilities to know about products, consider parameters of choice and make decisions based on a comparative understanding of product availability set against their own needs and financial circumstances. These might now be taken for granted but even today a considerable amount of effort goes into consumer information that enables consumerism to operate smoothly.

Second, *Which? Magazine* and other media like it provide the confidence to consume in an atmosphere that endorses and promotes consumerism as a normative part of everyday life and in this sense it was a liberating intervention. *Which? Magazine's* party trick was precisely to point up and put an end to the proliferation of exploitation through undifferentiated products. The lesson learned about aspirin tablets became a model line of inquiry and has remained so.

Third, although *Which? Magazine* always tested and compared a range of products at different quality and price locations in the market, thus enabling subscribers to optimise their buying, by doing so it also introduced consumers to products and qualities of products that they might otherwise not see. Although window shopping or the potential to see what one cannot afford (or reasonably acquire) was established long before, it is nonetheless true that shopping habits and intimate understanding of commodities remained more spatially differentiated, along class, ethnicity, region and income lines. In assembling a market range for any given product *Which? Magazine* detached class- (and region-) based consumer habits and created the potential for *desire* – desire if not for the most luxurious then at least a better, more desirable product. *Which? Magazine* also confused former class- or income-based decision making through its analysis of 'Best Buys'. Best Buys cancel out one-dimensional scales of choice based on ability to buy and introduce best choice (e.g. value for money, quality and longevity become considerations as well as price). Fourth, *Which? Magazine* promoted and in fact made possible the necessary development of *connoisseurship*. One of the core reasons why Young became interested in developing a consumer movement was that among his own circle of family and friends it was almost impossible to have sensible conversations about products. They didn't know what they were or even where to find them and if they did they had no way of knowing in advance what they were like, how they compared to rival products and so on. After the implantation of *Which? Magazine* and other consumer-lifestyle products and media, it became possible for people to become knowledgeable, to discuss products and manufacturers *expertly and therefore to judge how well consumer choices were being made by others*. As Bauman (2000) suggests, knowing what and how to consume began to confer status and position in a consumerist society but it is hard to see how this can develop if Miles' model of the design-duped consumer was ever true. Consumer choice magazines, whether in print or other media, were co-constitutive of the consumerism that eventuated in most Western locations. Apart from similar governmental organisations, these are indeed the only spaces where consumerism can generate its necessary appreciation of the choices at hand.

Consumer interest in and demand for information was one reason why people's consumption extended backwards, as it were, to second-hand goods, particularly for aesthetic and cultural goods that conjured up pasts, past fashions, prior art and design movements and periods, as well as furnish them with the necessary 'parts' and accessories for renovated and restored homes (particularly eighteenth and nineteenth century homes) in the inner city. The British TV comedy *Steptoe and Son* from the early 1960s is instructive for its setting in a time when things that are considered antiques and valuable today could be considered 'junk'. *Antiques Roadshow* did not air on TV anywhere until there was some considerable enthusiasm already generated in popular culture as a result of a renewed interest in history and heritage: it was first shown in the UK in 1977.

Retro consumerism

Although timeless, the origin of the efflorescence of contemporary second-hand markets and retro taste dates back to the immediate post-war period when Oxfam opened its first shop in Oxford in 1947. These days charity shops are an established and even fashionable feature of the urban landscape but they only sprang to life after the Second World War. And it was largely out of that wartime voluntary spirit of helping disadvantaged and needy people that the idea and enthusiasm for them grew. Oxfam was originally a wartime organisation (The Oxford Committee for Famine Relief) to help famine-affected people in Nazi-occupied Greece. After the war it continued to help Middle East refugees and as part of that campaign it had the crazy idea to take over a disused shop, fill it with donated clothes and objects (with a few celebrity items thrown in for good luck) and sell them for bargain prices. On its opening day it was inundated by a very excitable crowd of bargain hunters and sold out. The enthusiasm surprised everyone. The rest is history. That shop is still trading and Oxfam have added another 750 to their empire, powered by an army of 20,000 volunteers.

Charities carefully targeted their openings in those areas with the right demographics. Conservative taste eschewed the second-hand and used markets, particularly for clothes and consumer durables, and this included large sections of the respectable and affluent working class. Charity shops soon learned that their best opportunities were to sell to the younger educated and less conforming demographic who were filling university towns in large numbers and then moving into the inner city, often to former rundown areas of poor rented housing and industry. The geography of charity shops, at least during the 1960s to 1980s, was largely synonymous with the inner city, the counter-cultures and subsequently, key areas of gentrification. Aside from environmental awareness of the implications of rising consumption of new goods there was a coalescence of several important consumer-orientated factors:

1 A generalised suspicion of marketing-led consumer growth, especially for new factory-produced goods.
2 A consequent aesthetic for second-hand goods, recycling and restoration of usable goods (older houses, cars, furniture, clothes etc.).
3 A renewed interest in crafts and hand-made production, particularly pottery, fabrics, jewellery, gift wares and foods.

This counter-cultural constellation of consumption found specific and much repeated urban expression in particular 'opportunistic' spaces of the city. At Camden Lock in London there was a very early example of one such spark point of consumer/lifestyle-driven forms of urban regeneration.

The Camden Lock effect

In the late 1960s and early 1970s inner London was changing rapidly. Much of its former skilled working class had moved out of London and its manufacturing base had also begun to contract and relocate (Lawless, 1989). Warehouses and associated industries around the Regent's Canal at Camden Lock went into decline earlier as a result of increased road haulage in the 1950s. In 1971 three young men with an idea to develop this area leased some large buildings there, including Dingwall's former timber yard, and then began to sublet space, largely as traditional craft workshops. They opened a weekend market on the cobbled open yards in order to offer opportunities for the craft businesses to sell directly to the public, but the market also attracted businesses selling antiques, second-hand goods, clothing, food and drinks. Being close to the canal and the weekend barge activity, but also a colourful alternative cultural event to mainstream London, the market soon became very popular to the point where it was also a must-see tourist attraction, particularly because it offered a rare Sunday market.

The market also attracted like-minded people into the area to live, giving it a more cohesive or coherent cultural feel, but in addition to that it began to shift the character of business in the area. First, other markets grew up

Image 7.1 Camden Lock, London (photo Adrian Franklin)

in the immediate vicinity, but then the existing businesses began to change hands in the main Camden Town–Chalk Farm area. From largely generic stores serving a local population the new businesses, bars and restaurants began to cater mostly for visitors who came because this was now a fashionable cultural centre. Second, the studios of TV-AM, the UK's first breakfast TV station, were built in the heart of the Camden Lock area and this was followed by a third and consolidating group of international media companies.

Inevitably the market switched to seven-day trading during the 1990s, a time when the infrastructure of the entire area received a makeover and the market itself was renovated to become three floors of shops in the style of a Victorian trading hall.

The events at Camden Lock over this thirty-year period have been repeated in so many other British cities and cities in Canada, Australia, the USA and Europe that one can begin to talk about a nearly universal transformation of the inner city throughout the Western world, though initially it was noticed as a predominantly housing phenomenon (Ley suggests it was identified first in 1977), the oddly named 'gentrification' process. Ley quotes the Mayor of Baltimore in 1977 in what must amount to a prescient speech:

> people are beginning to come back and live here … they're beginning to find out that there is something alive here. They're coming back for … life, pride, and activity. (Ley, 1996: 33)

Ley also quotes the Mayor of St Pauls, Minnesota speaking in the same month. He said:

> Something is happening in our inner cities as a result of the fuel crunch, as a result of a new lifestyle, as a result of housing quality or residential qualities that cannot be matched by new construction ... there is a very discernible return to our cities. (Ley, 1996: 33)

According to Ley's definitive study of gentrification, and particularly as it played out in Canada, there were around 14 different descriptors of this movement by 1984 (Ley, 1996: 34) and although they ranged from those that emphasised redevelopment, those that emphasised renovation, those that emphasised cultural efflorescence and those that emphasised social displacement, none of these accounts makes any sense when taken out of the context of the thirty-year period in which they took place. Gentrification does not reduce to a primarily economic, cultural or housing event because all three are implicated and co-constitutive of a transition. On the other hand, from a historical-sociological point of view, it is fairly clear how the process tended to work out in most places: who colonised the inner city in new ways, who became attracted to the lifestyle that was established there, how such areas became epicentres of political and cultural change and whose cultural industries became expressive of an emerging lifestyle and modern stance, and finally why they became incredibly sought after as living spaces, investment spaces and new industrial spaces.

Of all the characterisations of gentrification, the one that stands out is contained in Ley's broad-brush chapter called 'Follow the Hippies': Cultural Politics of Gentrification'. Because it is less tied down with the taxonomic variables of housing analysis, something that tends to bog down and obscure as much as it reveals, it is able to make sense of the interrelationships between politics, culture, housing, investment, development and historical patterns of inner city social transition. However, it is fairly clear that the transition began and ended in a deliberate attempt to live a different lifestyle. Far from being derivative of economic and social processes, though of course intimately linked to them, Ley makes a convincing case that a new and experimental lifestyle took root in the relatively cheap, vacant and culturally permissive space of the inner city in the late 1960s and early 1970s and in many ways realised the dreams and aspirations of a large and educated generation.

If we are to follow the so-called hippies into their inner city adventures there is always the danger that they will seem to be the initiators of everything that follows, so at least some space needs to be dedicated to reconstructing the sort of inner city space they located to and also to ask what it was about this space that was commensurate with their own aspirations. At the time the

1960s youth cultures began to move into the inner city, its housing was on its last legs, its landlords having housed a sequence of poorer households on steadily declining rental incomes. Ley suggests that a turning point was reached: far from being the last opportunity to squeeze money from dilapidated housing before being sold off for development and more profitable use, the arrival of this group ushered in a new phenomenon. Unlike previous groups of the poor, new migrants and the underclass who lived there out of necessity and from a lack of choice, Ley argues that the youth culture of the 1960s constituted

> the first in a new sequence of residents for whom the inner city would not be the site of last resort for households with few choices, but rather, the preferred location of a middle class cohort with a rather different vision of the opportunities of city living, indeed a group whose residential location was part of the repertoire of their cultural identity. (1996: 175)

What was it about this location that attracted them? Undoubtedly the fact that it was available, cheap and central to the city cannot be discounted, but it was far more than this. Poor inner city neighbourhoods had long held a fascination with the social elites; not least for the *freedom* they had historically always offered respectable upper- and middle-class society. As Seth Koven reveals in his *Slumming: Sexual and Social Politics in London*:

> Upper-class men and women had long ventured into the low haunts of London in pursuit of illicit pleasure. In 1670, the Queen and the Duchesses of Richmond and Buckingham caused a public uproar when they disguised themselves as 'country lasses' at Bartholomew Fair to mingle undetected with the common people. (Koven, 2004: 5)

'Slumming it' is also related to the zoning of pleasure in the Elizabethan city: although the period of Shakespearean theatre in London was very prolific and popular, it was nonetheless not permitted inside the city itself. Because many of the theatres were clustered alongside pubs, inns and brothels in poorer areas on the social margin, they constituted a very specific 'pleasure space' where such freedom of expression and behaviour was sanctioned, if not fully approved. This set in train the habit of travelling out of everyday spaces to *ritual* spaces of sexual political transgression, personal freedom and self-making (see Rojek, 1995: 85–8; Shields, 1991).[2]

Although persistent and part and parcel of London's tourist trade, by the late nineteenth century slumming was being rivalled by a sincere and political wish to visit and mingle with the poor for philanthropic reasons.

> Slumming, the word and the activities associated with it, was distinguished historically by a persistent pattern of disavowal. It was a pejorative term used to sneer at the supposedly misguided efforts of other people. As a form of urban social exploration, it bore the obloquy of sensationalism, sexual transgression, and self-seeking gratification, not sober inquiry and self-denying service to others. (Koven, 2004: 33)

Nonetheless, as Koven argues, it is hard to distinguish the purely transgressive from the charitable and reformist, and in any case the sexual and moral lapses of the inner city slum permitted such issues to be discussed more openly, but more than that to be used as a theatre for personal experimentation:

> The metropolitan slums provided well-to-do philanthropic men and women with an actual and imagined location where, with the approval of society, they could challenge prevailing norms about class and gender relations and sexuality. These men and women may well have needed the freedom the slums offered them more than the poor in their adopted neighbourhoods benefited from their benevolent labours. Such claims capture the complex social dynamics of philanthropic encounters between rich and poor, as well as my own ambivalence about them. Reformers' creativity and passion, their sincerely felt and lived ethos of service, inspire admiration. At the same time, many were deeply invested in the titillating squalor of the slums, which they used as stages upon which they enacted emancipatory experiments in reimagining themselves. Synonymous with squalid tenements and soiled lives, the slums of London ironically functioned as sites of personal liberation and self-realization – social, spiritual, and sexual – for several generations of educated men and women. (Koven, 2004: 34)

Such places provided spaces of relative freedom, both from the norms of respectable society, church and state but also of specific moral communities. Inner London, like inner New York, was characterised by a social and cultural heterogeneity, diversity and difference and the familiarity and tolerance that this engendered. It might have been a spectacle to see but it was also a refuge from the requirement to conform. Such spaces, in the pubs, bars, coffee houses, brothels, clubs, speakeasies and theatres, provided a home for a range of non-conformists and non-conformist discussion and dialogue. Because they were the natural habitat of writers and artists, poets and students, musicians and actors they became places of creativity, challenges to the status quo and social, political and sexual experimentation. And, because most of these sociations were relatively public and performance-orientated, their presence in such places changed the atmosphere or social tone, drawing in crowds, audiences, followers, fans, spectators, fellow travellers and acolytes.

Chris Rojek (1995) usefully distinguishes between what he calls Modernity 1 and Modernity 2, where the former is the search for and imposition of order and where the latter expressed 'change, flux, de-differentiation, and metamorphosis' (1995: 79), where leisure lives were to be transformative, experimental, non-conformist and deviant. Drawing on Nietzsche, Rojek also argues that in modern societies the *Apollonian* impulse towards control and order is always in tension with the *Dionysian* impulse (Dionysus was the god of wine) towards sensuality, abandon, affirmation of life, intoxication and governance by passion. Nietzsche argues that the possibility of a total order is always an illusion, that 'change is inevitable and must be positively embraced' (1995: 81). Nietzsche argued for, and helped into being, the possibility of a new Dionysian age which must affirm a 'questing curiosity', avoid self-denial and search for freedom and desire.

Throughout the twentieth century breaking free from Modernity 1 and pursuing the Dionysian impulse of Modernity 2 was expressed in many places by many different people – but it was in the convivial atmosphere of inner city life that it was expressed most. The black jazz clubs of the USA in the early twentieth century provide an archetypal space of escape but also of expression for people who had suffered intolerable rejection and marginalisation as they became subject to an emergent (white) protestant modern order. The sociological interest in jazz is not restricted to its musical styles, its cultural forms and origins; it is also possible to talk of the social spaces of jazz as a counter-cultural space or deviant culture which had a very significant international impact on city life everywhere.

Jazz clubs emerged in the days of alcohol prohibition as sites away from surveillance and the policing of alcohol and drugs. They then became synonymous with a variety of counter-cultures (black, gangster, immigrant, youth) in which individual freedom and Dionysian values were cultivated. It is for this reason that jazz was often referred to as 'the devil's music'. Critically, jazz opened up spaces of cultural transition:

> jazz was welcoming, inclusive, open. It replaced minstrelsy with a cultural site where all Americans could participate, speak to one another, override or ignore or challenge or slide by the society's fixations on racial and ethnic stereotypes. Black Americans (and other ethnic outsiders) could use it to enter mainstream society, white Americans could flee to it from mainstream society, and the transactions created a flux and flow that powered American cultural syntheses. (Santoro, 2001)

In this way jazz played an important role in breaking down traditional lines of American protestant culture and paving the way for a more permissive, open (Dionysian) society. But not just in America.

Meller (1976) showed how jazz jumped the Atlantic to England during and after the First World War and the social and cultural impact it had. Up until then working class leisure culture was tightly organised around neighbourhoods and their chapels. Dancing was strictly supervised and limited and music styles conformed to the stringent moral regime of non-conformist (protestant) life. The arrival of jazz and watered-down dance variants reconfigured this completely. Coinciding with new public transport systems in the city, electrification and rising youth wages, the new music found expression in new inner-city centre dance halls. These were commercial and more permissive and as the possibility and styles of dancing (among unmarried young people) became more exciting (not to say intoxicating), so thousands of dance schools emerged to educate the new generation into jazz-inspired freedoms. Among other things, this ushered in more intimate premarital social relations between the sexes, the beginnings of teenage culture and more freedom for women, particularly to move freely and safely in public space unsupervised.

Popular and rock music followed hard on the heels of jazz, copying or merely inhabiting its styles, language and spaces – most of them in the heart and soul of the city. Here were the main centres of musical publishing, performance and organisation. In the post-war period the small club lands of jazz were no longer large enough for hugely expanded markets and so the larger mainstream theatres and cinemas, even sports arenas were encroached upon. All of these interpellated a growing educated, young generation whose cultural influences included the Beat poets, Bob Dylan, Dylan Thomas, the Beatles and civil rights.

The fashion world was also increasingly related to the leisure, artistic and performative industries of the inner cities and less exclusively to the wealthy elite. As with other areas of the arts in the post-war period it was both revolutionary and popular and through the performances of Jimmy Hendrix, the Beatles, Janis Joplin, but also new retailers such as Biba, and retailers in the Kings Road and Carnaby Street, the inner city began to take on a particular 'look', the so-called 'new look'. By the time the 1960s counter-culture was in full swing, the fashion/art/rock cultures were interleaved, evoking a transcendental, transformative and emancipatory culture that was focused on the inner city but few other (permanent) spaces. It eschewed the suburbs as 'straight', 'square' and 'dodgy' and these sites of 'straight' and 'oppressive' social reproduction remained tainted with boredom and a stultifying mindlessness. The country, particularly rustic lifestyles on communes, constituted a significant element of the generational experimentation; however, compared to city life it was less successful and enduring (Munro-Clark, 1986). Certainly the squatting and short-life housing collective lifestyles proved long-lasting and beneficial for other less affluent groups (Franklin, 1984). Many of these formed the bases for the third tier, Housing Association form of tenure.

While the mainstream relentlessly pursued a technical modernity, this culture reaffirmed a medieval orientated, crafts-based, natural material culture.

It reprised the Arts and Crafts Movement of the end of the nineteenth century, it embraced surrealism, transcendentalism, Buddism, yoga, meditation etc., and it championed the conservation and restoration of the old as against the relentless onslaught of the new.

While mainstream culture was future-focused the counter-culture concentrated on the past and the present. While the mainstream produced ever more disposable goods and convenience modern processed foods, the counter-culture produced things made by hand and favoured 'wholefood alternatives'. The wholefood store became something of a social centre to life in, for example, inner San Francisco, Bristol, Copenhagen, London and Chicago. Run often as cooperatives, they provided meeting, information and messaging space for entire neighbourhoods. Wholefood stores spawned new movements for real ale, real bread, organic produce, green milk and fair trade products. Famously, The Body Shop emerged from the efflorescence of these new business cultures in Brighton, UK.

Whereas the modern mainstream became an international 'Western' culture, the alternative counter-culture embraced and hybridised international peasant and indigenous cultural influences, bringing into view for the first time Indian, American, African and North African civilisations, culminating in the establishments of WOMAD international world music festival in 1980, styled after the fashion of most rock festivals. Indeed, their ultra public, communitarian ethos together with their belief in *staging* their lifestyle regardless of whether it was economic, artistic or everyday rendered city life into a generalised theatrical form. And the dominant form that it took was the festival, a postmodern return of the carnivalesque. As Ley argues, 'In their spontaneity and expressiveness, hippy subculture became the living out of a continuous festival. Like street players in costume, they have transformed the pavement into sort of "living theatre" (Ley, 1996: 180 quoting Stuart Hall, 1969: 70).

As early as the mid-1970s, the previously shocking, scandalous and counter-cultural lifestyle orientation of the baby-boom college leavers was becoming mainstream and fusing with or merging into the key new industries: mass media, retail, design and creative industries, welfare and caring professions. Clearly their artistic, experimental, change-orientated, self-determining, aestheticising and progressive qualities were not incommensurate with business success or the reconfigured commodification of more and more aspects of life in the city. Paradoxically, hippie culture championed another element of protestantism that was entirely consistent with capitalism: the elevation of the self as the centre of aesthetic, cultural, spiritual and everyday life. While their commune experiments at collective living failed, their unswerving attention to small business and self-advancement was remarkable. There were notable early successes that shared aspects of the Camden Lock effect: the late Anita Roddick opened her first counter-cultural Body Shop store in Brighton in 1976, but by 2005 there were 2045 stores around the world. The idea and significance of urban lifestyle was realised by Terence Conran's Habitat chain (first store in London in 1964), which currently numbers 74. Although associated with a relatively up-market urban gentrification, the store also owed its success to extending and making available values that originated in early counter-cultural circles. According to Habitat's Wikipedia page, 'Conran has said the main reason for the shop's initial success was that Habitat was one of the few places that sold cheap pasta storage jars just as the market for dried pasta took off in the UK'. Richard Branson also began his business career solidly within counter-cultural circles, starting a student magazine in 1970, establishing Virgin, a record retail business, in 1973, and signing the Sex Pistols to his newly formed recording company, Virgin Records, in 1977. Currently his Virgin Group is worth $3 billion and employs 24,000 people around the world.

Ley argues that those formerly run-down areas of the inner city that were initially colonised by the artistic avant garde/counter-culture became highly attractive to the more mainstream middle class home buyers once these areas had been rendered colourful, different, festive and community orientated through their new urban lifestyles. By comparison, the established middle class outer suburbs which were more quiet, privatized, conservative and exclusive, became less attractive. Ley makes much of the role of artists in this transition arguing that they form a 'priestly caste in a secular society' whose 'artistic aura has the capacity to transform the meaning and value of space – and thereby its economic values also. In deeply devalued districts in inner Chicago property prices inflated six to tenfold in a decade with the influx of artists and their followers' (Ley, 1996: 191).

I want to extend the idea that the new city life was far more than merely a cultural change in composition and activity. As Butler and Robson argue for the suburban-reared gentrifiers, 'the inner city provided the excitement and cultural buzz that had been so lacking in many of their childhoods and had been awakened by the experience of being at university' (Butler and Robson, 2003: 163). Of course, to unlock precisely what Butler and Robson mean by 'buzz and excitement' (though it is well taken) is the key to understanding contemporary city life. Certainly, those cities that have it have thrived while those that did not, have not. When we examine the constituents of buzz and excitement it is important to understand them as background ambiances that can be anticipated, lived in and embraced. Producing them required the sustained and intense presence of clearly new types of activity. Such cultures produced and supported highly ritualised performances of individual and group transition and in so doing they inscribed a transformative quality on both everyday life and the spaces in which it took place. They were appealing and attractive to outsiders not only because they were inclusive, inviting, communitarian and performative but because they offered a highly *interpellating* experience: something that hailed most if not all members of a generation and class. Of course, the cultures that took root in such areas were not content to merely change their own way of life. They saw their future as ushering change to society generally and so they therefore projected this culture outwards into public spaces of performance, and via those to a general public. What they offered was not a particular life but immersion in the transformative atmosphere of on-going change. The interpellation offered not only the transition from mainstream, conservative and quiet ways of life, it also offered transition itself.

This analysis has produced a 'stage theory' of gentrification in which mainstream middle class professionals, are eventually followed by the more conservative private sector managers, sales workers and financial professionals, but more importantly it demonstrates a more *general* transformation of taste, practice and culture. In addition to the terraced nineteenth century housing of the inner city, new build developments with slick, crisp architectural flourishes extended their cultural grip on the wider city – and elsewhere, e.g. O'Connor and Wynne's (2000) study of people moving into newly built development in Manchester (see also Butler and Robson's *London Calling* of 2003 for variations and adjustments to crude models of gentrification).

In the inevitable competition for residential demand and suburban renewal, the experience of gentrification and the ingredients of the city life it produced as benchmarks were drawn upon in so-called suburban retrofitting. Increasingly this involves securing hub areas that have critical masses of residents, lifestyle spaces (parks, cafés, restaurants, squares) public arts and performance (Garreau, 1992).

The habitus of gentrification

Gentrification is a highly ambiguous term, as it is uncritically applied to the renovation of older inner areas of cities. Its name suggests that new middle class groups are moving into working class areas of the inner city and displacing working class households. In some areas this has been true, although as we have seen in the case of Camden Lock it often takes place when working class inhabitants have already begun to vacate such areas in favour of the outer suburbs and new towns. Equally, when we look at who is moving in, it is often not the so-called gentry but the university and college educated children of working class and lower middle class parents. In many cases it is also households headed by affluent technical and trade-related occupations. Apart from those areas such as London, Toronto and San Francisco where inner city housing has been affordable only to the already-wealthy/advantaged, most inner cities have been renovated and transformed by a more mixed group of people and incomes. Indeed one of the distinct features of the renovated inner cities is mixture, diversity, difference and hybridization.

Restoring the past

As I have already suggested in Chapter 6, from the 1960s onwards the rejection of the past/tradition in favour of the future/progress was itself rejected. Why should the past, past identities, old buildings, old places and old practices be rejected in favour of something untried and untested? More significantly, in times where change is always undermining our sense of belonging and identity, traditions and histories provide, as Walter Benjamin observed in relation to collecting, a way of coping with 'the chaos of 'memory' that modernity evokes. In other words, collecting is very 'centring' and Walter Benjamin likened it to a coping strategy in the fast-changing and potentially fragmenting modern world. Collecting helps us to recover our past (and it is very often highly personal and biographical in its orientation but it can also be collective), organise and order our memory and transform the potentially shocking and disruptive procession of the new into looked for and aestheticised series of changes, innovations, progress and novelty. Those who bought and 'did up' inner city housing did not simply restore the houses to liveable states but went to great lengths to restore them to their original design, specification, appointment and character. To this end they became collectors, searching through renovation yards, skips, tips and dumps to find the correct doors, fireplaces, tiles, handles and chimney pots. And having restored to their houses an authentic set of structural items, this drive for authenticity often extended to furniture and fittings and even collectables themselves from the period.

Often such renovation/restoration projects had first to remove previous rounds of modernisation. In Bristol, where I observed and documented the minutiae of such renovations, original doors and walls often had been modernised in the 1960s by smoothing out decorative mouldings with vast quantities of hardboard. Even original Georgian and Victorian wooden fire surrounds were often boxed with hardboard and painted. Where the impulse to renovate came from is uncertain but it was certainly related to the heritage movement in old buildings of national significance, the renovation of disappearing technologies beginning with the steam engines and moving quickly onto veteran and vintage cars and motorbikes, boats, trains and trams, and to the National Trust, an organisation that had one of the largest memberships of any charitable organisation and whose mission was to conserve old and natural areas of 'national importance'.

At first, the renovators obtained a great deal of their original items from the modernisers, particularly those who were still buying old properties in order to let to the single and student market. They merely required the maximum number of rooms to let rather than original and authentic spaces and so many older features such as baths, fittings, tiles, fireplaces and cupboards were ripped out and replaced. Then renovation yards began to spring up in key gentrification hot-spots. The renovation yard in Bath Spa was perfectly placed to access, supply and sell on to renovators in Bath and Bristol, making good use of its location next to the central Saturday market. However, demand gradually outstripped local supply and new sources from continental Europe began to appear alongside a vibrant reproduction industry. Even so, there was still not enough of the original materials and shops such as Habitat began to manufacture fittings and furnishings that were commensurate with, if not identical to, the authentic. In this way few gentrified houses were museumised Victorian or Georgina dwelling but hybrids, drawing on a range of aesthetic traditions – something that the Victorian world had done in the first place anyway. However, this eclecticism did not stem so much from a wish to copy Victorian habits as to extend new values from within the ethical and political corpus. This included a great curiosity for 'the other', a desire to collect tastes rather than narrow and refine, a drive towards empathy and tolerance and a strong aesthetic for colour (Alan Warde et al., 2008 calls this 'omnivorous taste'). Indeed demand for tolerance and cohabitation was ultimately expressed through their collective identity with the symbol of the rainbow.

Gentrified houses of the 1980s thus began to take on the hues of plain primary colour schemes rather than the busy patterns reminiscent of the 1970s, relatively plain wooden surfaces rather than the busier lines of industrial design products and the eclectic mix of old and new. By the 1990s and the arrival of a more sophisticated appreciation of design and new design companies such as Ikea and Alessi, the eclectic look of the 1980s morphed into an eclectic ranges of possible looks. Ironically, even the ultra-modernist traditions from Bauhaus minimalism to 1950s Contemporary softened once they could be less threatening and in danger of being cast out themselves.

That sense of tradition and place

Beyond the individual home the same mentalities drove the wish to research and restore the memory and history of residential areas as places. In Bristol, for example, the Malago Society, a social history society dedicated to producing a history of the fast disappearing industrial/residential complex of Bedminster, became the focus of much research and writing and its publications became popular. There was a sense of urgency about this movement, not simply because old building and industries were being lost rapidly but because the memory of the past 100 years or so was being extinguished as the older generation died. Oral history was thus a way to stem the tide of memory loss but also as a means of producing 'people's histories'. So, for example, in 1983 a group of local historians and researchers, Bristol

Broadsides, produced *Bristol's Other History*, which reanimated the inner city landscape with stories from women, children workers, the leather industry, the slums, the mines, the docks and the workhouses.

Sentiments associated with place, identity and past showed their strength in relation to demolition and redevelopment of redundant infrastructure and very often these were very galvanizing campaigns. When Imperial Tobacco wished to sell off the long idle factories that distinguished the Victorian suburb of Southville, the new owner-occupying residents felt they were stakeholders in its destiny rather than merely bystanders at the march of progress. Old, decorative swimming pools that were produced in the late Victorian period were hardly practical in their design and technology but the new incumbents could not bear to see them removed. Ultimately, national organisations began to reconsider the industrial heritage of Britain alongside charitable organisations such as the Art Deco Society and later The Twentieth Century Society who had set about the preservation of early and later (1950s–1970s) modern architecture of note.

However, as we saw above in respect of the Camden Lock effect, former industrial spaces offered uniquely large and characterful spaces for a variety of activities, many of them entirely new to the area. In Southville, for example, the former Wills buildings became a successful complex of eateries, bars, cafés and theatre spaces, with sufficient critical mass to be both commercially and artistically viable. As with Camden Lock, the appearance of this calibre of entertainment space proved attractive to other businesses and enterprises, thus building further interest, investment and intensity. In a relatively short period places such as these changed from 'zones of transition' to a focus for city life once again.

Image 7.2 Former WD and HO Wills Tobacco Factory, Bristol, now a centre for arts, bars and restaurants (photo Lesley Sawyer)

Gay community

Although major gay centres such as San Francisco have always existed, the cultural and political realities of gay villages and territories in the city, and particularly the perception that their presence is a positive contribution to urban regeneration, is a relatively recent phenomenon and one that relates to the mainstreaming of counter-cultures in the manner described above. As an 'instant city' founded on adventurism and the goldfields, 'San Francisco was always a place where people could indulge in personal fantasies and a place of easy moral standards' (Castells, 1983: 140). However, the gay presence there was consolidated when it became the major embarkation point for the Pacific theatre of war and a place where those discharged as homosexuals were disembarked. While gay networks based on the bars of Tenderloin were certainly in existence before, it was the Beatnik culture of the 1950s and 1960s that encouraged them to 'come out' of hiding and live openly and confidently in the city and enabled them to negotiate a place alongside other different city cultures. As Castells wrote, the critical moment was 'the transition from the bars to the streets, from nightlife to daytime, from "sexual deviance" to an alternative lifestyle' (1983: 141). Nonetheless, the buzz and excitement of the gay villages derived also from their previous bar-based culture in which fun and humour were paramount. According to Castells, 'they relish the capacity to enjoy life, turn oppression into creation, and subvert established values by emphasising their ridiculous aspects. Bars, feasts, and celebrations should be, they believe, the nest of gay culture, as they are one of the primary sources of a vibrant city life' (Castells, 1983: 141).

According to Richard Florida (2003a), those cities that have performed best in terms of recent economic development are those that are very tolerant of cultural diversity, and in his view 'homosexuality represents the last frontier of diversity in our [USA] society, and thus a place that welcomes the gay community, welcomes all kinds of people' (Florida, 2003a: 256). Working with Gary Gates, Florida published data that showed that in the USA six of the top ten 1990 and five of the top ten 2000 Gay Index regions also rank among the nation's top ten high-tech regions. Florida argues that the relationship between concentration of gays and successful high-tech industries is that the key creative workers the latter need to recruit prefer those tolerant and diverse inner city lifestyles that have been particularly welcoming to gay and lesbian people. But it is more than that; more than mere tolerance.

Through their work in artistic, creative and performance-related industries, gay communities have clearly been significant in producing the buzz and excitement that marks out the city life that is attractive to the now dominant 'creative class'. This is very obvious in the renaissance of Manchester, UK, as a city where 'cultural industries' such as fashion, design, new media and music have helped to breathe new life into city centres, creating a performative space where previously it was industrial workscape. According to Justin O'Connor (2000), 'the cultural industries have been major players in the rejuvenation of the housing market and in economic renewal within the city centre and fringe districts of Manchester – particularly in the Northern Quarter, "Gay Village"/Whitworth Street, Castlefield and the University districts'. Even though gay populations have emerged spontaneously in such places as San Francisco and contributed substantially to both housing and economic development, in other cities policy makers have deliberately attempted to assist 'gay village' development. For Alan Collins.

> the recent development of Manchester's gay village ... took place within a wider discourse around the 'Manchester model' of urban regeneration – the Manchester script that has been ascribed to ... In this way, the Manchester model of becoming an erstwhile cosmopolitan and European city has become enabling and empowering in helping shape a sense of entitlement by many users of the gay village that they do have a stake and a voice. (Collins, 2006: 185)

Again, an important dimension of contemporary city life, as one encounters it in places like Manchester, is the sense of a lifestyle that is not merely consumerist but one that *matters* culturally, politically and economically. One soon appreciates the presence of people who have created a sense of place by themselves for themselves and in this way they have come to develop a sense of belonging and responsibility. In many ways, the grassroots city politics and economy that Castells sensed in the 1980s and which is apparent in most analyses of subsequent urban regeneration, has restored to the contemporary city many of the vital elements that distinguished the earlier preindistrial cities. As with the European tradition of the carnival, the consolidation of gayness in the city is expressed through the gay Mardi Gras in cities around the world, including Sydney, New Orleans, San Francisco and others.

Ethnic community

City life in the twenty-first century is particularly multi-ethnic but ethnicity alone is no guide to lifestyle. Richard Florida's index of immigration, the so-called Melting Pot Index, is also associated with successful cities, particularly those with vibrant high-tech industries, but it is a more complex relationship than with gayness. The melting pot index is not statistically related to innovation and job growth for example, suggesting that areas of ethnic density do not necessarily share, or take part in urban regeneration.

The inner cities of Western nations vary hugely, and often from district to district within them. Broadly speaking, central city life has always been about mixture, diversity and co-existence. In that respect, different ethnicity has been an important ingredient in the emergence of counter-cultures. However, the allure of difference and exotic diversity, while generative of pleasure and freedom, has not always successfully interleaved itself into the everyday. While London's historic slums were important places of sexual adventure, excitement and experimentation within an essentially white city, the experience of the arrival and concentration of other poor ethnic groups in Western cities has been mixed and there is no inevitable process of convergence or divergence. Certainly the arrival of South and East European, African, Latino and Asian populations to West European, Australasian and American cities has been tempered by a mixture of curiosity and attraction as well as rejection and revulsion (what Bauman (2003) calls mixophilia and mixophobia). Inevitably perhaps, the first generalisable process involved residential segregation. Historically the port areas of inner cities were places of arrival that typically offered a sequence of ethnic groups a buffer zone in which familial establishment, community development and the extension of economic ties and networks offered a degree of isolation from and protection against racist and discriminatory ethnic majorities. These were never desirable places to live or lifestyles but were transient, temporary and in flux, and many successfully negotiated their way into more desirable circumstances. Some preferred to remain together in city enclaves, forming tight economic and moral communities such as Little Italies, Chinatowns and Afro-Caribbean communities. By and large these areas have benefitted from the outmigration of working-class whites in the 1950s and 1960s and the influx of the more tolerant, curious and other-orientated middle class from the 1970s onwards.

Northern industrial inner cities of the USA offered Afro-Americans an escape from racial segregation and institutional racism, but while many have achieved social mobility and have moved into mainstream suburban life, a great many have not and remain the only group left in large areas of the inner cities. Castells (1983) was very careful to distinguish between San Francisco's vibrant Chinatown and the Latino Mission District from the black communities in the Western Addition, and the ghetto areas of Hunter's Point and East Oakland or Chicano Wards in San Jose. These latter black areas remain relatively isolated, poor and marginalised from the city's substantial urban efflorescence over the past forty years. Their relatively higher crime, gang and violence rates do not mark them off as attractive and if anything, neighbouring districts have developed a defensive overreaction with the innovation of cocooning, gated communities and enhanced surveillance and security (see Atkinson and Helms (2007) for a discussion of these developments). By contrast, the Mission District, while distinctly edgy, has been more embraced by the mainstream middle classes.

The Mission District was always a gateway into the USA, being the landing settlement of the first Spanish mission of 1776. Surviving the earthquakes and fires of 1906, it became home first to Irish and Italian working class families and when they moved out during the mid-twentieth century, to Latin and Central American migrants from Nicaragua and El Salvador. During the 1960s and 1970s its ethnic composition became extremely diverse, adding Samoans, Native Americans, Puerto Ricans, South Americans and Mexicans, Cubans and Filipinos. Its diversity became its most distinctive quality and because so many different people were packed cheek-by-jowl in a highly commercial street culture, it produced a lot of noise, colour, difference, grocery stores and restaurants and cinemas, but also bars, prostitution, fiestas, youth cultures and radical politics. Far from being inward-looking and exclusive, it was highly open and expansive and as a result it was, broadly speaking, popular, considered to be full of life:

> And yet unlike most American ghettos, this agitated ambiance has not discouraged white middle class people from walking around the Mission, enjoying its colorful life and even looking forward to their own life in the District. This urban vitality is not stage managed and organized behind the lights of the bars and Mexican restaurants, but is the expression, in spite of poverty and deficient public services, of a very diverse network of neighborhood-based activities, of a continuous flow of newcomers, and of an active community of businesses. In the same way that Chinatown highlights the Asian roots of San Francisco, so the Mission underscores the city's deep Latin American connection. (Castells, 1983: 108–9)

Since the 1990s, an independent young arts movement, the Mission School, with roots in street art, sculpture and graffiti, has emerged with interesting parallels with the 'Lanes Art Movement' in Melbourne, Australia. In both places the relative freedom for an essentially youth dominated culture to express itself onto the surfaces and textures of a formerly disused urban landscape has been an exercise in making themselves at home in the city, carving out a niche, but also embedding themselves alongside others. Their presence in the streets maintains that sense of a permanent festival, exhibition and performance as an outpouring of the Mission as a place.

Lifestyle on the doorstep

When Sally MacIntyre and her colleagues (2005) investigated the popularly held belief that out-of-home eating outlets were largely responsible for the new outbreak of obesity in deprived outer areas of the UK, she found that they were actually mostly concentrated in the inner city and the most affluent areas and relatively uncommon in the outer estates of Glasgow, where obesity was most alarming:

> restaurants and takeaways are likely to be located where there is most potential custom both during the day and evenings, and such demand is higher in retail, transport and commercial centres, areas with high density of entertainment facilities such as cinemas, theatres and pubs, and along arterial highways with much passing traffic. 'Gentrification' has involved the movement of socio-economically advantaged individuals into Glasgow City centre (e.g. 'the Merchant City') and the West End. (2005: 5)

The presence of so many activities and people in the inner city means that it attracts and concentrates a disproportionate amount of life there – and leaves outer areas almost devoid of anything. This is particularly true since suburban development took away the local strips of services and shops and located them in larger drive-in malls. The range of activities most inner city areas support, by comparison, is historically unprecedented and growing: there are extraordinary activities such as theatre and music, occasional activities such as carnivals and other festivals, and everyday activities such as eating out, going to cafés, taking in exhibitions in libraries and other centres and so on. While most shopping centres are open longer hours, they do not have the intensity of activity that the inner areas generate, especially with their unique night-time economy, and so the domestic-at-home and the public realm are not blurred in the way it is in the inner city. This was brought home to me most in London's West End where I was doing some observation of street life. New Bond Street is where I was hoping to observe elevated levels of excitement among ordinary shoppers and passers-by. This was the epicentre of fashion purchases, maybe for special occasions and many shoppers would only rarely shop there. Equally it was the epicentre of London tourism, a cross-roads between the shops and the museums, and something of a transport hub. It was also home to the main art galleries and leading auction houses as well as close to the public spaces of Hyde Park and risqué Soho. There was certainly no shortage of observable excitement and elevated emotion: there was more laughter, swaggered walking, smiling excited conversation, groups of friends and crowds of drinkers and revellers by the late afternoon than there was in the outer suburbs or smaller cities. However, what was most striking was not the crowds of incoming shoppers and tourists, but groups of local people often engaged in long conversations close to their homes, around parked cars, in cafés and bars. As with Paris, a lot of people live above the streets and a lot of streets are in fact purely (and fairly densely) residential. The demeanour of these residents was more relaxed, more everyday and quite clearly more at home than that of the crowd. Only they would bump into friends and neighbours; only they would stop in a purely residential street to have a chat. However, to live in the middle of the West End, or for that matter, any area of inner London, was to be surrounded with a quite extraordinary pulse of people and activity – right on the doorstep.

One of the most profound changes in these areas, and one that signals the more or less continuous presence of relatively affluent middle class people, is the growth of bistros, diners, restaurants and cafés. The amount of time that full-time workers spend eating out doubled between 1975 and 2000, while it trebled for the age group 51–65, students and part-time workers. On the other hand, the amount of time spent eating per se reduced across all categories over this period. This is only a very rough-and-ready indicator of de-domestication of contemporary life, but clearly the possibility to engage in more public fora is far greater in the inner city.

Lifestyle oases: city cafés

Cafés are now symptomatic of the new urban lifestyle, and again, their presence seems essential to contemporary city life. In the past ten years there has been a spectacular growth of lifestyle, branded cafés in the UK: between 1997 and 2005 the number rose from 778 to 2428, a rise of over 200% (IGD, 2007). Forty-three per cent of the UK sample regularly visited branded or independent cafés and 50% of consumers visited cafés for social purposes, to meet friends or family (IGD, 2007).

Over the past thirty years café spaces have changed considerably from basic canteen formats to cosy, high-design lounges on a par with airline club lounges: or as IGD put it, they have changed from 'sellers of hot beverages' to 'sellers of lifestyle' (IGD, 2007). Clearly they are working differently as social spaces, but in what way? Recently Eric Laurier and Chris Philo reported their ESRC-funded project 'The Cappuccino Community: cafés and civic life in the contemporary city'. Among other things they found that cafés provide for the encounter of 'people who are neither our private family and friends nor our colleagues from work'; that the barista has emerged as new form of public personality who de-anonymises our daily life in the city; that cafés are important places of both rest and work, the latter being a particularly important space for many major businesses to conduct important business and specific types of meeting (Laurier, 2004); that other social meetings (e.g. literary meetings) also take place in the spaces of cafés; that they are gathering places ('locals' almost) for business friends, women with children, older people, shoppers etc., and that cafés have specific crowds, ambiences and buzz. They conclude that 'in today's newly invigorated cities, the value of the ambience and daily eventfulness afforded to city residents, day trippers, tourists, and others by both staff and those already customers seated in the café should not be underestimated'. Somehow cafés form an important link between the individual and the collective city life: 'the British people are enjoying the buzz that we get, not from the coffee, but from being in a place with people we have things in common with and people we don't. The buzz of an intimate occasion that makes the collective space of our cites into a place that is temporarily our place' (Laurier and Philo, 2007: 1).

NOTES

1 See the various works by the Centre for Contemporary Cultural Studies in the 1970s and 1980s.
2 This carnivalesque space can be analysed in much the same way that the carnivalesque and the seaside has been (see Rojek, 1995: 85–8 and Shields, 1991).

8 Cities of Spectacle and Carnival

In this chapter I am going to make connections between spaces of travel and tourism and the contemporary city that are seldom made, and link these to the transformative powers of ritual and earlier forms of ritual in the city. In a way I will be arguing that the renaissance of an enervating and ritualised city life in contemporary cities is something of a restoration also. It was quite explicitly evident in Roman and medieval times, as we saw in Chapter 1, and was expressly banished and suppressed through Protestantism and the Victorian legacy – a period that in cultural terms only terminated or at least abated in recent years. Although the carnivalesque and pilgrimage were in many ways suppressed, they were mostly banished to spaces beyond the respectable city heartlands and it is here beyond city walls, out in rural sites and especially on the coast, that they maintained some forms of expression. They became increasingly popular places of desire and release, and eventually their cultural forms began to be imported back into city life once more – but only under quite specific social circumstances.

The story of this reintroduction or reinvigoration is the substance of the first part of this chapter. In the second part I will consider how new forms of spectacle and ritual emerged in the modern city through the medium of sport, music (jazz was critical, for example), festivals, entertainments and tourism. Without these cultural foci the modern city would be unrecognisable and, to use a more recent term, 'unliveable'.

The story that this chapter tells modifies the notion, relatively common in the urban literature, that contemporary urban regeneration and its spectacular forms has been the result of investment and policy; of purposive recent innovation and creativity. There has indeed been a great deal of this, but without knowing its longer cultural trajectory, its home in popular culture, its development through ludic and ritualised form and the *anthropology of ritual*, the entire picture is missing vital elements. Worse, one is left guessing as to what, exactly, city life, its atmosphere and buzz, its seeming aliveness and attraction, is all about. A lot of money hangs on making cities work on these terms and this chapter seeks to contribute to that analysis.

If we return to the Roman and medieval cities we considered in Chapter 1, we find cities where work, domestic affairs, ritual and leisure were all prominent, interleaved and related components of city life. Work and home life were for most people indistinguishable in the everyday round while leisure and pleasure were often organised around highly ritualised and seasonal festivals, the ritual calendars of the gods and organised religious life. We can be sure that in Roman Canterbury, as in its previous life as the capital of the kingdom of the Cantiaci, ritual and religious life was very rich, with a large temple building and precinct built at the epicentre of the city (Detsicus, 1983). There was a theatre opposite the temple (a usual Roman arrangement), which also seemed to be both central and important. Formed in a semicircle with a 70m diameter, it was surrounded with an auditorium superstructure of at least four storeys and capable of seating an audience of more than three thousand. Plays, performances and religious rituals and festivals would have formed its main repertoire and it would have been a key gathering place for the entire community. In addition, Vespasian constructed a colosseum around AD 80, at which point Roman games and gladiatorial contests would have added to other entertainments (Lyle, 2002). Hence, even though it was a relatively small town, barely a city even, one can easily imagine that life there was far from dull. Music, literature, ritual ceremonial and sport were all clearly regular and important elements of this life. Indeed, the Romans created a familiar and pleasure-rich city life in almost all of their provincial centres and outposts, a fact that changed the future of European cities for all time, setting down important characteristic structures and expectations, norms and cultures.

Much the same might be said of the medieval Canterbury that emerged out of the Dark Ages. It too had substantial religious houses, including a major cathedral and monasteries, theatres and also many inns where music and plays were performed. From the twelfth century Canterbury was also a busy pilgrimage town and catered to large numbers of visitors. There were many inns, accommodation houses and hospitals built by the Grey Friars, Black Friars and White Friars for a growing pilgrim trade over the next two hundred years, and one can tell from Chaucer's *Canterbury Tales* that life in the city was pleasurable and lively. However, because pilgrimage also involved the creation of *liminal spaces* of ritual in which individual transformations can take place, such as revitalisation, healing, redemption and purification, city life was also 'charged', atmospheric and magical, with a strong sense of communal and group solidarities added to the mix. Unlike the everyday, one did not know in advance what was going to happen on a pilgrimage to Canterbury; it was what Goffman calls an 'action space' full of performative potential, slightly scary, interpellating a different, a new or a longed-for self.

Later in this chapter I am going to argue that one of the key characteristics of successful cities in the contemporary period has been their ability to remake the city into a place of exploration, personal transition or growth, in which one can indulge in self-making and in doing so search for salvation or redemption. This is not so much an innovative new 'turn' (although it has been realised through a great deal of creativity) as an *artefact* of the sort of society we have become – in what Bauman calls the liquid era of modernity. Despite often being rejected as a shallow, individualist and consumer-orientated society it actually generates and even depends upon a great deal of cultural and ritualised ferment. Certainly we can say the city has been transformed by this long process with its origins in the late 1960s, although the sociology of the city that ushered it in is often lost through the economic, political and policy orientated discourse of urban regeneration. This chapter will marry these two together so that the cultural and the social, the economic and the political, can no longer be considered apart. It is an exercise in interdisciplinarity.

The city and pilgrimage

Apart from their defensive, industrial, residential and administrative functions, cities were historically also ritual and religious centres, places of intellectual and political transformation and ferment, the birthplace of cults and followings as well as important contexts in which personal biographies were shaped and reshaped. I am also going to argue that a number of ritual-like or ritualised activities that were richly performative, communal and public made this possible and that these were in many respects similar to the sociological work that pilgrimage and rituals of pilgrimage performed. It is therefore worth considering how pilgrimage worked, sociologically, as a benchmark and baseline by which to understand subsequent urban forms.

In its classic form pilgrimage can be defined as journeys away from the everyday, mundane world of work and home to specific sacred sites formalised, recognised and maintained by major religions and princely kingdoms, often at tribal or national centres. The type of pilgrimage that prefigured tourism in the West belongs to the same social order of feudal or semi-feudal rural societies that characterised much of Christian Europe from the fifth to the sixteenth century. Places such as Glastonbury in Somerset, UK, or Cloagh Patrick in Ireland were centres of religious pilgrimage prior to Christian adoption, and although they remained principal places of pilgrimage, they were joined by a much larger number of pilgrimages to the shrines and other sites associated with saints and kings, such as at Rocamdour, France, from 1193; Canterbury, UK, from 1170 or Loreto, Italy, from 1294. Even before the Norman conquest of England, the Anglo-Saxon kings of England and others who had the resources to undertake such journeys made specific pilgrimages to Rome, to the Catacombs and St Peter's (Wood, 2000). Even though most people during this period were tied to a local economic and religious life,

'Christianity developed its own mode of liminality for the laity. This mode was best represented by the pilgrimage to a sacred site or holy shrine located at some distance away from the pilgrim's place of residence and daily labour' (Turner and Turner, 1978: 4). These proliferated across Europe and were based on shrines of saints, the Virgin Mary and sacred relics.

What were the rationales and anticipated benefits of such arduous, extended and dangerous travel? First, pilgrimage offered an alternative to, and the chance to get away from, the mundane world, its 'small grievances over trivial issues [that] tend to accumulate' or the 'store of nagging guilts' (1978: 5). At the same time, the trials and tribulations of the journey provide 'a release from the ingrown ills of home'. Second, pilgrimage offered an initiatory quality, a chance to leave the profane world for the sacred, a dimension guaranteed by the holy objects and spaces. Third, the individual moral unit of the pilgrimage 'seeks salvation or release from the sins and evils of the structural world' (1978: 8). Fourth, the pilgrim receives a powerful inspiration or guidance into the future.

In the final stages of pilgrimage, in or around the shrine centres, the pilgrim is bombarded with 'religious buildings, pictorial images, statuary, and sacralised features of the topography. Linking these together are often the essential thoughts and feelings of a founder's religion or those of influential followers, but in combination they permit the exhausted but receptive pilgrim to receive 'the pure imprint of paradigmatic structure' (another structure of feeling) which gives 'a measure of coherence, direction and meaning to their action' (1978: 11). Finally, of course, pilgrimage offered healing, or at least *transformation* from a state of affliction.

As Chaucer's *Canterbury Tales* makes abundantly clear, although pilgrims may have started off on their own, with their own reasons for completing a pilgrimage, they very soon found themselves on the busy highways of pilgrim's ways, staying at inns along the way and frequently forming parties of fellow travellers. First it was safer to do so, but second, part of the liminal space and culture of pilgrimage was characterised by play, games, drinking and merry-making – things, one suspects, that made these journeys all the more compelling and attractive in the first place. In other words, ritual is frequently constituted in and through a public realm, and this is something that cities would later offer to modernised forms of ritual.

One of the intriguing elements of the history of European pilgrimage was its banishment in the major protestant countries as they emerged from the religious grip of Rome. Religious devotion was not the object of these bans so much as the decorative use of idols and images and the confusion of cults before which the pilgrims bowed and devoted so much time. It was of course associated with Roman Catholicism, but also in the minds of its protestant detractors was its association with ludic play, which to them was a dangerous distraction for the solemn business of prayer and work. The pilgrims in

Chaucer's *Canterbury Tales* mixed serious religious and spiritual intent with a great deal of leisure and play, and that play was of the ritual kind described above, tending towards an especially heightened form of excitability, aided by drinking, sexual freedom and generalised merry-making. Associated with the pilgrim trail was what we might call today 'disorderly conduct' – and this was of course part of its liminoid phase, forcing a break with the quotidian; a social space or journey betwixt and between the orders of daily life.

The attempt to prevent such lapses of order, and indeed to introduce a total regime of protestant/capitalist social order marks the beginning of what Rojek (1995) has usefully called Modernity 1. Essentially what Rojek argues, following Nietzsche and perhaps also Elias, is that the passions and tension of life that gave rise to ritual institutions such as carnival or pilgrimage could not be swept under the carpet by the instigation of bans and the introduction of more approved diversions. Crudely, we might say that with pilgrimage banned in the seventeenth century and the carnival banned in the early nineteenth century, 'tourism' (very much after the innovation by the religious enthusiast, Thomas Cook) and 'leisure' emerged soon after to fill their place.

There are good reasons why this came to happen, though the innovations that Cook was to make were hardly inevitable. The approved leisures of protestant cultures (reading, poetry, art, crafts for example) that resembled more work than pleasure and release, specifically avoided addressing the inevitable tensions and pressures of daily life and of the life course. In Protestant religion, the salvation offered by work and the need for recognition of success added to the pressure to succeed in daily life and to secure a strong, upwardly moving career trajectory. Rojek argues that these passions, tensions and pressures gave rise first to a secretive world of desires and illicit behaviours tolerable only if practised away from the centres of civil society, hence the development of what Rob Shields (1991) identified as the connection between tourism and 'places on the margin'. In addition, of course, such a pressured life produced tensions that were not easily resolved in their place of origin; hence we find the huge popularity of therapeutic spa travel in the eighteenth century.

In a different context, why did Thomas Cook get the idea for tourism, the notion that travel *itself* might have cathartic and useful properties? Again, we find it close to the world of ritual. He found himself increasingly drawn into his amateur life as a preacher in the religious revivals that accompanied the most pressured and difficult times of the hugely expanding British industrial towns of the early nineteenth century. These religious revivals of nonconformist religiosity existed outside the established churches and as if to emphasise their marginality and potency, these were often held a long way outside towns in the country, on temporary greenfield sites. People travelled long distances to them and there was something about the large numbers of the congregation travelling and assembled together at the destination (as well as the

Salvationist tones of the preaching) that produced a powerful liminoid ritual effect. Cook had the germ of the idea of 'a tour' when walking to one such revival on a very hot day. Why not hire a steam train and several coaches at a discount price, and then sell individual tickets to the revival? This proved profitable, but Cook noticed something important: the effect of forming a touring party was immensely enjoyable in its own right; he observed a special effect about the collective nature of the journey itself but also the 'machinic' pleasure of trains. As Cook elaborated on the revival tours by organising new destinations to other sacred sites of the day – the Romantic Lake District, the Scottish highlands, or the Great Exhibition of 1851, he made sure that they maintained that essential ritual form, with himself (and others) as the guide officiating, rather like a priest. By 1869 Cook had initiated tours to the Holy Land, largely for people like himself, but in this case the difference between tourism and pilgrimage was particularly blurred:

> Low Protestantism did not make much room for traditional notions of pilgrimage; so perhaps being a tourist might actually have been a new, acceptable way for Evangelicals to express a widespread religious impulse. Chaucer has planted in the popular mind the notion that people who were officially pilgrims might have hoped to gain some pleasure from the journey. These tourists, conversely, were people who were officially pleasure seekers, but who longed to derive some spiritual benefits from their travels. (Larsen, 2000: 341)

So the point is that tourism mimics pilgrimage (and vice versa); it was a novel form of ritual that used the performance of travel to secure the liminal spaces of personal and group transition. This helps us to understand some if not all aspects of the *seaside*, a phase of tourism in which pleasurability and rituals of transition were once again reasserted and gained a new universality. However, in so doing, and this is a point that makes reference to the discussions of the nature of contemporary tourism (see Franklin, 2004), the conditions were established for the movement of the ritualised pleasure peripheries to return to the centre, or more correctly perhaps, to lose the necessity for spatial distanciation or differentiation. This is the essential point about Rojek's definition of Modernity 2. Spatial escape attempts become an illusion under the generalised distribution and economy of leisure, and here we might say that new technologies of (urban) leisure were called into existence by this desire rather than the other way around. This is particularly the case for a society that, during the heyday of seaside, was progressing from a producer to a consumer society. Here the distinction of work/everyday and leisure/holiday is significantly blurred by the distribution of consumerism into both.

Some of the aims and desires of contemporary consumer society are also embodied in the lives of celebrities, and celebrity itself is a predominantly *urban* phenomenon deserving serious sociological attention (but see Rojek, 2001). Think for just one moment how much of our time is wrapped up in seeing their images, watching them, reading about them and talking about them. We are fascinated by their working lives (e.g. the Cavern club in Liverpool where the Beatles played in their early days), their homes (e.g. Elvis Presley's Graceland), where they died (e.g. where John Lennon was shot outside the Dakota Building in New York) and their graves (e.g. Jim Morrison's grave in Paris). All of them have become sacred urban sights and places of pilgrimage for modern tourists.[1]

An interesting connection to make here is the assertion that much popular culture, of the type created by Elvis, the Beatles and the Doors, is a recomposed form of carnivalesque:

> Again, much popular culture explores the margins, the inversions, the not barely respectable, the out-of-bounds. In short, much of this is carnivalesque, challenging the harshness of fate and history. The grotesque body returns, for example in forms of popular humour, in wrestling, in advertising. ... Hence carnivalesque parody, inversion and grotesque humour retain an ability to unsettle both the defenders of the rational, disciplined zone of project, and the modern avant-garde, revealing the truth in Shiach's observation that 'Basically "the popular" has always been "the other"'. This may be even truer, though, of those elements lying on the far boundaries of popular culture itself, or beyond: the hippies, the crusties, travellers, ravers, eco-warriors, and other denizens of the nightmare world of the respectable middle classes ... (Jervis, 1998: 330–1)

When we considered the renaissance of modern cities during the 1970s it was precisely this aspect of city life, long repressed by the disciplines of capitalism, that was restored and which is now considered desirable and increasingly vital for the contemporary cities. This forms the very substance of a revived, literally a regenerated city. This is what *was* regenerated or revived; not only a structure of feeling, an economy and market but also a structure of expression and the space in which it can be performed, seen and have an impact.

Protestantism and the city

In addition to banning pilgrimage, the extent to which Protestantism also curtailed the pleasures of the city was very significant. Protestants objected to much about the lively, political and risqué nature of sixteenth century renaissance plays but especially the fact that boys played women and that the plays were often performed in or near pubs and/or brothels. The rich period of theatre during which Shakespeare had flourished came to an end in 1642 with an order to close all theatres and it was not until the restoration of the monarchy in 1660 that they opened again (Bryson, 2007; Wood, 2005).

Protestantism asserted itself on city life once again through its later captaincy of industrial capitalism in the eighteenth and nineteenth centuries. Meller (1976) shows how, in the case of Bristol, the major industrial companies owned by such Quaker families as the Wills and the Frys had a profound impact on traditional city leisure and thus the kind of life and culture the city supported. Alongside similar demands from Methodism and other non-conformist sects, they undermined and discouraged the drinking of alcohol and life after work in public houses. Through new instruments of urban governance they also effectively removed the rich life of street trading, work and play (including gambling, horse and dog racing, bull and rat baiting) that had characterised Britain's street life. Their own highly paid workers were discouraged from traditional games and pastimes, such as pub-based skittles, and given new approved leisures, often in purpose-built, employee-only facilities. As the influence of the Anglican church waned and that of the non-conformist sects rose in the first half and middle of the nineteenth century, local leisure lives, especially among the morally-at-risk young became highly organised around chapel halls where new activities could be tightly controlled and watched over. Mixed sex dancing was effectively curtailed and a full and extensive programme of 'improving', useful leisures was inserted in its place.

At the same time, the last vestiges of traditional seasonal ritual and sporting life were gradually closed down and banned. In south Bristol, as we saw in Chapter 2, the week-long festival or fair known as the Bedminster Revels was terminated in 1830, an act that effectively ruptured the city's carnivalesque tradition dating back to before the Norman Conquest. 'In the tenth century, gatherings on the big festival days ran into hundreds and sometimes thousands of people, all descending for a few days on to a small royal estate for a particular saint's day, or for a lawmaking jamboree, or to witness the hegemonic rituals by which kings kept their thumbs on recalcitrant vassals' (Wood, 2000: 196). So, even before the Norman Conquest in 1066 we can say that carnivals and pilgrimage were central to English culture at all levels of society – as elsewhere.

Carnival

'Carnival' is the generic name for that group of ritual festivities all across premodern Europe that are variously called *festas* (Italy), *fiestas* (Spain), *fêtes* (France), festivals/carnivals/fairs/revels (Britain) and so on. There are of course many other synonyms for the same basic activity in other European countries but they all refer, as we have seen above, to quite specific forms of celebrating and performing holy days, particularly saints' days. Rather like the Aboriginal songlines that describe the places of emergence of totemic ancestors and their subsequent journeys in the Australian bush (see Chatwin, 1987; Fullager, 2004), inscribing a sacred cartography on the landscape, the saints of the early medieval period also left traces or paths of their saintly lives throughout Europe. These were often former archbishops or priors of monasteries or other noted holy individuals, and their careers and teaching described specific life routes – where they worked and lived, where they stopped, preached, prayed or performed some miraculous transformation. As with Aboriginal totemic ancestors, their journeys and their presence at particular places were believed to hold some continuous significance for the living: some of their saintly power and affect continued to reside in these places but *particularly* in their relics, objects associated directly with their life. Again, in common with Aboriginal totemic cults, these powers seem to be most concentrated in particular places and perhaps even more so in artefacts or relics associated specifically with them. While these sacred sites and collections of artefacts became the places of pilgrimage, very often they coincided with trade and annual fairs held in their name. So there is clearly an overlap between pilgrimage and carnival. However, while pilgrimage had very wide catchments of followers of particular saints' cults (a good example is Thomas Becket, murdered in Canterbury cathedral in 1170, who attracted vast numbers of pilgrims from all across the UK but also from France and Holland), the carnival was a ritual belonging to and defined by the restricted congregation of a *locality*.

The carnival is always identified with a particular town, especially in Italy or Spain, or a particular rural district (which often included a local town) as in the premodern carnival in England, and in this way it was a ritual occasion performed by and for a specific local culture. The carnival was, like the social composition of its congregation, an inward-looking, insular and self-sufficient affair. As Bakhtin argued, carnival comprised

> forms of protocol and ritual based on laughter and consecrated by tradition ... which were sharply distinct from the serious official, ecclesiastical, feudal and political cult forms and [ritual] ceremonials. Carnival is a spectacle lived by people who are all participants, actors, not spectators. [They] offered a completely different, non-official ... extra political aspect of the world, of man and of human relations; they built a second world and a second life outside officialdom. (Bakhtin 1984: 5–7; quoted in Shields, 1991: 89)

It had a number of common characteristics that established it as a liminoid, ritual activity:

1 It typically began with a procession to the special place on a specific local saint's day (importantly it was an annual, one-off event), a day (or two) when the hierarchical nature of these localities was made manifest, particularly through ritual robes and vestments. At the head of these processions were the ritual objects, typically statues of the saint and objects and representations of his/her life.
2 Over a specified number of following days, carnivals involved an ordered or ritually proscribed disordering in which there were considerable inversions of roles and practices. There was a heightened party atmosphere generated by more excessive drinking, feasting, dancing and music, but also theatre and games or sports. Critically, much of this behaviour would not be tolerated during the rest of the year.
3 Characteristically, carnival involved a ritual language, often derived from market argots and gestures 'permitting no distance between those who came in contact with each other and liberating them from norms of etiquette and decency imposed at other times' (Bakhtin, 1984: 10; quoted in Shields, 1991: 90). Similarly, normal observation of low and high culture within the community was undermined and inverted through the use of the grotesque body, which lowered 'all to the material level of the earth and body, asserting the primacy of life'. This offers a critical clue to understanding Carnival: it is a celebration of 'the collective, ancestral body of all people' (Shields, 1991: 93) and in the specific case of the medieval carnival, the relative isolation and interdependence of the communities that gathered to perform them.
4 The invocation of a primal grotesque body was achieved partly through a language of lewd gestures and slang and ritual plays, theatre, games and foolery, but also through objects, grotesque statues, masks and costume. Adding to the performance of the grotesque by local people was the mysterious presence (turning up on time and melting away afterwards) of migratory professional entertainers, owners of grotesque side shows (who offered glimpses of freaks of human and other nature, exotic wild animals embodying the idea of monsters, anomalous and mysterious objects), travelling theatre companies and so on.

By the mid-nineteenth century the rural communities that had supported these very old festivals and revels were largely urbanised. Those festivals that continued into the nineteenth century, such as the Bedminster Revels near Bristol, were, as we have seen, gradually terminated by statute. As Meller (1976) makes clear, the Revels had always attracted an international and national travelling group of entertainers, sideshows, musicians and theatrical performers whose annual economy was based on the cycle of festivities and carnivals all across Europe and beyond. When the rural English carnivals dried up many of these travellers stopped coming and confined their attentions to Europe, where they were still tolerated and continue to perform to this day, e.g. at Pamplona etc. However, the geography of leisure and entertainment in England had already shifted and differentiated – towards, for example, medicinal spas that had become important exclusive foci for the affluent aristocracy and emerging commercial classes. These had begun in a rudimentary way as early as the sixteenth century (Shakespeare had played at Tunbridge) but by the eighteenth century and the building of elegant centres and cities such as Bath Spa, the leisure industry was becoming more urbanised, if still seasonal. By the early to mid-nineteenth century most seaside towns such as Brighton, UK, had accreted a considerable semi-permanent assembly of carnivalseque entertainers and sideshows, and as Shields argues, the carnivalseque itself had shifted or displaced to the seaside. In this new space, away from the stratified rural societies that gave it meaning and function ('an unlicensed celebration of a socially acknowledged interdependence of all people'), the seaside carnivalesque was nonetheless similar:

> The realisation, rehearsal and celebration of this same interdependence are at the heart of the scene of holidaying Commoners who shifted aside the weight of moral distinctions of the Sabbath and propriety to practice carnivalesque forms of unlicensed, commodified, leisure 'attractions' that lined the beach. Particularly through humour, such transgressions deny class barriers founded on moral reasoning. The rowdy fun and mockery of the holiday makers instigated a heightened level of reciprocity within the crowd from which it was difficult to withdraw and from which no one was exempt. (Shields, 1991: 96–7)

Note that Shields has used the word 'carnivalesque', meaning carnival-like. Seaside was not the same as carnival but its form and ritual nature had evolved into the new spaces and socialites of modern urban cultures. This involved one further elaboration, the new idea of the spectator at the carnival. Jervis puts it well:

> When Goethe, discussing the Roman Carnival of 1788, claimed that one participated as 'both actor and spectator', one was perhaps witnessing the fate of Carnival in our own time, the transformation of Carnival into carnivalesque, into spectacle, but nevertheless still a resource for popular appropriation; not so much the people's second life, but still a distinctive aspect of culture, embodying a distinctive 'form of critical reason' ... (Jervis, 1998: 331)

Jervis cites Docker (1995: 284) who argues that 'the flow of mass culture may possess its own forms of reason, not reason in a rationalist sense, of attention to discrete ordered sequences of information and interpretation, but of sudden juxtapositions, swift contrasts, heterogeneity … carnivalesque remains an always dangerous supplement, challenging, destabilising, relativising, pluralizing single notions of true culture, true reason …'.

In sum, the carnival was a ritual (or as Shields called it, an anti-ritual) of annual renewal of collective social life in the premodern period. It was not simply functional to the power hierarchy of its day in allowing the otherwise common people their day to let off steam, it was more complex. Carnival stressed the necessary interdependencies, duties and mutual obligations and social contract of the feudal and post-feudal order; in mocking the existing hierarchy, and posing its hold on power as contingent it asserted the universality and commonality of the people. It pointed always to higher powers, saints, kings, god and the sacred, but reminded everyone of their essentially corporeal life on earth. The notion of collectivity which the carnival embodied was at odds with the emergent individualism of capitalist society, which is one underlying reason why capitalist nations such as Britain gradually suppressed them in that form. The Bedminster Revels showed that they were bad news in theory and in practice. However, carnival belonged to the common or popular culture and it could not be silenced or banished. Rather, we can say it found new forms of expression in the emergent mass society and popular culture. One of these was the arrival of soccer as spectacle; another was jazz.

Soccer becomes spectacle

The pubs, inns and alehouses fought back against the non-conformist protestant ordering in a number of ways. They became, for example, the centres for urban working class club life, often based around the more approved leisures. Franklin (2002: 124–31) shows how pubs developed their own angling clubs and became the principal organising vehicle for the expansion of urban-based working class rail excursions into the countryside. Another opportunity came with the advent and dramatic expansion of modern sports, especially soccer. After a period of anarchic and asymmetrical development, a modern form of soccer emerged in 1866 and with it the Football Association and its governance over a universal set of rules. Many English city clubs formed between 1855 and 1871, when a knockout cup, the Football Association Cup, was mooted. Whereas earlier, traditional forms of football were rooted in rural inter-village competition, modern soccer became focused and representative of the modern city.

Thereafter, soccer became a firmly entrenched, though seldom acknowledged part of city life. Again, there was always a feeling among the respectable middle classes that this was a louche, rude and disordered element of city life, to be confined to the social margin (Cashmore, 1990: 216). But the rise of soccer was later consolidated by two very important developments. The first was the establishment of the Football League in 1888, a premier national league consisting of the twelve most prominent clubs. The spectacle of critical weekly games proved to be intoxicating, and by 1893 a second league was added. A year later, the two divisions between them had thirty-two clubs, representing most cities of England. The second development was the proliferation of lower leagues, local or district leagues that spread like wildfire across every city. Because soccer was organised around clubs and they required a base for meetings, they were typically organised where much other working class leisure organisation had taken place, in pubs, often taking their name from the pubs themselves. During this period every city in England, Wales and Scotland began to expand the number of playing fields on the edges of town and in existing parks. It created large expanses of green (together with the pavilions, clubhouses, changing rooms etc.) that would otherwise not exist (and most still exist, even if a few have grown into colosseum-like stadia). With only a few exceptions the main city club stadiums were built away from the hubs of cities, and although they became the shrines to their travelling fans, there was typically little other development – and thus not much city life – around them, in stark contrast to the relationship between theatres and temples in Roman cities. Typically the grounds were sited near nineteenth century terraced housing well within the industrial factory landscape (Rowley, 2006: 393). Even as late as 1980 the *Guardian* newspaper could write 'there is a sparseness, a meanness about the ground. It is like a grey snapshot from the thirties ... the rawness of it proclaims a football town ...'.

Although soccer and the other football codes of Europe, America and Australia has remained dominant over other modern sports that emerged over the same period, sports such as ice hockey, athletics, cricket, rugby, basketball, hockey and others have continued to provide an all-year round focus for much city life, developing spectacular forms around inter-city national and international competitions. FIFA, the governing body of international football, was founded in 1904 and the popularity of international competition provided the impetus for the building of major stadia in most capital cities throughout Europe. This, together with the commodification and modernisation of soccer into an entertainment industry, became grounds for moving it back into the cultural centre.

The spectre of jazz

The advent of the First World War ended the domination of city life by the non-conformist chapel operating in the working class suburbs and introduced new rivals. Church- and chapel-going declined rapidly after 1918 (Bruce, 2001) and as the tight bond between chapel hall and working class leisure loosened, new forms of leisure that were ushered in by the war shifted the emphasis of city life, particularly *night life*, from working class neighbourhoods to the city centre and from surveillance and discipline to freedom.

Meller (1976) shows how jazz jumped the Atlantic from the USA to England during and after the First World War and the social and cultural impact it had. Up until then working class leisure culture was tightly organised around neighbourhoods and their chapels. To repeat, dancing had been strictly supervised and limited and music styles conformed to the stringent moral regime of nonconformist life. The arrival of jazz and watered down dance variants of black American jazz reconfigured this completely. Coinciding with new urban public transport systems, electrification and rising youth wages, the new music found expression and a home in newly built city centre dance halls. These were commercial and more permissive and as the possibility and styles of dancing became more exciting, so thousands of dance schools emerged to educate the new generation into jazz-inspired freedoms. Among other things, jazz ushered in more intimate premarital social relations between the sexes, the beginnings of teenage culture and more freedom for women. Critically, jazz was not merely music but also the beginnings of counter-cultures and their take-over of the city centre.

Jazz is a musical style that developed from both African and European traditions, emerging around the beginning of the twentieth century in African American communities, particularly in New Orleans. While there are now many styles, they all share some or many of the following musical qualities: syncopation, swing, improvisation, 'blue notes', call and response, sound innovation such as growls and stretched notes, and polyrhythmic structure. Jazz is one of the most interesting sources of counter-cultural fusion between black and white cultures in the West and is frequently used as a metaphor for openness, cool, equality and freedom of expression – often expressed in an embodied way through dance.

The origin of the word 'jazz' is controversial but the most likely genealogy follows *jasm*, an American English word (first seen in print in 1842) for semen that also meant vitality and virility, through *jazz*, a slang term for copulation used among dice players (both black and white) in San Francisco some seventy years later. The word 'jazz' first appeared in print in San Francisco baseball articles in 1913 to describe a player's magical qualities of life, vigour or effervescence. It was then used to describe the music of a ragtime band who entertained players at a training camp and from there it spread through musician networks to Chicago and New York by 1916. It was not until 1917 that the term was used in New Orleans, where the music style had its origins (Quinion, 2004). Its dark, potent, sexual and life-affirming qualities provided the perfect antidote to the tightly controlled protestant city ordering and provided perhaps the licence and permission to dismantle it.

The earliest forms of the music in New Orleans arose from marching bands where brass instruments and African rhythm and beat fused to form 'raggedy' or ragtime music. Ragtime was quickly absorbed into early twentieth century mainstream white musical cultures (for example in Irving Berlin's songs), where black music and dance had been influential and popular since minstrel shows and public dance hall music. But as the New Orleans ragtime moved north through California and up river to Chicago and to New York, new variants appeared and with each variation there was both the commercial forms of the major clubs and hotels and the purer musician forms in the bars and speakeasies (Becker, 1973). Becker shows how jazz musicians (and jazz itself) were formed into cultural groups and social cliques and how individual musicians negotiated careers between the poles of pure (uncertain and poorly paid) and commercial (secure and affluent) jazz.

The sociological interest of jazz is not restricted to its musical styles, its cultural forms and origins. It is also possible to talk of the urban social spaces of jazz as a counter-cultural space or deviant culture. Jazz clubs emerged in the days of alcohol prohibition as sites away from surveillance and the policing of alcohol and drugs. It then became synonymous with a variety of counter-cultures (black, gangster, immigrant, youth) in which individual freedom and Dionysian values were cultivated. It is for this reason that jazz was often referred to as 'the devil's music'. Critically, jazz opened up spaces of cultural transition:

> jazz was welcoming, inclusive, open. It replaced minstrelsy with a cultural site where all Americans could participate, speak to one another, override or ignore or challenge or slide by the society's fixations on racial and ethnic stereotypes. Black Americans (and other ethnic outsiders) could use it to enter mainstream society, white Americans could flee to it from mainstream society, and the transactions created a flux and flow that powered American cultural syntheses. (Santoro, 2001)

In this way jazz played an important role in breaking down traditional lines of American culture and paving the way for a more permissive, open society. But not just in America, as we have seen.

Jazz is also significant in developing a form of individualism commensurate with its counter-culture aspirations and planting it in central city club sites away from the institutional heartlands of conservative discipline and surveillance. It inspired the personal politics of 'cool' and 'hip', which, as Pountain and Robins (2000) maintain, now dominate contemporary forms of individualism everywhere. *Cool* is now a generalised expression of opposition and defiance to a variety of authority figures, especially the state and its agencies and agents, but most importantly it stands for freedom of expression and action. It has become a permanent stance to the world, not necessarily a life stage that one will grow out of. Cool also registers the new significance of individualism and individualised, as opposed to collective, politics. For these reasons, cool is no longer the preserve of the young but is distributed across large sections of urban society, particularly among those who have lived in the post-1960s counter-cultures and its natural environment is still the city centre. Most of the counter-cultures that gave rise to the specifically spectacular form of urban revival after the 1960s are directly descended from the sub-cultures of jazz. In many ways its cultural home in New Orleans provided a model for later urban renaissance in the North American and European city, notably its emphasis on racial tolerance and cultural diversity, its melting pot culture, the appreciation of fine food and music, plus encouraging a generalised atmosphere of carnival.

Cities as places of visitation and play

The arrival of jazz music and dance in the city centre confirmed a trend that had actually started long before. The hubs of cities that had once been traditional residential and industrial areas were being transformed into places of visitation and play. Nation states that had emerged in the eighteenth and nineteenth centuries created massive national shrines in newly revamped capital cities, which included new forms of public architecture (houses of assembly, museums, universities, theatres and operas) often in campus-like central plazas. These buildings and the public art (especially sculpture) that typically provided a narrative of nation formation were explicitly spectacular and were fully intended to be visited in order to coopt, interpellate and recruit raw nation-pilgrims into the emotional and exciting space of nationalism. This was made possible by new forms of connectivity between cities and regions that broke down the dominance of district and regional life and created a more cosmopolitan national life. Railways brought large numbers of visitors and revellers into the very hearts of cities for the very first time, creating at the same time new opportunities to feed, water, entertain and educate. This was a new role for the industrial city and is an early starting point for the development of culture industries.

Beginning with the Great Exhibition of 1851 in London at the spectacular Crystal Palace, the major cities of the world began to vie with one another to lay on ever-more elaborate shows. The exhibitions and expositions, showcasing new industrial products, new design and technology became a regular feature and a regular draw and became a model for yet more major spectacular events. These included the biennales, which showcased art (the first being the Venice Biennale in 1895); the (modern) Olympic Games, beginning in 1896; the Grand Prix motor races, beginning in 1901 at Le Mans; film festivals, beginning with Venice in 1932; and international fringe comedy festivals, beginning with Edinburgh in 1947.

City life has also been embellished and enriched by the proliferation of new carnivals as well as the revival of old ones. The model for the new carnivals is the carnival in Rio de Janeiro which, in its modern form, has taken place every year since the 1930s but it draws on earlier, flamboyant festivals in Rio dating back to 1723. The Rio de Janeiro carnival is less a procession than an all-night parade of dance and its composition is made up from large numbers of formal and informal Samba Schools. It is not only the major show in Brazil but it has become a major international tourist attraction, bringing millions of participants and spectators into the city.

According to Pelan (2005), modern forms of carnival emanating from such places as Rio and Trinidad can be considered subversive and emancipatory versions of the Christian carnivals to celebrate the beginning and end of Lent (carnival literally means 'to mourn meat' and rich foods):

> Trinidad, in fact, is known as 'the Mecca of Carnival,' and the event itself is a bringing together of Trinidad's mixed religious heritage: Roman Catholicism (French, but some Spanish and Irish), Anglican, Islamic (primarily Sunni), Hinduism, the Church of Scotland, the East Indian Presbyterians, African religions, Spiritual Baptists, Pentecostals and fundamentalist Christians ... Central to its development was conflict among the elites of Trinidad, especially the ruling Anglicans and the Roman Catholic (largely French) planters who owned most of the estates. The European theory of carnival in Trinidad suggests that it is a pre-Lenten festival of the elite French and French Creole population, who permitted African and Afro-Creole masking and costuming, but only as part of the dominant Christian festival. After emancipation, Africans celebrated their freedom in the festivity known as *cannes brulées* (canboulay), which ultimately became central to the carnival space, resulting in a withdrawal by the white elites. Carnival in Trinidad today, then, is a form of cultural coup by Africans who changed what had been a Euro-Catholic festival into an Afro-Trinidadian one. (Riggio, 1998: 26, 30)
>
> Pelan 2005

The parallels with jazz seem clear enough.

The Notting Hill Carnival in London, which attracts up to two million people a year, is the second largest street party in the world (after Rio).[2] Critically, its first manifestation was a relatively low key affair, staged in 1959 as a community festival in St Pancras Town Hall. It was designed to create better race awareness and relations following the UK's first race riots of that year, and eventually it moved to a carnival format on the streets in 1965. Like Rio, this form of carnival is a music- and dance-based parade that showcases soca, calypso and several other musics and dance styles, but it is also a more confident assertion of West Indian presence in the streets of London and has contributed significantly to the renaissance of Notting Hill as a *cultural* area. It encouraged music publishers and record labels to move there, including Ndebele, Notting Hill Music and Rough Trade, and it has since developed a major night-time economy with the number of bars, clubs and restaurants growing each year. The efflorescence of Notting Hill as a cultural area can also be attributed to other literary and artistic currents that had very little to do with 'urban development' or 'commercialisation'. The 'cool' novels of Colin McInnes were of course set in Notting Hill and these established its credentials as formative of the culture that was to remake London as a cool place to live or visit. Critical here, as we have seen above, was the role of jazz and particularly the jazz clubs. The hero of *Absolute Beginners* takes us to the dark and fuggy world of 1950s Notting Hill jazz clubs, which he sees as his university. The club was a place of learning, where learning was not impeded by the judgement of others or where racial, class or gender discrimination operated. Jazz was the great leveller, it was mind expanding and a respite from the 'uncool' world outside.

These are precisely the reasons why jazz can be seen as one of the founding counter-cultural antecedents of contemporary city life since it is not only about tolerance and diversity. It is also about personal transformation and self-making under the ideal conditions of diversity of cultural possibilities and tolerance of personal outcomes. These are places where this can happen which makes them places of transition and ritual and marks them out as more exciting than the everyday.

Notting Hill was also the setting for some of Martin Amis's novels, and although these were not the sanguine, stylised work of McInnes, they did establish it as an edgy place, an unpredictable mix of migrant cultures, traditional market places, greed, poverty and affluence, but above all a place where people seem to mix promiscuously on the street and where cultural difference is bridged, albeit imperfectly. In other words, it was a perfect 'action space' in Goffman's terms.

Other cultural endorsements continued to build in Notting Hill, and included a major film feature starring Hugh Grant and Julia Roberts (which was also curiously concerned with how a place like Notting Hill facilitates the meeting or reconciliation of difference), the involvement of modern artist Damian Hirst with the restaurant 'Pharmacy' and the arrival of Tina Turner as a resident.

One-off or annual festivals have proven to be major crowd-pullers and a central element in the economic and cultural development of cities in the twentieth

Image 8.1 Taste of Tasmania food festival, Hobart, Australia (photo Adrian Franklin)

century. A rough and ready guide to their significance can be appreciated by the number of times the word 'festival' occurs in a Google search, against the first year of each decade since 1950. From 1950 until 1980 there was a gradual increase in the number found for each year (from 58,000 in 1950 to 74,300 in 1980), but the numbers rose considerably between 1980 and 1990 and even more so in each of the next two decades, reaching 32.2 *million* by 2007 (Figure 8.1). In part this is because festivals became a dominant model for event organisation (from formal to ritual forms) but it is also true that more and more cities and towns organised festival events as a means of concentrating and maintaining a high level of interest in what came to be called inner city regeneration that climbed on the back of the gentrification phenomenon. However, one of the more important reasons for the proliferation of festivals is their adoption by special interest and local community groups as a principal form of extended meeting, and as we saw in Chapter 7, this was a characteristically new feature of the counter-cultural groups who first recolonised crumbling city centres.

The rise of festivals as a form of assembly is critical to understand here. Festivals are particularly open, informal and unstructured events permitting a range of ways and intensities of engagement. Festivals are also more ritual-like than concerts: they do of course allow a purely spectator level of engagement

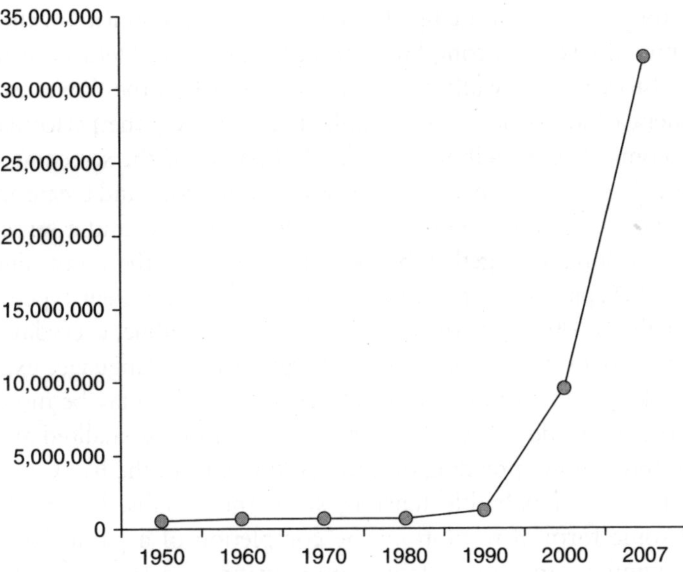

Figure 8.1 Number of hits for 'festival' by decade on Google (27 December 2007)

but they also invite participation, performance and delegation at a range of levels. Since many if not most of the festivals have a specialist interest, they become important foci for communities of interest that may be very widely, even internationally scattered. Such interests and events can easily transform into organisations with conventions and conferences as their main meetings and these have also grown incredibly since 1950.

The trend continues, A 2007 Google search using the word 'festival' resulted in 266 million hits, of which some 200 million were associated with a city or town. By comparison, there were only 314 million hits for 'cafés', 148 million for 'resorts' and 218 million for 'museums'. While this is only a very blunt measurement it does at least show the scale and significance of festivals relative to other important leisure spaces; a rough and ready guide to the increasing presence of more performative, ritualised activity as a component and proportion of city life.

Taking part in festivals, whether as a spectator or active participant, is unlike other forms of engagement with the city. For most it involves all of the stages of ritual discussed above. It involves preparation for and travel to the site of the festival, often a journey from the everyday to extraordinary spaces, spaces that are often dressed and decorated specially, spaces where special music, rhythm and dance form the background steady state. Then, festivals also typically draw participants into a range of special objects, objects that have particular significance, aura, association and transformative powers. These objects assist in the construction of a liminal space of the ritual, whether it is the Samba that is continually danced and processed in Rio (or the Calypso or the ethnic floats in Notting Hill, the Furry Dance in Helston or the Obby Oss in Padstow in Cornwall), the competitive space of the flower exhibitions at the Chelsea Flower Show, a Formula 1 motor race, the performance of a stand-up comic at the Melbourne Comedy Festival or the screening of a film at Cannes. These liminal spaces compress time and space and create among the participants a temporary community of fellow travellers and a sense of communitas or belonging together bracketed away from the constraints of the everyday. This space permits and even encourages a different type of excited behaviour that is often otherwise sanctioned in the public, everyday realm. It is characterised by playfulness, more energised body language, exaggerated gestures, joking and role inversions. Drugs and alcohol may be more permitted (at more or at odd times) and there may be a more sexualised atmosphere and tone (this is now spreading out, for example, from the Rio Carnivals).

There is often a palpable tension, since the ritualised festivals always involved some form of resolution: the completion of a parade or task, the resulting winners and losers from competition, the transformation from one state or place to another. For example, the May Day rituals sing and dance in the liminal space between spring and summer, the resolution being the safe arrival of summer. In the art biennales the liminal space consists of the massing together of the works of thousands of artists normally working and exhibiting alone, the resolution being that only a few will be chosen as winners and it will therefore be their work and their names that will define the art of the ensuing period. Whether one is the artist catapulted into a new status or part of the audience who witnessed the birth of a new style, trend or movement (and often they can be involved in public forms of judging and awards too), everyone is implicated in transformative processes that tend not to occur in the everyday. Thrift (2001) has argued that in addition to festivals individuals have become far more involved in rituals of the body, ritual techniques that induce trance-like states, create liminal periods of quiet and extended moments, stillness and slow time.

Arts festivals and the renaissance of cities

Arts events and arts festivals are an expensive and risky business to inject into a new place no matter how artsy the place thinks it already is; the graft is never guaranteed and the expense normally falls on the public purse unless there is already a grass roots art movement of international interest to hand – which of course there rarely is. So why are arts festivals such a strong part of every urban renewal strategy? What is so important about art?

Part of the reason lies in the relationship between art and governance and especially the relationship between art and the creative class. Art is rarely about producing a likeness of the world, a technique merely to mirror what is there. Art is all about changing the world; finding a way to imagine a better or at any rate a new world. It is what might or could or should be; how things might change – or have changed, rightly or wrongly. This is certainly true for modern art, which maintains a critical stance to modernity as well as being its vanguard (it maintains its bailiwick over the shock of the new). Keeping things as they are does not generate excitement but changing them does; some (the most successful) cities become spaces of change and so therefore share an affinity with modern art in general. The creative class *create* new things, their lives are predicated on change: art speaks to them.

Modern art has never been more popular and it is entirely down to the emergence of this new class. Leave a city untouched by modern art and it will wilt. Thirteen of the 15 core industries of Richard Florida's creative economy include art, i.e. design, film, advertising, architecture, performing arts, crafts, toys and games, video games, fashion, art, publishing and TV. Art is a core dimension of these workers' working lives, important in their lifeworld and therefore critical to any would-be creative city. Art is also widely diffused as a leisure interest and a key element in their touristic taste and therefore critical to policies to attract them as visitors.

So art is always the preoccupation of those in positions of governance and change. When art was a more restricted practice of the courtly social elite it performed an essentially similar role, confirming the projects of the elite or perhaps permitting them to imagine beyond the present. They could express what often could not be said or even thought, but through art the expression and reception of new ideas could percolate and infuse.

In Australia art played a key role in permitting people to imagine an Australia, and actually more than just one subsequently. At the same time the unveiling of new art caught up in fresh imaginings is always exciting, cathartic and therefore not surprisingly highly ritualistic. I am reminded of a truth from the pen of the playwright Alan Bennett, who talks in his biography (1998) of his limited stamina for new art exhibitions, by which he means that they are capable of generating intensities of mental and emotional involvement; churning, jarring, changing and confronting him, leaving him exhausted.

In Australia there is a track record of excitement at the reception of new works of art as well as a ritual regard for the Australian art canon. It was important long before café society and the small gallery scene emerged recently. Even before national state galleries, major works of art would travel by cart across most of Southern and Eastern Australia. The Pre-Raphaelite Holman Hunt's masterpiece *The Light of the World*, for example, toured small-town Australia alone in the mid-nineteenth century. It was unpacked, and hung in a town or church hall and advertised as a spectacle. Long queues formed to see it and a small entrance charged levied after the manner of the peep shows at fairs and carnivals. It was billed as an uplifting and moving experience and no doubt many received it as such. In 2009 Salvador Dali's art toured Australia in a major exhibition. As the Premier of Victoria said of the exhibition in his opening speech, 'It now ranks alongside other major events such as the F1 Australian Grand Prix, the spring racing carnival and the Australian Open Tennis as a tourist drawcard for Victoria'.

The Great Exhibitions of the nineteenth century heralded the arrival of national art, design and industrial life as a *national preoccupation*, which is to say that it ceased at that time to be the concern *solely* of the ruling elite, of the court and courtly circles (Prior, 2002). From then on it became part of the imaginative dream world of the masses. The defining moment was probably the first major international exhibition, the 1851 Great Exhibition in London. Originally it was not conceived to be a mass spectacle but a showpiece of British ingenuity to a world stage, a marketing device, especially. But the visionary Thomas Cook conceived of novel, unthought-of ways of taking ordinary working people by rail to see it. The logistical problems of establishing a mass excursion in a country where such a travel culture did not exist were as overwhelmingly difficult as persuading a non-travelling public to do so. Cook made a breakthrough in the sense that once popular travel had been experienced it proved to be addictive and the very quality that Cook observed in his first ever guided excursion of 1841 was a strange state of excitation that accompanied them (Withey, 1997).

Towards the end of the nineteenth century permanent art exhibitions, national and state galleries, were founded across the world, and while they too generated visiting as a practice on an unprecedented scale, they were permanent collections and did not systematically perform the new. The innovation that was to keep art on the leading edge of change was the biennale movement, beginning with *La Biennale di Venezia* in 1895. As early as 1910 this festival was testing the boundaries of modernity: the Secretary General, Antonio Fradelletto, 'had a work by Picasso removed from the Spanish salon in the central Palazzo, fearing that its novelty might shock the public' (www.labiennale.org).

The Venice Biennale has always dominated the art world, particularly the modern art world, and its leadership of a *revolutionary*, future orientated art force can be gleaned from its themes over recent years.

- 1979 Postmodernism: *La via novissima*
- 1990 Future Dimension
- 1994 Identity, Prospects, Reform
- 1995 Identity and Alterity
- 1997 Future, Present, Past
- 1999 Over All
- 2001 The Plateau of Humankind

- 2003 Dreams and Conflicts – The Dictatorship of the Viewer
- 2005 Tipping Point

Today, at the last count, there are 17 other biennale cities in the world (Montreal, Sydney, Kyoto, Zagreb, Berlin, London, Istanbul, Paris, Munich, Johannesburg, Prague, Varna, Shanghai, St Petersburg, Guangzhou, Beijing and Chengdu). These in turn have inspired arts festivals outside the major capitals and created a second line of arts cities, all of which, as Florida discovered, become attractive homes for contemporary elite workers. One thing they have in common is their place on the social margin, in places that are worth travelling to. Here the excitement generated by art and tourism combine.

The model for the provincial arts festival is the Edinburgh Arts Festival, but especially the comedy fringe festival. Edinburgh festivals started in 1947, in a city with a population of around half a million. While the main festival was decidedly an event for Scotland, even if it was an international festival, the fringe has become something more than that, with large numbers of small companies and their associated audiences travelling great distances to be there. It is now, for example, one of the key comedy institutions of the world. The population of Edinburgh doubles over the fringe period, the fringe provides employment for 4000 people and alone raises nearly seven million pounds.

The Adelaide Festival began in 1960 and in recent times, when Adelaide's population is around 1.1 million, it attracts something just over half a million paying visitors. The point is cities do not have to be central to be successful and some central biennales, such as the Sydney biennale, can be decidedly humdrum and lost in everything else, as I discovered myself in 2005.

How seaside came to the city

> Seaside towns and inland spas have, under local Acts, extensively developed municipal services [sports and other leisure facilities]. The object has been, of course, to make staying in these resorts pleasant for visitors. Is it not reasonable to suggest that the same efforts should *everywhere* be directed towards making a place attractive to its inhabitants? (Henry Durant, *The Problem of Leisure*, 1938: 255)

The sociologist Henry Durant's observation made in the mid-1930s is not merely a utopian socialist sentiment. In his consideration of leisure at the mid-twentieth century, particularly his assessment of the impact of the cinema and glamorous Hollywood movies, it seemed that there was a worrying disjuncture between the possible lifestyles portrayed in films and the somewhat grim reality of city life among cinema-goers. Most industrial cities offered a life of unremitting toil and boredom (see for example Stan Cohen's interview transcripts with Mods on Brighton beach in the 1960s: boredom and 'nothing to do' appeared to be the characteristic reported experience of London life at that time) and it must have seemed incongruous for there to be such a gap between the experience of the everyday and the holiday. However, the holiday, particularly in its mass manifestation as 'seaside', was never likely to remain on the social margin. The experience it provided in terms of excitement, reinvigoration, 'action spaces', freedom and redemption was not understood as simply the opposite of the industrial everyday but the very direction the future was taking everyone; it was the way modernity was heading (Franklin, 2003). As such, the early formative experience of seaside is as important to understand as its gradual adoption into city life. Beaches become special liminal places rendered ludic and festive by the new economy of national holidays in most Western nation states in the early twentieth century. Some companies began suggesting a seaside break for their workers, but then it was encouraged powerfully by national organisations and finally legislations.

To what extent did the experience of the seaside holidaymaker replicate the experience of pilgrimage? It is clear that the intentions of the holidays-with-pay movement and other organisations promoting the seaside and other holidays identified the importance of getting away from the everyday world of work, neighbourhood and city. An unremitting life of work was seen as unhealthy and unproductive; simple time off work would still leave the individual vulnerable to other obligations and chores and the city at this time was particularly polluted, dirty and for many a grim environment. Simply to get away, to do something different, even to face different challenges on the tourist road, characterised the sentiments of the seaside break.

While holidays were certainly approved by the legislators among industrialists and the professional middle classes, they were probably basing their judgement on the largely sedate and improving nature of their own tourism and resorts more than a deep understanding of the sociology of *working class* seasides. They were almost certainly not aware of forms of direct participation in crowds that Irving Goffman (1967) called 'fancy milling':

> [the] mere presence in a large, slightly packed gathering of revelling persons can bring not only the excitement that crowds generate but also the uncertainty of not quite knowing what might happen next, the possibility of flirtations, which can themselves lead to relationship formation and the lively experience of being an elbow away from someone who does manage to find real action in the crowd. (1967: 111)

Fancy milling has been considered an important ingredient of life at the seaside by many analysts of seaside behaviour, whether it is associated with drug taking (Uriely and Belhassen, 2006), casual sex (Wickens and Sönmez, 2007) or gang fighting (Cohen, 2002).

Although the seaside holiday of the interwar and post-war years can be seen as artificial, shallow and insubstantial – by its very nature – we need to appreciate that in fact it was an *exciting* experience. Pure pleasure spaces such as these, spangled and noisy and designed to deliver you into a state of elation, contrasted so dramatically with the industrial landscape of work. It is instructive here to think of the introduction of stained glass windows in medieval cathedrals and churches. To us now they seem unedifying and perhaps a little serious, if not moody even. However, when they were first innovated and built into the medieval cathedrals they took people's breath away; the spectacle produced excitement and the sensation that this was a very special, exalted place. Seasides buzzed with these special objects: magical piers, amusement arcades, entertainers, funfairs, coloured lighting twinkling at night, parks and gardens, monuments such as Blackpool Tower or the Winter Gardens at Bournemouth. But was this a deeper level of existence? In some ways it was. As Eugenia Wickens and Sevil Sönmez argue:

> several researchers reporting on tourists' hedonistic and self-indulgent lifestyles have argued that tourist resorts are 'liminal' spaces that provide the hedonistic tourist with opportunities to step outside of social conventions (Ryan & Kinder, 1996; Shields, 1991). While liminality describes the sense of in between-ness involving a temporary loss of social bearings, 'liminal space' refers to an area where 'strict social conventions are relaxed under the exigencies of travel and of relative anonymity and freedom from community scrutiny' (Shields, 1991, p. 50), whereas tourists are viewed as "free of all constraints ... to do as one pleases, to dress ... celebrate and feast ... they break the fetters of everyday rules ... have-a-good-time ideology and the tomorrow-we-shall-be-gone-again attitude sets the tone' (Krippendorf, 1987, p. 33). This perspective of tourism echoes others' views of it as an escape from everyday life into a free area – a notion that is isomorphic with the concept of 'liminal space'. (2007: 202–3)

Uriely and Belhassen (2006) also mention the importance of 'fancy milling' to behaviour in cities during festival times/atmospheres. They cite a study by Redmon (2003) 'who depicts the event of Mardi Gras in New Orleans as a themed backspace offering liminal license for people to participate in temporary forms of transgression, including public exposure of sex organs (flashing breasts, penis, etc.), masturbation, oral sex, and penetrative sex in public with strangers. Clearly, the tourists examined in these studies are depicted as uncontrolled action seekers' (2006: 345).

The material life of an industrial worker through the first half of the twentieth century was extremely basic. Sophistication and depth could be measured by access to luxury and the time to luxuriate. The seaside had depth and excitement for those who craved and dreamed of consumption and the things money could buy. It was no accident, for example that the giant Woolworths super store (the very first supermarket in the UK) was situated across the road from the central railway station of Blackpool, nor that this was the first port of call for most arriving by rail (Cross, 1990). Further, the seaside had depth in terms of social activities that could not normally be considered: café lunches, hotels and guesthouses, sports, such as tennis, swimming, clock golf ... In a consumer society fixated on the luxurious lifestyles of celebrity Hollywood, it is quite easy to see that all this was more than charming; it was sacred, magical, amazing; but also personally transforming and therefore similar to salvation. Turner and Turner (1978: 3) argue that liminoid rituals of this kind are about transition, what is 'going to be' but also 'what may be'. It is hard not to imagine tourists of the mid-twentieth century as being excited by the speed of technological and consumer change. Real wages did grow, consumer power grew dramatically even during the 1930s, the world of goods expanded and it was possible to be drawn into utopian dreams of a consumer future. For all its kitsch glamour and carnivalesque borrowings it still held the promise of a leisure future that was more fun, more exciting. Indeed Durant's (1938) discussion of leisure in the late 1930s reveals that government and planning rhetoric contained a clear intention to model new urban leisure policy on the seaside. In other words, the seaside was a metaphor for the consumer society just around the corner; a world (later dubbed 'the leisure society') that might be ...

During this period the numbers of people who could imagine the fixed place of holidays and leisure in their lives steadily grew. For many of these their first glimpse of a more pleasured life was made at the seaside; the seaside was replete with symbols, architectures, objects and texts that provided an imprint or paradigm structure of a new kind of lifestyle based more on leisure and pleasure. The sheer proliferation of exhortations and encouragements of these objects interpellated a leisure subjectivity and this was confirmed through *devotion*, and the crowds of fellow passengers. So much of this seaside consumer excitement relied on the imaginative and speculative world of the future; in this sense we can understand seaside as the promise of a brighter dazzling and more techno-pleasured future.

So developed new 'spectacular' seasides; large centres with a very considerable emphasis on spectacular pleasures, entertainments and elements of fantasy. These include the major seaside towns of Blackpool, Morecombe, Margate and Great Yarmouth in Britain and Coney Island, New York and Redondo Beach, Los Angeles in the USA and the Luna Park under the spectacular new bridge in Sydney. They were predominantly mass holiday and play venues and largely, although not exclusively, working class. If they were not exclusively working class, we can say that they were inscribed with a populist social tone, and as such they maintained a claim to being a ritual spectacle of the common people. These were the forerunners of Disney-styled theme parks[3] and in many respects these aspects of seaside are now detached from the sea and the beach, and the rituals of health and restfulness that they grew from. They are still very often on coastal sites, as in Florida and San Diego, USA or the Gold Coast in Australia, but they are clearly also separable and placed in major inland cities.

Theme parks

City-based theme parks are now so normative and their fantasy component so widely diffused in the city (from theme parks to theme malls to theme shops, eateries and cafés, entertainments, and so on) that Hannigan (1998) is able to suggest the notion of *Fantasy City* as a metaphor for the contemporary metropolis. As a result, tourism, or at least the pleasures it used to deliver, has become an everyday experience, and even though we now make many trips away from home they are no longer confined to 'holidays' or what Rojek (1993) means by 'escape attempts'. As he argues, 'the distinctions between the world of duty and the world of freedom have lost much of their force experientially and therefore are of dubious analytical value' (Rojek, 1993: 169).

The Mass Observers (see Cross, 1990) did indeed anticipate the way spectacle display parks were heading. Increasingly these parks were attentive to the worlds of modernity and modern consumerism, in other words these parks were related not to rituals of social reproduction and renewal as with the carnivalesque, but to rituals of transition: *the experience initiates the participant into the new themes, technologies and experiences of a changing modernity*. If day-to-day life in modernity was a line of flight towards multiple other 'future' worlds, the idea of *an* (i.e. singular) other world lost its currency: from now on the other world came at us from the future and via channels of technology and consumerism. In Tony Bennett's later (1983) analysis of Blackpool this point was made of the pleasure Beach – for almost all of its twentieth century history:

> From its earliest days as a seaside resort the by-word of Blackpool, recurring again and again in its publicity brochures, has been *Progress*. In the Pleasure Beach ... pleasure is resolutely modern. Its distinctive 'hail' to pleasure-seekers is constructed around the large mechanical rides, unavailable elsewhere in Blackpool and packaged for consumption as a manifestation of progress, harnessed for pleasure. (Bennett, 1983: 146, 140)

But it was but not only the exciting rides that made their way into city life. Other forms of 'action space' entertainment also became part of a common experience of life in the city with similar effects. As Lewis Erenberg shows, these types of action spaces were gradually recruited into the city and participated in the modernisation of self and sexual relations. The cabaret, for example, ploughed new ground:

> By the 1910s the cafes served as settings for action and vitality for both sexes, allowing them places to question limitations over their personal lives. The cabaret thus represented two major conflicting trends in twentieth century life: an impulsive self-fostered style for individual living and an institutional and rational specialization of social roles. ... the cabaret represented institutional spontaneity. Here in the breaking of barriers between actor and audience, men and women had the chance to risk their selves, to be expressive, to be a vital part of urban life. In fancy milling ... one is brought together with others, those who are famous, who appear glamorous, above the controls of social life, sometimes even above the law, who seemingly live a life of constant excitement and danger. (Erenberg, 1984: 133)

At one level tourists seem abundantly happy to visit theme parks such as Disney World or other film studio theme parks where the exhibits and worlds are nothing other than the characters and things that they already know and where a major attraction is the 'opportunity' to purchase associated merchandise, a means of deepening and concretising their association with transcendent consumer brands and products. Is there much of a difference between a Disney key ring and the tin–lead ampullas of holy water sold at Canterbury in Chaucer's day? Probably not, except that the modern consumer of a key ring is less prone to the sensing of aura than the fourteenth century pilgrim, even though in both cases what is purchased is a copy of the original. The modern consumer makes up for auratic quality deriving from a limited number of wonders with an unlimited supply of consumer creations and their reproducibility. In the case of celebrity, which is increasingly itself the object of themed attractions, the auratic possibility is far stronger, as indeed the zeal for it is more religious and 'devoted'. Its current voguishness may be understood in relation to the collapse of aura in consumerist societies: Marilyn Monroe, Princess Diana and John Lennon are refreshingly one-off.

Several authors, including Harvey (1989) and Rojek (1993), argue that the seemingly absurd eclecticism of those theme parks that mix or compress space and time by having mixtures of historical moments and geographical domains jammed together on a small acre site, are nothing other than the way the world is experienced by modern consumers – the way London is compressed, for example, through its mediation by the Underground. As Rojek (1993: 164) says, 'simultaneity and sensation are at the heart of the postmodern experience': the world we live in *is* simulation or a world socially constructed for tourists (and others) by what Rojek in a later paper has termed indexing and dragging. Indexes refer to the set of possible visual, textual and symbolic representations to an original object, while dragging refers to the agency by which elements from different indices may be assembled to create a new value (Rojek, 1997: 53–4). Places, for example, can now be evoked as much by novels and films set in them as by what actually happened there.

So these are strange new worlds that are not Other to us but symptomatic of us as an essentially transformative culture, and these sites are compelling because they interpellate new subjectivities, that can yield to and participate in a more simulated, negotiated and constructed world. We would and do soon tire of these worlds given to us as attractions; they must continue to usher in novel interpretations, technologies, information, acts, simulations and hybrids: they must relate powerfully to us as consumers and provide, as Rojek argues, a sense of who we are becoming in a concentrated form. This was the challenge to developers who would transform city life into excitement, leading edge experiences and embarkation points into brighter futures.

The planning of urban regeneration?

In the 1980s and 1990s urban regeneration was taken a step forward through major new developments and cultural projects by partnerships of business and local government. As Ley (1995) argued, however, we must not lose sight of the fact that it was only after counter-cultural and middle class transformations of the city had often already taken place, making them first and foremost into attractive *cultural* spaces, that more significant capital was invested in them by other groups and corporations. The renaissance of Manchester, for example, particularly its Northern Quarter, seems to have relied heavily upon the development of the typically small/medium businesses of its vibrant culture industries (many of which developed within counter-cultures such as music, design, fashion and food) and rather less on the local city council or partnerships with government and developers (Brown et al., 2000). Indeed, as these authors show, in the case of Sheffield, without prior spontaneous informal development from among the culture industries, occupying new spaces and clustering in colonies, subsequent new organised development may not always work. However, these developments did catch the eye of both central and local government and major developers who could spot the basis for a sustainable or at least relatively long-lived investment potential in the spaces of the central city. Even the small-scale businesses characterising the culture industries realised that only they could guarantee a sustainable future:

> The early 1990s saw cities linking 'quality of life' issues and tourism which used a wider notion of culture – the 'feel', the 'atmosphere', the bars and restaurants, the night life. Cities became 'European cities' – a strangely mythical, amorphous notion involving cafe bars, cappuccinos and late licences. This image and facilities based approach, linked to the attraction of real estate investment in the central sections of the city, was part of an 'urban regeneration' model drawn from North America. Culture renewed the built stock, revived the image, created a tourism infrastructure and underpinned the vibrant, late night 'European city'. (Brown et al., 2000: 439)

The so-called American model or urban regeneration based on the realisation that cities had now become 'fun' or could be made more fun has been well documented by John Hannigan (1998). Beginning in the 1980s with the astonishing transformation of Baltimore, for the next twenty years other deindustrialised American cities tried to work the same magic. In recent years, especially through the work of people like Charles Landry and Richard Florida, the ingredients of this magic are being sifted through; how a city space dominated by innovative energy can be assembled or planned for (Landry, 2001: *xv*) and how to combine the three key ingredients (technology, talent and tolerance) that constitute the attractor for its social base, the so-called *creative class* (Atkin, 2003; Florida, 2003a). However, while technology, talent and tolerance may be critical taxonomic variables that all successful contemporary cities share, it seems that none of them stands a chance of developing unless it is a fun place, a place that is not only innovative but invigorating.

With some notable exceptions, such as New York, London and Paris, many mid-twentieth century modern city centres were practically dead after office hours and on weekends; and many still are. They were mostly redesigned for the massive post-war consumer retail boom combined with the centralisation of major businesses and corporations. The result was the removal of less profitable residential, particularly working class residential, property and the building of shopping centres and office blocks. These bustled between eight and six o'clock during week days but were quiet at other times. City life at this time was more dissipated across wider cityscapes; it was less intense and set around more low-key activities. Most new leisure development, with an emphasis particularly on sport and country club development, followed the more affluent into the suburbs while at the same time, the same industry concentrated on building holiday resorts on the coast, in the mountains and lakes and in the overseas 'pleasure periphery'. Generalising, we can say that city life oscillated between work and light leisure modes that contrasted strongly with more intense and excitement-driven experiences during vacations. Under these conditions in the early 1970s, the development of city centres was 'not viewed as an attractive proposition' (Hannigan, 1998: 51).

The spark for renewal came from a number of sources. First, during the 1970s, as we have seen, the inner city areas began to gain in popularity, house prices were being driven up by the early gentrifiers and they were considered fashionable, artsy, quirky and attractive places to visit. Second, their docklands, industrial and warehousing areas were run down if not standing idle, thus providing a once-in-a-lifetime possibility for major redevelopment. Unlike other spaces in the city they were only lightly populated and were unlikely to generate stiff opposition. Third, a new type of multi-function pleasure space was envisaged that would draw large crowds of visitors and trippers into the city centre on weekends and during the night. Calling for 'flagship destination projects ... that were safe, exciting and not available in the suburbs' (1998: 51), these cities began to build a raft of new and interrelated spectacles: new convention centres, casinos, exhibition centres, museums, entertainment facilities and centres, open plazas, art galleries. These were rendered coherent spaces by redeveloping scenic wraparounds out of the large former industrial spaces, waterways and docks, riversides and parklands. Now it was even desirable to envisage building major sporting stadiums at the very heart of the city and these were built in the centre of Cardiff, Manchester and Sunderland, for example. Barcelona and Sydney used the opportunity of the Olympic Games, and Manchester and Melbourne their holding of the Commonwealth Games to build sporting infrastructures upon which a sustainable sports *tourism* industry could be based (Hall, 2004). And it is not only the super cities who can do this: Indianapolis turned its economy around from 'smokestack to stadium' according to a study on sports fandom there by Roan in 1998, and Sheffield remade itself as Britain's first 'National Sports City' (Hall, 2004: 195).

Very rapidly, sufficient of these cities became tourist destinations in their own right and vied with the resorts that in many ways could not compete with their star attractions (major art galleries, museums, sporting clubs and national associations and cultural centres were very loath to move to the coast, for example). Developed in partnerships between city government and (nervous) private investors, these 'destination spaces' created a new image for central districts which had previously suffered from the negative image based on crime, insecurity, graffiti, vandalism and gangs. And while one of their great (and sustained) criticisms is that they failed to deliver economic fortunes to the urban poor (see Atkinson and Helms, 2007), and even that poverty in such areas deepened, the widely shared perception was that they were miraculous transformations, and transforming, often turning around, a city's fortunes by making them more attractive to the high-tech industries and their all-important employee base, the creative class (Florida, 2003a).

Hannigan shows how the urban regeneration model emanating from the United States originates from a relatively small number of 'maverick developers' such as James Rouse, who introduced the first closed shopping malls and later festival market places which had a Disney-like feel to them. Eschewing further replication of collections of major chain stores, Rouse kept the level of novelty and interest high by restricting their number and introducing high quality speciality shops and pushcart sellers – even circulating such businesses through short-lease arrangements. Instead of a guaranteeing standardisation and quality, he provided variety and surprise – and in addition the shoppers were treated to liberal amounts of entertainment and the possibility of eating in the heightened atmosphere.

In all of the cities I encountered while doing fieldwork for this book the centrality of shopping to the vitality and energy of a city seemed very obvious. Without good shopping, exciting shops, arcades and squares none of the regeneration would come off. It is one of the reasons why regeneration often seems such a poor deal for the city's low-income groups; why, even when they live very close to the shops, it is as if they are on a different planet.

Into the 1980s and 1990s the Rouse formula extended across the Western world, though by the 1990s it was looking somewhat tarnished and overexposed. Although it is still commonplace in shopping areas, the general trend from the 1990s onwards was for a greater cultural component to be added into the mix, more serious festivals and rather less entertainment. As in the case of Sheffield, city governments could use its ownership and control of remaining unused space to encourage neo-bohemian quarters relatively cheaply.

These were not only linked into the more developed and institutionalised inner city arts community and scene, they were also working in situ and selling directly to the public. Such developments were not always guaranteed to succeed and, as Brown et al. demonstrate in their comparison of cultural quarters in Manchester and Sheffield, the successful developments, as in the case of the Camden Lock example, are often more spontaneous and driven by the artists and businesses themselves rather than through the application of facility- and grant-led development models. Joost Smiers (2000) agrees, arguing that a palpable atmosphere of creativity needs to well up from the city as it does in many successful instances as opposed to where money is simply thrown into arts projects to 'bolster prestige, aid urban renewal or promote tourism' (Smiers, 2000: 111). In a similar vein, Andreas Wiesand argues against the European Cultural Capital model: 'Marketing does not suddenly make Glasgow the cultural capital of Europe. In itself it is an interesting city, but it would be better if it would refrain from promoting itself with all that rubbish you are obliged to put out when you are selected to be "European cultural capital" for a year. It costs money and helps nobody' (Wiesand quoted by Smiers, 2000: 112).

> In Glasgow ... one should delve back into the history of the city and the region. There you can find many sources of inspiration – in design, in furniture, for instance. Let the sources that are actually there express the role they want to play in the artistic field. (Smiers, 2000: 113)

The spark may not always originate from the past, however. Some of the more interesting cultural quarters have sprung from *young* artists wanting to produce new works, styles, designs and performances, often not home town kids but graduates from elite institutions. Cities really do take in, transform and provide opportunities to their vast array of migrants. Examples include the artist-bar enterprises that make up a lot of the city life in Melbourne's Lanes district in the heart of the city. The Lanes had previously served as the service conduits for the major retailing stores and retail-orientated small industries. When much of this space fell vacant and the rents crashed in the 1990s it became possible for young Melbourne artists, many of them graduates of nearby city art and design institutes, to rent these spaces for workshops. Owing to the relatively liberal liquor licensing laws in Melbourne, these artists were also able to subsidise their art by developing café, food and bar businesses on site. The importance of having the right conditions to grow such impromptu colonies or quarters was illustrated by a TV programme on art [Not Quite Art, 16 October 2007; www.abc.net.au/tv/notquiteart/]. The Melbourne Lanes phenomenon was contrasted with the absence of anything like it in nearby Sydney. In inner Sydney rental values prohibit anything other than established businesses from taking root and local liquor licences are more difficult to obtain and jealously guarded by vested interests. These enterprises were instantly more appealing than the more commercial inner city rivals; they combined bar space with gallery and even retail space and they were cheap, plus their number grew rapidly creating a critical mass that could be and was added to the city's cultural itinerary. Their presence has also made the night-time economy of Melbourne more varied and interesting, especially given that they are not all reproducing essentially the same product. One of the more interesting developments are bars that feature wrap-around screens showing locally produced video films, or small screening spaces off from main bar areas. These provide income not only for the bars but the growing number of film- and video-makers who, because of their concentration in this area, gain by being networked into financial and exhibition organisations and venues.

So, why is it that cultural quarters and other cultural developments, particularly indigenous, named or spontaneously generated accretions and movements are such important contributors and maintainers of that crucial urban buzz or 'aliveness'? And how does that relate to the overall health of contemporary cities?

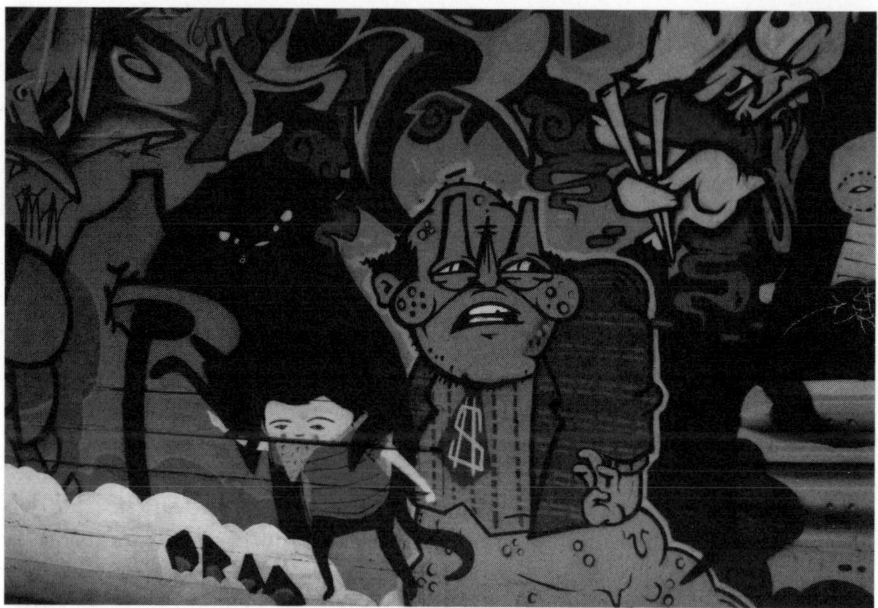

Image 8.2 City Art, Melbourne Lanes, Melbourne, Australia (photo Adrian Franklin)

The most obvious answer stems from the new and enlarged role that culture plays in contemporary societies and economies. As we saw in the previous chapter on lifestyle, contemporary societies do not feature stable and enduring subjectivities and identities and therefore cultures. Individuals live in a constant state of self-making which involves remaking themselves, reinventing themselves in a constant steady state of flux and change. There is now a new and barely acknowledged group of cultural leaders who have largely replaced what Bauman called 'legislators'. Rather than mobilise expert knowledge to set down codes, laws and norms about how people are to live, in the contemporary consumer choice economy expertise is not legitimating so much as 'offering alternative', 'providing advice', 'creating new solutions', 'advancing new therapeutic regimes'. Owing to the extraordinary range and potential for cultural expression, culture generally, and especially perhaps urban culture has become highly fragmented, specialised and ephemeral. As such an enormous thirst exists for new practitioners, new products, more frequent shifts in style and fashion, new ideas, new techniques and technologies.

Secondly, words like 'buzz' and 'atmosphere' refer then to the concatenation, circulation, clamouring, hectoring, and interpellative noise and ferment of this new creativity. It cannot rest, it has to be on the front-foot, heavily marketed, up-sold, hyped, reviewed, evaluated, sold with the accompaniment of music, and wherever possible, endorsed by celebrity – with food ... Therefore it exists in a state of commotion and disturbance which becomes the looked-for background hum of interesting cities and in its absence the defining feature of dull or dead cities.

Thirdly and relatedly, it entails a great deal of movement and mobility. So much of this culture is embodied and performative: inscribed on the surface and layers of the body; directed at its health, fitness and look; choreographed through kinaesthetic, sensory and prehensile techniques; aimed at producing health, vigour, vitality, well-being, sexual fulfilment, happiness, ecstasy and joy; requiring new discipline, application, connoisseurship and of course *practice and training*. A feature of cities that are 'buzzless' is their relative stillness [unless that, of course, is offered by way of therapeutic solutions to the near-universal problem of fast time and fast culture], their predictability, their acceptance of things as they are. It is not only in the more informal culture spaces that this has become characteristic. Even in the major galleries, if successfully managed, this can become a defining feature.

The fourth reason why these cultural quarters produce a feeling of aliveness is that they produce ritual-like states and stages in personal and social transition. No longer do we metamorphose through predictable universal age-related stages of a life cycle; through known stages prefaced by ancient *rites de passage*. In many pre-industrial, premodern societies these form a large proportion of the events that mark the annual calendar and the content of sociability and exchange. In contemporary societies the passage from one stage to another has been replaced by a proliferation of states or manifestations of the self in an open-ended procession of self-making. All of the excitement and effervescence that Durkheim related to occasional states of ritual transformation are now supercompressed into an eternal ritual present. Precisely because our metamorphoses are never completed, because we never want to be completed and because no end-point is ever envisaged or desired, we are left with desire itself – the desire or wish to be other than we are. This means that the buzz and atmosphere relates to the permanent presence of rituals of self and group transformation. Such states are always present; life is always provisionally and ritually entailed away into something else. I have observed this at what might be called the trivial level (though I anticipate others' comments here rather than describe my own thought on the matter) in the buying of fashion accessories, clothes and shoes, for example, and at the profound level as when people engage in neo-paganistic magic, or ceremony, as when they convert to a new lifestyle movement or credo. In the context of our consumerist society, where incredibly finely tuned degrees of taste are routinely exercised and *matter* materially and tangibly in other ways, a new pair of shoes can be an important choice and affect important transformation. I am alerted to and take very seriously the seemingly throw-away complaints of parents about their children's heightened concern to be bought the right type of trainers, for example. I have watched children studying shoe-shop windows and their manner often betrays great excitement mixed with great concern: it is clear that they judge themselves to be at a critical point of change, not simply a change of footwear. Although it might seem trivial, the difference between the right pair of shoes and the wrong pair may have very profound effects on the child's social status, position in social groups, evaluation of their taste and connoisseurship and their general competence. Therefore, those who successfully position themselves as design innovators, artists, creators of new products etc. find themselves at the centre of unprecedented attention and need.

A fifth reason is that by and large the culture industries uphold a *critical* tradition and new works typically attempt to engage critically with contemporary society, economy, politics and ecology. The cultural industries therefore exhibit leadership in the *translation* of critiques and the new ideas that spring from them in accessible *forms* or at least, the objectification of these ideas. Their products therefore tend to be less consumer durables than positional goods; compressed ideas expressed through artistic, craft or design registers. Like other significant, individual or group-defining objects, or sacred objects, they tend to command a higher or heightened reverence, higher prices, greater respect and interest. Collectively they express the new ideas of the moment, the here and now and challenge in exciting ways, existing practices, attitudes and values. Because they do this they are always more than merely *new*. Examples of this in London alone include the Carnaby Street of the mid-to-late 1960s, Biba, Heals contemporary style in the 1950s, Kings Road punk fashions of Vivian Westwood in the late 1970s, the design leadership of Terence Conran through his Habitat stores in the 1970s and 1980s, Twentieth Century Design (Kensington Church Street) in the 1990s. We should also include other areas of creative challenge in change: for example in the area of food and body. Here we might include fusion, vegetarian and seafood innovations, real ale and wine makers, and hair and body products. The London vegetarian chain Cranks is an archetype here; or Moosewood in California.

Sixth, since cities are so dependent on the social relations of tourism, cultural quarters or districts have greater appeal when they contain an ethnos or ethnographically specific or coherent content or movement, rather than the mere repetition of chain stores or international styles. This links the experience of the city with the specific people or cultures of the city in a way that grander, more prestigious international art and design collections cannot. Having a natural habitat in the city allows what Malcolm Miles calls 'the social life of small urban spaces' to develop and thrive because it concentrates a particular group of people both working and hanging out in its space. It is curious how the development of ethnos can become touristically interesting to cultural outsiders. One thinks here of the straight presence at the Sydney Gay and Lesbian Mardi Gras, the otherwise very unspecified presence of different West Indian island communities in London at the Notting Hill Carnival, Rusholme's south Asian 'curry mile' in Manchester, or the huge attraction that central London punks (ironically) provided during the 1980s. I would argue that these are socially transformative, ritual-like spaces rather than merely places to shop, buy or eat. This is why they have to have spaces to gather and assemble, places to share food and drink, places for dancing, sex and meeting.

Of course, much does depend on the key social groups that different cities deem to be critical to their regeneration. Much has been made of Florida and Landry's work on the defining qualities of the top cities in the USA, notably their reliance on attracting the high-tech industries and the creative class who work in them. Here the anthropology of the city becomes a critical thing for companies to think about in their location decisions. However, not all cities can be top American cities and almost all of them will not aspire to attract large concentrations of hi-tech industries. Nonetheless, for the very reasons outlined in the six points above, there is something *generally* important about cultivating, encouraging and maintaining a critical cultural mass in most cities and finding ways of creating spaces of spectacle, excitement and ritual.

NOTES

1 See Anthony Elliott's *The Mourning of John Lennon* (1999) for a sociological account of Lennon's appeal to mourners and pilgrims.
2 According to Sky News (http://news.sky.com/skynews/article/0,,30100-13609012, 00.html).
3 For a good discussion of these see Bennett, 1983; Hannigan, 1998; Rojek, 1993.

9 City Natures

In *Soft City* Raban made the case for the magical, mysterious and unfathomable *natural* qualities of cities as opposed to their typical sociological characterisation as the rational, antithesis of nature, as pure culture, machines for living, the result of 'urban policy'. Humans may always try to order their world (they are destined by nature to do so perhaps), and their actions are often intended to achieve *an* order (for this *can* be conceived in the abstract realm of thought and fantasy and imagination and occasionally realised, for a while outside of these realms) but these are only ever imaginings and (often failed) ordering *attempts*, and they become absorbed, twisted, confounded and entwined as they collide with the great many other non-human orderings. As Raban (1974: 159) put it, 'For most of their inhabitants, cities like New York and London *are* nature, and are as unpredictable, threatening, intermittently beautiful and benign as a tropical rain forest. That they are in point of fact *constructs* is a mighty and deluding irrelevance.'

Some of these non-human orderings are the great pulses and waves of nature, its weather and climate systems, its unfathomably complex configuration of species and genetic materials (many of which have co-evolved as symbionts and parasites of the human), others are the technologies and materials already circulating from past human ordering attempts (deep, invisible and unpredictable sediments and layers of potential as the sociologist Ulrich Beck characterised them); some of these are benign, not as yet clearly connected to human orderings and others arise as serial rounds of direct responses to human interventions (the Mississippi to the multiple [often failing] concrete and steel structures of the Corps of Engineers at New Orleans, for example). We should not therefore confuse *attempts* to purify or distil a human order, or pure culture from nature with the *existence* of a pure human order, separable from nature. This is the deluding irrelevance of which Raban speaks and the profound truth contained in Bruno Latour's *We Have Never Been Modern*. As Latour (1993) argues, the more we try to purify ourselves from nature the more we produce human–nature hybrids.

Cities are inevitably natural configurations and operate in ways that are similar to other ecologies. This is why they present themselves to their human inhabitants as a challenge every bit as great as any other environment; and why they continually appear as problems, rather than solutions, to the question of *dwelling* (see Ingold, 1993). Two things flow from such a view. The first is that city life is composed of such a complexly and richly intertwined assemblage of objects and beings, so shot full of intended and unintended consequences of their association, and such mangled lines of flight that it can never be entirely predictable, knowable or static.[1] As Raban says:

> to live in a real city is to live in just as indomitable an environment as any valley full of rocks and stones and trees. Streets, shops, cafes, houses, underground railways and office blocks are not, for most of us, matters of choice and reason merely because someone built them out of bricks and mortar and decided that they would be useful there. The city dweller is constantly coming up against the absolute mysteriousness of other people's reasons. (1974: 158)

But also relevant here is the way they are themselves configured and reconfigured as networks and associations with objects, technologies, texts, signs and systems. Thus modern urbanites cannot be distinguished from pre-industrial people on the basis of a more rational mentality and stance to their world because even their world cannot be apprehended as such. Both are as magical and as rational as each other; which still leaves the city magical. Yet until recently, few urban studies scholars have attempted to probe and reveal this quality, preferring to distinguish cities and culture from nature and environment. My notion of city life and ecological cities attempts to reverse this nonsense.

Secondly, in the minds of its human and perhaps non-human subjects the city thus presents itself as *strange*, seemingly having a life all of its own and one that requires the development of techniques of prediction, sense-making and control. Sociology is but one of these techniques. As Steve Pile argues in his *Real Cities* (2005), '[s]omething about city life lends itself to being read as if it had a state of mind, a personality, as having a particular mood or sentiment, or as privileging certain attitudes and forms of sociation'. He agrees with others who write in this vein, such as Amin and Thrift (2002), that this is how most modern cities can be distinguished from each other; on *these* sorts of terms rather than on their putative rational structures of buildings, communications and landscape. Pile argues that what is real about cities 'is as much emotional as physical, as much visible as invisible, as much slow moving as ever speeding up, as much coincidence as connection' and he suggests that by seeing it as *phantasmagoria* we stand a better change of grasping it.

The term phantasmagoria captures the way real city life is experienced as movement rather than fixedness; 'of a procession before the eyes' and of things beyond the visible or tangible. In other words, cities are also necessarily comprised of projections, fantasies, imaginings that are ghost-like and dream-like. Through this emotional work the city street, the crowd and the cityscape become enchanted and therefore add up to something that can be thought about, written about and talked about. Seen in this way the city can perhaps be accurately described, though possibly novelists and poets have had an advantage over most sociologists and anthropologists who have been bent on uncovering their blueprint social system. But because cities just don't have one, most, like those of the Chicago School, are merely beautiful fantasies. Because novelists need to explore how characterisation is formed they are more open to the *potentiality* of cities and the necessary way in which individuals conceive of their mysteries, powers, characterisations and narratives. In the hands of writers London is a mighty natural phenomenon, as significant as any forest, cyclone or infection.

Like all major cities London has been the setting for much writing and the Great Wen itself and/or its distinctively different districts, typically seem to appear as characters in them. As Will Self wrote about his own tales, 'I don't mean simply that they were set in London, I mean that the city was the main – and possibly the only protagonist' (Self, 1999: 122). One is strongly reminded here of James Joyce's *Dubliners*, where Dublin seems to be alive and active/present in the lives of its residents. 'Through a process of secretion and compilation, Joyce builds up the geography of his nighttime world to describe the transcendent city that stands at last as the simulacrum of the twentieth city.' Cities fascinated Joyce, but not just as symbols, as summations. For him they were alive. According to Potts (1979: 261) 'they appeared to him as collective individuals, history turned into shape and space, large reservoirs of *life*' (my emphasis). Thus, as Begnal (2002) writes, 'When Anna Livia Plurabelle addresses her husband Earwicker, he becomes a living urban presence, a city, inseparable from the place where he exists' (Begnal, 2002: xx).

The city or its multiple parts therefore *act* on the human characters and the landscape in which they live in tangible, tacit and profound ways. In fact it seems to dominate and overshadow whatever agency mere individual humans can muster against it, to make ground against its *push*. And it is in this sense that cities appear as colossal ecological entities whose only cognate form is nature itself; but then again (let us remind ourselves) they are, after all, nature itself.

London surely is one of the world's most astonishing epicentres of symbiosis, of myriad relationships between living organisms and their material cultures, black holes of global energy and materiality, giant nodes of things and beings in choreographed (albeit loose and chaotic) movement and circulation. It is no wonder that the city itself appears god-like or nature-like or enchanted to its writers. This impression is an old one. Daniel Defoe visualised London as a great body that 'circulates all, exports all and at last pays for all' (Ackroyd, 2001: 1). Ackroyd, thinks of it as a labyrinth half of stone and half of flesh ... experienced as 'a wilderness of alleys and passages, courts and thoroughfares' (2001: 2). By comparison, even the planners and architects of change pale into insignificance, their bickering and debating missing by a long way the terms and conditions that really matter. It is always the case that their buildings and even their connecting technologies of roads and rails are less important than the specifically complex ecology they have to work on, through and with. A tall tower block of apartments is never a universal habitat; does not specify an ecology or habitus. It will succeed or fail as any one of these depending on the confluences, junctures, habits, weather, pulses, beats and narratives that are always already in train in any given city.

Novelists whose stories have been based in London seem to share this realisation, despite differences of history and generation and despite disparities of literary style. Commenting on Virginia Woolf's essay 'Street Haunting', Jervis (1998: 71) argues that 'There is a sense in which the city as experience returns to nature'. Jervis contends that Woolf is not using nature merely as a metaphor but as a descriptive reality: in her case an especially gendered imagination of it. 'Street Haunting' is not the only place where she makes such observations: 'Elsewhere, in *Orlando* (Woolf, 1977: 183–5), for example, Woolf is energised by the natural throb of the city; its pulse and life force; her so called 'thick stream of life', (cited in Jervis, 1998: 71).

John Betjeman's London poems are set in this 'thick stream of life' and are as often about movement and connectivity as about place and character. In his 'Middlesex' he reminds us that London's suburbs were sold first as countryside and that the outer suburbs were villages whose spirit was kept alive by surviving (i.e. maintained) hedgerows, the practice of gardening and the railways that still run through their heart. A lot of poems such as this one have the rhythm and movement of a slow suburban trail that stops at each suburb and village, but they are not a celebration of the machinic triumph of humanity but an awkward, messy but none-the-less comfortable accommodation between the march of human technology and a resilient nature. For the human inhabitant, London is a procession of movement before the eyes as well as a structure of feeling. 'Parliament Hill Fields' portrays a world that can only be apprehended in the endlessly repetitive suburban train and tram journeys where the aesthetics of signage and adverts blur into those of shrubbery and park.

Londoners are networked into the mysteries of its public transport system every bit as much as they are into its housing market (which other city could give rise to the Radio 4 panel game 'Mornington Crescent'?). London's technical connectivity, through its pathways, routes, maps and diagrams, provides for many the only coherent way of knowing its shape and character. Its tempos and termini seem to count out the very pace and direction of life, providing continuity and movement even in times of difficulty. This is captured by Betjeman's poignant poem 'Devonshire St W1' (Betjeman, 2003: 177), where, at a physician's rooms, a couple have just learned of the husband's terminal illness. In the face of this personal catastrophe and death, their composure is temporarily restored in the last few lines, through their reconnection to life: their joint calculation of the best journey home by bus and tube. Against the frailty and ephemeral nature of the human condition, Betjeman's characters seem to take solace in the enduring flows of the number 19 or 22 bus.

Colin MacInnes's 'London Trilogy' was set in the 1950s, a time during which major shifts in social composition, industry, culture and relative wealth produced a simmering tumult of civil and racial unrest. MacInnes's London was tense and unpredictable and the scenes of *Absolute Beginners* were set using jarring language and symbolism. London was experienced as disorientation and contrast: a volatile place where disasters were immanent and imminent. MacInnes did not see modern London as a socially ordered, or a civilising space. Rather, in places like Notting Hill different clannish urban cultures were mostly tribally organised and territorialised through ethnic affinities; co-existing like ecological communities. They were knitted together but only tenuously and dangerously. Elsewhere, in Kilburn, the 'primped up exteriors' of the lower middle classes concealed the dark, dubious and 'occasionally horrifying' mix of lunacy and violence. There was an overarching, irreducible and palpable perception of London as wild, dangerous and unpredictable; it seemed to have its own mood and manner. On balance it was a dark, corrupting force and was 'unleashed' and 'at large' rather than emanating from specific circumstances.

Martin Amis's London of the 1980s seems to develop even further MacInnes's perceptions. For Amis, London encourages, is in fact ordered around, an economy of excess, ugliness and sleaze: indeed the action in his books often takes place in the same postcodes, W10 and W11, or roughly speaking where Amis once lived, in Notting Hill. Amis does not take his eye off his characters very often but when he does, the London around him is systemically disordered and this systemic disorder extends seamlessly between its social and natural coordinates, the one seemingly co-constitutive of the other. The scale of London and the necessary coexistence of social isolation and fragmentation with opportunity and freedom mean that London is a bastard assemblage but that it generates an energy, something somehow coherent and knowable, something that strikes you as completely London-like – and unlike New York and LA, the two other cities in *Money* (1984). These London conditions and orderings are always relentless, monumental, colossal, total. In *Money* the overarching disorder is sensed by Amis in the traffic, in the crowds and the weather. Amis reserves the metaphors of a failed nature–humanity rather than a disordered machine for the city: 'Blasted, totalled, broken-winded, shot-faced London, doing time under sodden skies.' Such ugliness and squalor circulates, reproduces itself everywhere, morphs into more squalid forms and inscribes itself on everything including its human inhabitants, none more than the anti-star Keith Talent ('a murderer's dog more than a murderer') who features in *London Fields* (Amis, 1989: 9). Although exaggerated for comic effect, the pulsing circulation of Londonness as a life-form and its inscription on urban surfaces and symbionts is a strong feature of Amis's writing. Although in *Money* the Thames is likened to a human brain, perhaps the living, pulsing epicentre of the organism London, it is also vulnerable, delicate and mortal: 'it can die' (Amis, 1984: 167).

And it is not just 'natural' things like rivers that can be considered as alive (and dead). To Londoners obsessed with the housing market and its effect on their physical and psychic well-being, it is as if they are subject to a force every bit as natural and unpredictable as weather or infection. House price inflation and deflation washes over London creating sudden, dramatic changes of fortune. Cultural and physical efflorescence can be followed suddenly by cultural and physical putrescence, catastrophe. For those in the core areas these movements are like tides in the middle of great oceans: the ups and downs of its ebbs and flows are nowhere near as severe as they are on the outer edges. Being on the outer or less fashionable edges can bring fundamental change to life chances and life forms. The way a fresh pulse of rising house prices wells up, deluges or inundates is, for some, every bit as palpable as a bumper harvest. Equally, rapidly receding house prices that ebb away from wannabe suburbs create feelings of being left high and dry, wrung out; every bit as palpable as a lengthy drought. In Amis's *The Information* (1995), for example, Richard and Gina find themselves first of all blessed by rising values, happily listening to the sound of gentrification all around them, and then cursed as both housing equity and 'nice neighbours' move away. This was bad enough but nothing compared to bad neighbours, including whores, moving in.

By contrast, Doralee and Peter from Fay Weldon's *Mantrapped* (2005) are winners in London's house market, but to be a winner is not to be left without anxiety because the ebbs and flows are never finished; their consequences are the stuff of doubts and disappointments, shattered dreams and living nightmares. A siege mentality pervades everywhere. Londoners live in fear of house price fluctuations just as coastal cities once feared Vikings. Doralee and Peter's 'High View' teetered on the edge of respectability and council-underwritten gentrification. Would the local tax base support 'development' or would it 'withdraw supportive funding at any moment, and then the windows will start to get broken as the Goths and Vandals sweep in, and the barbarians take back what was so long theirs (Weldon, 2005: 61).

For Will Self, London is also inscribed with memories that stalk the streets like ghosts, forcing him into detours to avoid enemies and even to develop a fear of the streets themselves. In his essay 'Big Dome' (1999) he paints a personal biography of 'becoming London' where, as his biography unfolds, more and more of the city's districts and backwaters become inextricably interleaved with the events, deeds and networks of his life. He suggests that an individual becomes written across the city just as the city is comprised of, is written by, the narratives, texts and stories of its inhabitants (1999: 118).

In yet another way, therefore, the city becomes more than its human designers could ever intend. It takes on a life of its own and it impacts on the lives of those who live there in the same way that other environmental forces do. The city is confronted as nature and constituted as nature, or, if we were forced to retain the humanist insistence on separable realms and categories (as opposed to seeing the cities as heterogeneous assemblages), as a complex of human and non-human entities and relationships. It seems to be transcendent, to have a totality that is greater than the sum of its parts; it has rhythms and pulses; its own weather systems and vascular-like systems that feed and starve, and it has pasts: multiple and overlapping pasts, reputations, alliances, narratives and antipathies. It's life is always already constituted in this becoming, just as we are with it.

So far this chapter has focused mainly on human perception and experience of the *city as nature* but it is now time to look more specifically at non-human natures and especially at what they *do* in cities as opposed to what they represent or feel like to human inhabitants (Pickering, 2008; Thrift, 2000). This has become a growth area of scholarship in the past ten years or so, ever since the idea of a sociology of nature (Macnaghten and Urry, 1995; Murphy, 1995) and nature/animal geographies (Braun and Castree, 1998; Clark, 2000; Whatmore and Hinchliffe, 2003). This has been developed theoretically from actor-network theory (and its later iterations as relational materialism) (Latour, 1993; Law, 1999), an interdisciplinary posthumanism (Gill and Anderson, 2005; Haraway, 1991, 2003, 2008; Pickering, 2008) and non-representational geographies (Cloke and Jones, 2001; Thrift, 2000, 2001).

Nature in cities

It is not only novelists who refuse to treat or reduce cities to rational, sanitised human systems. In recent years several sociologists and geographers have attempted to restore nature to cultural themes and space from which it had been mysteriously detached, although within urban studies this trend has been slow to catch on. As Wolch et al. (2002: 396) argue: 'Most urban analysis incorporates no theory of nature or else relies on weak, often unidimensional characterisations of nature and nature–society relations.' Nature may enter the picture, perhaps, as 'land' or 'property' but not as an agent in urbanisation or a resource appropriated by urban lifestyles and consumption practices. But even when urbanists more explicitly consider nature, the portrayal of the natural environment is typically limited and based on faulty, outmoded assumptions.

Non-human natures have been remarkably quick to inhabit almost all surfaces and spaces of the human built environment, as they had in fact throughout history. In some cases the cohabitation started almost immediately, carried on from previous, rural associations (martins, swallows and swifts have lived in human habitations for millennia, for example), but in others it took a while to learn how and where to live in the modern city. Fear of rural humanity must have played a part in the reticence of some species to commence some form of cohabitation. Rural ways of life both of the wealthy and the poor meant that few creatures were not hunted or trapped as vermin or for the table, but rapid urbanisation in England meant much of this abated in the country and, at the same time, rural habits and tastes were lost or modified in relation to new labour and food markets. Cheaper meat from the colonies and fish from steam trawling meant that countryside species were not always 'squeezed' so hard or so often. However, as urban populations grew in size and wealth, demanding ever more food, and as farming modernised to facilitate it, the amount of habitat in the countryside changed and shrank. Over roughly the same time-span, suburban development on the fringes of the great cities matured and because so much of this was influenced directly or indirectly by the garden city ideal, by the growth and development of gardening as an approved leisure and by the continued planting of parks, cities ripened into suitable habitat for the rehousing of non-human species of plants and animals in less than a hundred years after they were initially sequestered.

These species made their way into the city along the same conduits, the train lines, tunnels, canals, roads, motorways and ships that allowed the cities to grow in the first place and in many cases their arrival took a long while to be noticed. However, once there, their own lifestyle changed in relation to new conditions, not least of which included an urban culture that was very appreciative of nature and concerned for its future.

This cohabitation was not without a considerable amount of encouragement from city dwelling humans themselves. Almost as soon as super-sized cities such as eighteenth and nineteenth century London emerged, it seemed unbearable to live without trees, birds, plants and open natural spaces for walking, playing and contemplation. As we have seen in Chapter 3, the expansion of Paris's densely built and populated medieval city created a feeling of unhealthiness and claustrophobia and Napoleon III and Haussmann borrowed the idea of building countryside into the modern city from London. In fact very few have ever viewed living completely divorced from nature as a positive thing. Romanticism and the aestheticisation of nature grew as a response to the growth of the modern, potentially overwhelming city. Nature became associated with health and well-being while the city, at least initially, became associated with ill-health. It was therefore logical to build cities that did not cancel nature but in fact encouraged its presence and the continuity of human associations with it.

Although health continued to play a role in the association between nature and cities, it was enhanced and consolidated by what can be called 'city nature practices' that were encouraged by it. Because nature was never taken for granted by urbanites, because it was always vulnerable, because they were placed in protective and custodian-like roles and because they tended to produce a biopolitics of care and conservation, education and popular recruitment, they have developed a curiously intense love affair with what little nature they have and whatever nature exists beyond the city boundary. In this way nature was always politicised in cities and because it was never considered in isolation from the loss of habitat and endangerments that occurred outside the city, because in fact it was their demand that drove nature practices in the rural and city hinterlands, and very often in suburbs, they experienced a personal loss of connection as the built line encroached further and further into what had once been their nature playgrounds. Because of all of this, cities became the main source of support and activism for environmental and ecological movements. The embodied and close relationship between city dwellers and their urban natures and the development of their environmental sensibility is completely lost in much of the dualist literature on nature and environment with the consequence that cities and city natures become written out of the equation as they become 'other' to the at-risk true natures. This is unfortunate because nature has been extremely influential on city life. However, these dualisms are beginning to be challenged and in recent years the challenge has come not so much from academic research as from drama and natural history where observations and stories have faithfully respected what happens rather than what should happen.

One senses, from a number of diverse sources, that older relationships and the boundaries between humans and non-humans have been *questioned* and are now being rejected in theory and practice. Two major television productions, one a drama the other a natural history documentary, illustrate this shifting terrain.

Nature Boy was a drama set in a northern British town featuring all of the grime and grimness of a former industrial landscape and all of the social pathologies of deindustrialisation, mass unemployement, community collapse, familial mayhem and neighbourhood chaos. Against this, the hero, David, finds beauty, friendship and order among the animals, birds, fish and flora in the nearby wastelands of the local estuary sandflats. Flashbacks establish that as a young boy he was first introduced to the techniques of fishing and trapping and to a nature aesthetic by his now estranged father, and these continue into the present with his friend, a local hermit who lives on the estuary. David finds escape and solace in nature. His natural relation with non-humans directly descends from local rural culture via his father and it highlights the continuation of such links and the persistence of nature even on the edges of former industrial zones and inside urban cultures. *Nature Boy* challenges therefore the putative boundaries between urban and rural, nature and culture, and true nature and sullied nature. David's 'nature' is sullied, polluted and problematic, rather like his family and domestic circumstances, but this is all the more reason to maintain a moral connection with it and to cherish it. David's search for his father and his persistence in trying to feed his hopeless heroine addict mother with fresh fish makes a powerful but seamless link between the human and the natural world. This story reminds us that imperfect natures of this kind are the backdrop to the lives of most people, that their closest and strongest dealing with the natural world are through their gardens and backyards, through allotments, pigeon lofts, dog walks, through the scraps and bits of nature along railway lines, roads, old industrial zones, canal banks and coastal wastes. It reminds us that it is only on rare occasions that we travel to the so-called 'natural' areas, wildernesses and places of outstanding natural beauty. It reminds us also that we are never properly at home in such places; their natures are unfamiliar to us, the land belongs to others (notably to the rural gentry and the middle classes, who can afford the necessary dress codes for countryside leisures), the touristic pathways are restricted by rules and practices that discipline the body to keep to paths, not to touch, pick, take or otherwise disturb. It is a nature inaccessible in a fully sensed manner.

When we reflect on *Nature Boy* we must surely conclude that the academic accounts of the relations between the human and natural world are lacking this anthropological depth, this ethnographic sense of practices on the ground or its variable and contested nature in complex nations such as the USA and Britain. Certainly there has been little focused research on the everyday relations, beliefs and practices. To begin with, for obvious reasons to do with the dramatic impact of the green movement in the 1980s, many recent books *conflate* nature and environment. The outstanding political and scientific issues have driven sociological interest here, so that the natures of sociological interest are not, paradoxically, those of the disciplines primary focus, modern urban cultures, but those of the scientists, the political economists and geographers. So, sociologists have embraced the global changes in the environment both in terms of their social construction in the media and through science, and in their impact on civil society through such inquiries as Inglehart's postmaterialism thesis. Sociologists have also paused to consider very fully Beck's concept of the *Risk Society* and the range of environmental issues and environmental changes that allegedly create such a phenomenon.

Conflating nature with the environment also means that the agenda for research becomes driven by what environmentalists decide is important and what scientists deem is of environmental consequence (Wynne, 1996). Increasingly, the science–environmentalist discourse on nature has taken on a very unified content and agenda, with environmentalism itself very strongly directed by science and scientists. Hence, we have witnessed an endless interest in the actions and activities of environmentalists and environmentalism and, although this is important, the unintended consequence is to skew the research and publication effort in favour of a highly selected subset of natures. Environmentalists are much like romantic writers in the nineteenth century in that they tend to identify, promote and defend areas of pristine wilderness, and of other pure natures such as forests, areas of sea, wetlands etc against destruction rather than the already spoiled areas closer to human habitation, including urban areas (see Williams, 1972). Theirs are the truly scandalous coalfaces on the human–nature boundary. Urban cultures are of interest only in their capacity as a danger to these fragile marginal natures through tourism and leisure and perhaps as a warning of what we need to avoid in future. Even here the practices, beliefs and conceptions of people come a poor second to what is deemed to be their impact, usually adverse, on the natures they insist on visiting. Hence, the social issues tend to be the demographics of ecotourism, the impact of ecotourism, and especially questions to do with management and control of visitors. Urban cultures are also of interest, again, not for their actual relationships with the natural world but for their expressed *values* in relation to extant environmental issues. These are significant only in the sense that they are the most powerful electoral force in most nations, and such studies drive, as Macnaghten and Urry (1998) argue, a very one-sided and abstract knowledge of nature and modern cultures.

Cities themselves are also of interest but the extent to which it is a social interest is also very limited. Thus, one of the most staggering nature–human interfaces, gardening, has been ignored almost completely. Of more scandalous importance are issues to do with pollution, cities as sources of environmental problems or the brown environmental agenda: car usage; heating and pollution; emission of CFC gases from domestic appliances; suburban sprawl and invasion of bush and countryside; pollution of waterways by dog and other pet faeces; water usage and conservation; introduced pest species (pets, plants etc.) escaping into the bush and threatening native species; gardeners poisoning the environment; metropolitan effects on weather patterns. Again, people tend to be cast as the cause of the problem for nature with research tending to focus more on management and control issues such as the collection of dog faeces, recycling behaviour, environmental action groups, changing uses of domestic cleaning agents and so on (Baldassare and Katz, 1992; Derksen and Gartrell, 1993). As such a misanthropic gloom pervades the entire research enterprise on nature, Schama's (1995) reassurance wrought from his long historical overview that nature will be looked after ultimately because it is central to all Western cultures' sense of selfhood seems somehow lost on these authors. By contrast, Schama's optimism provides something of an inspiration to a new generation of urban anthropologists, geographers and geographers concerned with city natures.

Living Britain (1993) was a radically new departure in natural history documentary-making in that it avoided the fiction (and ideal) of a separated humanity from the natural world. Indeed it showed for the first time how in a small industrial island of 65 million people, nature *and* humanity combine to form a set of distinctive and historically specific natures/ecologies. In this film, nature is not made to seem primordial, steady and good nor is humanity made to seem modern, destabilising and bad. Nature is whatever happens to result from the interaction between species, including the actions and designs of man; it is a result of history unfolding. What is so striking about this documentary is the *hybridity* of nature, how impossible it is to disentangle the human from the non-human. When film-makers do not insist on entirely human-free shots to depict nature it is surprising how much nature and humanity comes into view – together. Hence one of the strongholds for the otter in Europe is close to the oil terminals of the North Sea oil industry in the Shetland Isles. Wild otters and seals are seen in symbiotic relations with the local fishing industry. Wild foxes that have been endangered in the countryside and set aside for the sport of the gentry are seen playing, hunting and rearing their young in the peaceful haven of a municipal rubbish tip. The more the camera looks at towns and cities the more wild life it picks up. City dwellers are not, nor have they ever been, separated from the natural world, this is the fiction of urbanisation and the mythology of modernity (Latour, 1993). *Living Britain* shows a very close relationship between suburban Britons and a very wide and growing range of animals and plants. Indeed one of the most important natural habitats for a large number of rare or declining animal and bird species is in British gardens. These include the hedgehog, weasel, dormouse, badger and fox, the red kite, owls, the wren and many others. In the USA we find a similar hybrid history unfolding. The white-tail deer, the icon of American deer hunting and role model for Disney's star Bambi, has made huge population gains as a result of tolerance and protection by suburban gardeners and residents, but there is also a long and rich history of animal and bird feeding in the USA that is conveniently forgotten in the misanthropic views of recent environmental history (see United States of America, Bureau of Census, 1998 which has data on these activities going back to the 1950s).

Outside of the gardens of concerned nature lovers, industrial and commercial landscapes are just as much habitats to animals and birds indifferent to the social spatial classifications of modernity. Disused factories provide abundant new nest sites for rare birds; the most forbidding prospect of myriad pipes in an oil refinery near London provides the perfect setting for migrating birds; the rooftops of the CBD provide nesting sites and hunting grounds for several urbanised hawks. However, it is not only the animals and plant species that have discovered these new, albeit strange habitats, their urban human enthusiasts have tuned into their presence in an individual and organised manner. In addition to the attention paid to wild animals naturalising themselves into the city, to join with those plants, trees, shrubs, lakes and animals already naturalised by city builders, we can now add new and recent additions: city farms, suburban nature trails, city pond and wetland reserves, city bird watching hides, suburban and inner city clean-up days, organised care activities such as the 'toad crossing teams' assembled to help migratory frogs and toads cross roads safely on their migration to spawning ponds, the planting in Australia of native plants designed to provide needed habitat and food for declining native birds.

Nature Boy represents the sort of enthusiasm and attachment to nature that can occur in a declining industrial urban complex. David, the hero, may not be an exaggerated figure in late-modern cities, since we know that extraordinary passions and enthusiasms for bird watching, fishing and wildlife do develop, especially in urban centres. The assumption has always been made that their enthusiasm grows in relation to the poverty of city wildlife, but this is unlikely. It is just as likely that such passions grow in relation to the *diversity and colour* of city and city edge natures.

My case that the 'modern' boundaries imposed between humanity and the natural world have been breached, if not in places dissolved, is also manifest not in political and environmental activities that always claim some pragmatic, instrumental base, but in a new religiosity of nature. There is something new about our relationship with non-humans, and with life itself that has convinced a growing number of urban people that humans and non-humans exist on a common and intimately connected, moral, physical and spiritual field. Combining aspects of animism, ancient pre-Christian religion in Europe, religious traditions from the East and more recent Christian and secular rituals, neo-paganism is reckoned to be one of the fastest growing religions in the West. Neo-paganism belongs to a wider set of cultural drifts in later modernity that are placed in bookshops under the heading New Age, although again there is nothing particularly new about them except that they hybridise hitherto separated categories such as nature and culture, that they seek to enchant the world once more with putatively neglected powers and spirits and that they wish to take control over their lives and their world by tapping into those forces through a new raft of technologies (crystals, witchcraft, possession dancing, shamanism and so on). We meet some of this in the colourful bands of nature protesters, but it is not their beliefs that are of interest so much as their political campaigns and their role as catalysts for wider political support. David, aka *Nature Boy*, follows a girlfriend who has joined a tribe-like band of road protesters currently in full campaign against a road development. David, the ordinary working class teenager, is not impressed with the tribal posturing of the protesters, their inability to feed themselves from the woods and streams where they are camped, or their camping and tunnel making on a flood-prone site. Here the makers of *Nature Boy* are underlining the point being made, that for all its fanfare and colour, environmentalism does not exhaust or even tap into the more embedded natures of modernity, that there are beliefs, practices, knowledges and histories that are more important to understand even for the narrower focus of environmental politics.

This is particularly clear in the historical development of the growing love affair the British developed for their own bird population. Again, city life is always specific, always accretions of practices and subject to historical continuities. So, British cities have a special relationship with birds that is often completely absent elsewhere. In 2003 comedian and birder Bill Oddie hosted a live BBC television programme from Bristol, *Wild in Your Garden*, that demonstrated an extraordinary bond between the suburban British and their birds. The programme grew into what is now an annual festival of live television birdwatching, *Springwatch*. Not surprisingly, very few urban sociologists have examined this relationship as a feature of urban life.

Birdlife, citylife

By international standards British city dwellers have been extremely sensitive to the moral and welfare position of animals *generally*, being the first to establish anti-cruelty legislations (in 1842), the first to establish a Vegetarian Society (1847) and among the leading group of nations seeking anti-hunting legislation in recent years. The political clout of urban Britons was recognised in London on 1 March 1998 when the biggest political rally ever recorded in British history, an organised assembly of 25,000 rural people, clubs, estates and organisations, came to protest at legislation planned to implement an anti-hunting bill. London looked on, baffled, at this rally as if a herd of dinosaurs had materialised from somewhere. As far as they were concerned the hunters and anglers from the rural backwaters were anachronistic and muddle-headed. In their view (as with those in other major cities such as Sydney), the time had come to protect what wildlife was left rather than endorse older relationships based upon sporting and consumptive practices (Franklin, 2008a).

It is over the past thirty years that profound changes can be discerned, particularly with regard to birds. In 1971 the Royal Society for the Protection of Birds (founded 1889) had a membership of 98,000. But over the next ten years the membership quadrupled to 441,000 and, astonishingly, between 1981 and 1997 their membership topped one million and has continued to rise. To put this in perspective, none of the other major wildlife-oriented organisations had anywhere near the same membership or expansion: in 2004 Friends of the Earth had 114,000 members, Greenpeace had 194,000, WWF had 240,000 and the Wildlife Trusts had 320,000. The conclusion from this is undisputable: there was something about birds that caught the attention of the British and their imagination. What could it be?

In comparison with most other forms of wildlife, birds are more plentiful, more visible and more accessible. Most British native mammals are nocturnal while almost all birds are diurnal. So even if the highly secretive, long persecuted native mammals could be found, they are always tricky actually to see with any clarity. Birds on the other hand are not only plentiful they are evenly distributed across just about every space and ecology, including the cities and suburbs. Birds were also less affected by the main barriers into cities for ground dwelling animals: busy roads. So a love affair was distinctly possible but what made it happen?

First, there was increasing scientific evidence during this period that the British bird heritage was under threat: the numbers of the most common bird of all (and symbol of city life itself), the house sparrow, were declining rapidly in relation to overly restored and bird-proofed house renovations, and many countryside birds were declining as a result of changing farming practices such as ploughing into banks, burning of stubble and removal of hedgerows. Hence there was a growth in those activities that promote and protect: joining an organisation that uses its funds to protect birds legally; feeding birds; installing bird nesting boxes; maintaining and extending habitat and watching birds (and a lot of birdwatchers take part in bird surveys that monitor population). So birds became a register of a more general concern with the demise of nature. Nobody, it seemed, wanted an invigorated city life without an equally secure nature.

It is estimated that there are now between five and six million bird nest boxes installed in city gardens throughout Britain (one in four households have one) and there is a national nest box week in February every year to encourage the installation of more.[2] The bird feeding industry was estimated to be worth 180 million pounds in 2004 and to grow to be worth 500 million by 2014.[3]

Second, in many ways birds are proxies for the nature of Britain and are very expressive of national identity. Certainly, like most totemic animals they are very effective symbols for their human neighbours.

Garden natures

In all sorts of ways nature itself became commodified and aestheticised in the affluent, leisured and mobile mass cultures of the twentieth century. Although we are used to imagining the modern consumer in the archetypal role of *flâneur*, as a metropolitan phenomenon, the modern consumer was just as keen to consume the natural world outside and inside the city limits. With the building of modern cities, garden suburbs, metropolitan railway systems, together with the revolution in personal transport, the relatively brief separation of nature and metropolitan culture in the nineteenth century was ended. From then on nature was scattered, fragmented, visible, transportable, relocatable, visitable, modifiable and interspersed with the artificial. It was intimately bound up with our everyday life, our everyday spaces, our aesthetic and productive projects and hobbies, even as an order that recommends itself for society. Essentially it was only ever in hybrid forms with the human. It entered a realm of significant controllability, simulation, manipulation and management across a wide range of different human projects. Globalisation rendered the world's natures highly accessible, first for the consumption of the exotic other, then as resource and soon after for tourism and other leisures. Television and computers rendered it virtual and produced and copied it at accelerating speeds. The ultimate hybrid of course is the modern garden. It is full of objects that are the result of an original natural object and human mental and physical labour, the exchanges and networks of horticultural knowledge, the fashions that select first this colour and then that, the work of plant collectors and botanists who throw yet more species into the melting pot, local networks of gardeners who produce gardens that work in particular soils, pHs, rainfalls and microclimates but can be recreated elsewhere where similar conditions prevail. Gardens have become like domestic interiors, spaces filled with decorative creations, and like most domestic spaces they are neither nature nor culture but hybrids.

Modern gardening: the universal leisure

Don Burke's primetime Australian programme *Burke's Backyard* was not exclusively about gardening, but it was exclusively about what happens in the urban garden, or as Australians call it, the 'backyard'. This top-rated programme (ranked 15th out of all TV programming in Australia and 1st in terms of infotainment programming, with viewing figures of 1,735,000 nationally) became popular in the UK and USA for precisely the reason that gardening (and doing things in one's garden) is among the most significant leisure activities in the Western world (*The Australian*, 31 December 2005). This has remained the case for at least the past 30–40 years when leisure data have been collected.

According to Young and Willmott (1973), about 14 million of the 18 million homes in Britain had a garden. Altogether this accounted for around 620,000 acres, a land mass the size of the county of Dorset. On the basis that gardening was more popular among the higher socio-economic groups, and that embourgoisiement (growth in the middle class composition of society) was spreading, it was predicted that gardening would become even more significant by the end of the century, heralding a rise in the demand for gardens and garden products (1973: 124). Subsequent studies in the 1980s confirmed this prediction. For example, in 1984 Ray Pahl showed that expenditure on gardening equipment rose from £235 million in 1974 to £600 million in 1980. It is most likely that this growth was associated with the aesthetic appeal of gardening rather than with instrumental reasons such as producing food. The Thorpe Report on vegetable growing in allotments, for example, showed that over the period from 1944 (when around 10% of British food was grown in allotments) to 1969, food growing for household purposes was in decline. Allotment holders were getting decidedly elderly, their associations were not recruiting younger people and they were finding it more difficult to let vacant plots (Pahl, 1984: 99).

The aesthetic gardening traditions of Britain focus around the Royal Horticultural Society. It has encouraged not merely the art and passion for gardening, it has promoted new plant development, more gardening activities (such as gardening courses for children) and the opening of more private gardens for public access. As free time becomes more pressured than ever the growth of its membership from 114,500 in 1914 to 250,000 in 2000 demonstrates the robust place of gardening in British culture. According to *Social Trends*, by 1994, 51% of British men and 45% of women had participated in gardening in the four weeks prior to interview. After the age of 30 British men and women participate more avidly: 62% of men aged between 45 and 59 and 65% between 60 and 65; 57% of women aged between 45 and 59 and 54% between 60 and 65 (Office for National Statistics, 1996: 218).

A mid-1990s survey showed that 37% of their London sample had done some gardening recently in comparison with less than 10% of New Yorkers (Stockdale et al., 1996: 7). New York is not typical of the USA of course. However, a 1998 survey by Leisure Trends Group found that gardening was the tenth *favourite* activity (6.9% of the sample said it was a favourite leisure activity) (Leisure Trends Group, 1998).

According to *American Demographics* (June 1996: 7), around 40% of American gardeners in their sample grew flowers and 33% grew vegetables, although lawn care is the most significant gardening activity. By the year 2010 the number of gardening households is expected to grow by 17%, a projection that correlates with America's aging population. In line with the general shift away from gardening as a form of household provisioning and towards more aesthetic criteria, we should not be surprised to see that women gardeners in this American survey outnumbered men gardeners. Such a view is also suggested by the *Better Homes and Gardens* (a DIY/gardening mix) readership survey that found that 71% were women. In a survey conducted for the US *Organic Gardening Magazine*, 34% of respondents planned on doing more gardening over the next few years while over half intended to maintain their current effort. According to *Marketing Tools Magazine* (May 1997: 3), the most avid and high-spending gardeners are white, university educated and middle class, a group that is represented substantially in the baby boom generations. Their survey found that contemporary US gardeners considered gardening to be most unlike housework and garden predominantly for aesthetic reasons (70%), because they find it relaxing (66%) and because they enjoy being out of doors (70%). A 2006 study found that gardening was among the two most preferred leisure time physical activities in all sub-groups of the US population (Crespo et al., 2006). According to a survey by British gardening magazine *New Eden*, one in four women prefer gardening to sex and 4% admitted having had sex in their garden (*Daily Telegraph* online, No 1420, 15 April 1999).

It is not only in the Anglophone world that gardening is a principal pastime. In Belgium, for example, a 1983 survey found that gardening was the mostly popular hobby, practiced by 40% of the sample (Govaerts, 1989: 80). Despite the general shortage of land in Japan (or perhaps because of it?) gardening/horticulture has enormous and stable appeal, with over 40% of the population participating in it through the 1980s (Koseki, 1989: 129).

Although we are able to find evidence for sustained if not rising interest in gardening it is clear that what people mean by gardening and what they find appealing about it has been subject to many changes over the second half of the twentieth century. In the next section we will shift attention to the changing nature of gardening in the early twenty-first century, in particular by considering aspects of its political economy and shifts in its styles and fashions. In doing this we will see that a gardening relationship with the natural world does not exist independently of social and cultural contexts, even if the generically *active* association that gardening encourages has remained relatively constant.

Gardens, nature and the city

In my book *Nature and Social Theory* (Franklin, 2002) I explored how gardening developed historically *alongside* rather than prior to urbanisation. It is very hard to find any period of British urban history that does not include a substantial emphasis on the importance of gardens and gardening. Nonetheless, at the risk of generalising, one can argue that from the Romantic period onwards, urban parks and gardens aimed to mimic a separable wild nature as the antithesis of cities. Bringing such garden ideas to the city was intended to bring the benefits of wilderness nature to the denatured state of most city experiences. In this way modern urban parks and gardens were in, but not of, the city; they were if anything an antidote to the evils of city life. Suburban gardens, even down to the very smallest iteration as fronts to terraced housing, were separate spaces, and categorically 'other' to the domestic sphere. In this way gardens reached fairly standardised form with relatively fixed semiotic meaning relative to the city 'proper'. However, in the same way that other former boundaries and dualisms were broken down during and after the 1970s, it is possible to see a dramatic change in the way gardens figured more in city life. They left their own spaces and merged more with the everyday living spaces.

According to Wilson (1992: 101), the garden first became an extension of the living space in the designs of modern architecture, particularly those designs that were closely linked to the character and needs of clients. Thomas Church's Californian designs made connections between the garden and the home, blurring the boundary and smudging lines. In his work we begin to see the origins of architectural plants, plants that have strong structural and aesthetic kinship with built structures. Such gardens de-emphasised the centrality of blooms, and used plants to create moods other than the picturesque: shade gardens appear, minimalist gardens and gardens that link the home to the surrounding environment both built and natural. Critical among this movement was borrowing and hybridisation: influences came from Japanese and Muslim gardens, from the Mediterranean and Mexico. Sensitivity to form and locality produced the work of Frank Lloyd Wright, a rejection of European orthodoxies and the introduction of indigenous plantings. His work in the prairie region attempted to blend built form into natural surroundings and the garden was a significant means by which it was achieved. From there an interest in native gardens developed in the USA and was later adopted with great enthusiasm by Australians and New Zealanders. Garrett Eckbo extended these ideas to a more rigorous use of ecological principles in landscape architecture. While much of this modernist movement in gardening remained avant-garde in the 1950s and 1960s and of little influence over the mainstream, it did slowly gather support and provide leadership for the destandardising movements of the 1970s onwards. This ecological way of thinking has been extended in recent years to acknowledge that combined city gardens form large habitats that can be managed to create better ecologies for wildlife (Cushing, 2005) and this has been popularised in attitudes, for example, to birds and the notion of city forests. New urban gardening sensibilities therefore do not continue to mimic nature *for* the city but create nature *out of* the city, realizing that the separation is false and that cities are every bit as much 'natural habitats' with even greater potential for life.

More and more garden designs, at all scales and income levels, now seek to render garden spaces into extensions of the home and in this way the stricter separation of nature and culture has more or less vanished. This is very evident in the garden design sections of the Chelsea Flower Show in London. In recent years it has become less and less clear whether the spaces designed are works of art, architectural spaces or natural plant communities.

Cities in nature

We are so very easily duped by our own bureaucratic and taxonomic fictions of the world we live in that we actually come to believe in such things as the sign that announces or welcomes you to New York, Melbourne, Oslo or Jakarta. We somehow believe that behind the sign lies the self-evident ordering of the city and that before the sign lays the disorder of nature. As we saw in Chapter 1, this sense of a protected, walled and safe space goes back to the very first idea of the citadel. At least then there was an intimate, consciously conceived connection between the city and its surrounds, whereas in the modern period, cities seem in our minds to float in abstract spaces, spaces of little major consequence, where fewer and fewer people actually live and where we imagine nothing much happens. Railways that delivered passengers right into the heart of cities ushered in this fracture and air travel these days has compounded it. The audacity and arrogance of much city life, conceived of as islands, and the world as an archipelago of cities, stems from the growing importance of the city centres as the centre of gravity pulling everyone and everything towards it. Yet every now and again we are reminded not only that this is not true, but in very real ways, cities are seamlessly connected to much larger natural configurations. The recent globalisation of news on such channels as Sky and BBC World have made us far more aware of this rather promiscuous relationship with nature and of the rather commonly held view in individual cities that specific natural phantoms are only ever lurking around corners and waiting for an opportunity to pounce.

Increasingly, the world's human population is coming to live in one of the 200 supercities of the world (defined as having more than 2 million inhabitants) and this historically unprecedented concentration makes many more people vulnerable to natural disasters. For example, 40 of these cities are located within 120 miles of a major tectonic plate boundary or a historically damaging earthquake. According to Professor Roger Bilham at the University of Colorado, 50% of the world's supercities now are located near potential future magnitude 7.5 earthquakes. From 1998 to 2002 earthquakes have caused approximately 10,500 fatalities per year and 100,000 Indian people were killed in 2000 alone (Colorado University News Centre, 24 April 2003). Far from protecting people against earthquakes, cities increase the risk they pose by concentrating people in vulnerable places and housing them in large, fragile (often jerry-built) structures. It is the bricks and mortar that kill most earthquake victims, not the earth.

Between them earthquakes, tsunamis, cyclones, landslides, floods, bushfires, volcanoes and severe weather can threaten most of the supercities and indeed some have argued that cities are especially vulnerable places; vulnerable to what Clark called the 'pervasive ordinariness of natural diasters' (2000: 182). Major cities often develop on the great trading rivers, on alluvial soils or rich volcanic soils, under mountain lees and on the coast, making them at least vulnerable to several major risks. As Olivier-Smith (1999: 26) pithily argues, 'proximity to resources also involves proximity to hazard' (cited in Clark, 2000: 186). Other combinations abound. As Mike Davis has revealed in his *Ecology of Fear* (1998), Los Angeles 'places its citizens smack in the path of flood, tornado, wildfire, drought and even puma attack' (cited in Clark, 2000: 182), aside from placing them on top of an earthquake epicentre. Clark alerts us to some of the implications from the recent study of disasters, the most important of which seems to be that disaster is less an occasional and rare phenomenon and more a regular and common state of nature and one that in fact is formative of most ecologies to some degree. According to Alexander (2000: 55), 'environmental extremes are powerful enough to exert a strong and consistent influence upon social and cultural systems' (cited in Clark, 2000: 185).

Although Londoners may not fear natural disaster as much as terrorism, few cast a glance at the Thames Barrier, a flood control system not far from the city centre, without a frisson of concern. The combination of extremely strong tides, a large and powerful river and potentially rising sea-levels always risks taking the specifications beyond those planned for in the Barrier. Such a tipping point was reached (finally) in New Orleans in 2005, an event that not only seemed to surprise a rich superpower like the USA but to demonstrate just how unprepared it was, just how little nature is taken seriously – even in a city whose entire history has been a dance of agency between the Mississippi river and the Corps of Engineers (Pickering, 2008).

In recent years bushfires in Australia and the USA have ripped through some of the most valuable real estate and deep into city centres with consummate ease. While we get used to seeing these events wherever we are it is a very different story on the ground. In cities such as Hobart, Canberra and Sydney, smoke is a regular feature of all summers and thick, sun-blocking palls are frequently the first sign of single or multiple 'events'. At such times, a ripple of anxiety spreads across these towns and the everyday is placed on hold, at least while those in the path ready themselves individually and communally. However, it is never just a question of humans mounting a defence against fire. Fire and humans are connected in complex ways, for example through both fear and excitement, community solidarity and individual heroism and reward. These high-level emotional exchanges lie behind the curious way some people become interpellated by fire; at the most extreme, they are recruited to light fires deliberately.

Cities on fire: a case study in co-constitution

Of course we tend to think of the evolution of pyrophilia as an entirely natural phenomenon, a response to the presence of natural fire in the landscape in places such as Australia, and to a degree this is true. But it is only part of the picture. This evolution and the spread of eucalypts to become the dominant vegetation in Australia was profoundly influenced by the hand of humanity in the form of the Aboriginal fire torch. As Aboriginal people spread across all areas of the continent they managed their landscape, keeping it clear for movement and burning it to encourage new growth and to concentrate game animals. As they maintained the regular presence of fire in the landscape they created a mosaic of patches, patches of very specific plant communities in specific geological and geomorphological conditions. 'As the environment changed [over the past 10,000 years] and changed again, a new, precise and fragile interdependence was established between eucalypts and fire. Most gum trees need to burn at some stage during their seed-bearing life. Some need heat to release their seeds ... some – it's only recently been found – need smoke to activate them. Most need the ash to provide a soft bed for the seedlings, free from competing plants' (Hay, 2002: 222). Like the landscape of any human nature manager, whether pastoralist, agriculturalist or hunter–gatherer, the resulting landscape is neither natural or entirely man-made. It is always a hybrid, co-constituting entity. Did such a relationship end with the effective removal of so many Aboriginal people from Australia? No.

White settlers who took over the management of the landscape came with ready-formed management strategies that did not include nomadism. It generally implied two major immobile entities: permanent fields for livestock and crops and permanent settlements, some of them large cities (and despite the myths of a golden rural past Australia is a history of major urban settlement in the six state capitals). Since for at least the first one hundred years they did not manage the forests as Aborigines had, by regularly burning off the build-up of fuel that eucalypts drop as part of their nature, the forests changed. They became denser and the resulting fires became more ferocious, less manageable and with different environmental consequences. If no fire came through specific tracts of land, rainforest species would begin to take over as the gum trees died out. Settlers noticed this substitution very early on. They also noticed that the charming park-like look of the original landscape changed, becoming more tangled and tightly clustered; riding became difficult and then stopped. This was not a major problem for most people because they sought to build lovely cities, and in the main they did.

The problem came when the new fashions for garden suburbs swept the world. It was one thing for Americans on the east coast and the English to seek the company and poetics of trees; in Australia (and the western USA which introduced the gum tree widely) it was quite another ...

In this final section I want to demonstrate, using the example of this relationship between bushfires and cities in Australia and the USA, a more general proposition, that nature and cities are not separated but intertwined and this intertwining is so momentous that it becomes possible to talk of their co-constitution. Many other examples could be given, for example Pickering's (2008) analysis of the relationship between the Mississippi and New Orleans, or the relationship between San Francisco and the San Andreas fault (Bolin and Stanford, 1998). However, even though it is hard to think of anything more significant than these three examples, the point is that they are routinely ignored by urban studies, which has remained resolutely humanist. What follows therefore is an attempt to demonstrate how and why a posthumanist approach ought to be part of the toolkit for urban studies.

Bushfires in Australia

After the effective removal of Aborigines from most parts of rural and wild Australia during colonial times, bushfires became more explosive and dangerous and a litany of major disasters were experienced: Black Thursday 1851 (Victoria); Black Sunday 1926 (East Melbourne); Black Friday 1939 (widespread in Eastern Australia); Black Tuesday 1967 (Tasmania) continuing to the present time with the Canberra Holocaust of 2003.

It was only after the major 1939 fire that systematic burning-off policies and strategies were widely used but even then, in very recent years around Sydney, Canberra and the most devastating fires of all that hit Melbourne in 2009, Australia's major capital cities are not insulated from risk from fire, or is it eucalypt trees? Peculiarly, the fires seem to be getting worse and more frequent.

The fiery dance of agency between white settlers and the gum tree began to take on an altogether different form. At one level it places the gum tree and dry sclerophyll forest in an ambiguous relationship with modern urban humans, but at another the dance is one of a series of non-dualistic defining features of Australia as a nation.

White Australia is and always was an essentially urban social formation, so why should there be any major concern about trees and bushfires? The answer here is that urban development in Australia is not the building of great cities of apartments but the sprawl of great suburbs. As with the UK, the best sorts of suburb are those that combine proximity to urban amenity with proximity to nature, which in Australia means forest or bush through most of south-eastern Australia (and that just about includes all of Melbourne, Sydney, Canberra, Adelaide, Hobart and all of the other country towns in between). These suburbs have been spreading out ever since they were founded in the nineteenth century and in this way each generation creates itself after the same manner by seeking to build a new home on the rural fringe. This is still true today. In Hobart where there are all manner of second-hand houses for sale in the city, new couples tend to favour building their own on the city fringes – extremely close to the bush. From the 1960s onwards some suburbs changed their character and aimed to be permanently 'in the bush', an unlikely and dangerous hybrid called 'the bush suburb'. Canberra fulfilled the more extreme aim of a 'bush city', with results in 2003 that few could have imagined. The small satellite overspill towns to the west and north of Melbourne provided relatively low-density bush living and village-like communities. They were living on borrowed time.

Image 9.1 Gum tree forests grow (and burn) close to the city. Hobart, Australia (photo Adrian Franklin)

The essentially Romantic love of trees and forests and even, perversely, demonstrations of nature's awesome power, established not only the arboreal aesthetic and, in city design terms, a return to a more treed living space, but also the desire to save the great forests through the creation of national parks. The economy of national parks dictates that they be within a reasonable distance from the major population centres, and most cities have encouraged extensive tracts of bush to abut the city perimeters for leisure and recreation. In the case of the 2009 fires in Victoria, Australia's worst ever, the people who lived in the satellite towns most affected by it were subject not only to forms of human settlement governance (which included the norm of staying on a family property in the event of a fire in order to fight it), they were also subject to, fatally as it happened, the governance of forests in national parks. Hence, large areas had not been back burned near the settlement and fallen trees and dense growth close to roads had not been cleared. In a way then the disaster that occurred was not a natural disaster about which nothing could be done. It was the result of a series of interlocking, largely human governance and aesthetic factors that combined to trap a large number of people in the face of the sort of fire that cannot be fought.

In a profoundly consequential way it was the result of humanist thinking, that fire has been controlled and can always be controlled, but also that fire is a rather unique and abstract substance that does not relate in a direct way to the trees that produce it. Australians do not say they are fighting eucalypt trees, but if it is not the trees what is it? While they acknowledge they are fighting a fire and acknowledge that the fire seems to have agency, they do not appear to relate this to the trees that are doing the burning. At the same time they do understand the biology of eucalypt trees and especially how to manage their presence as a fire hazard. They seem to be caught up in a strange humanist logic that runs something like: trees are vulnerable and should be preserved and saved by our own actions; it is natural to live near trees; fire on the other hand is a separate unique thing, one of the basic elements that represents a threat to life and property as well as the forests. Fires have a life: they can reproduce themselves by spotting new fires ahead of themselves; they can 'jump' roads and rivers; they can defy their normal behaviour (e.g. by running *downhill*); they have to be managed and fought, eliminated from posing a risk (Hay, 2002: 218–19). In a profound way this failure to connect eucalypt trees to fire is one of the things that proves fatal. In fact, fire is part of eucalypt trees, nature. They not only need fire, they actually generate *exactly* the sort of fire they require.

Hay summarises the architecture, morphology and chemistry of the fire-producing agency of *Eucalyptus*. The trees drop 'between a third and half of their leaves annually with their "peak drop" in late spring, early summer – perfect fire season time, in most places' (Hay, 2002: 211). In addition, gum trees regularly drop large amounts of boughs, branches and twigs that build up something of a pyre around the base of the trees.

> The trees' litter dries out and covers the ground as ready fuel (three centimetres of leaf litter can cause the kind of conflagration you get from a centimetre of refined gasoline) and most of them have a kind of open crown that can whip up an enormous updraught in no time. Some gums have shreds of hanging bark – stringybark or candle bark 'filigree strips – that dangle like firebrands and can be carried ten, twenty, up to thirty kilometres ahead of a firefront by the wind to spark new flames. (Hay, 2002: 211)

Even the asymmetrical morphology of the gum leaf seems designed to create fire: once lit and detached they can spin like a propeller high into the air above the fire front and then speed downwind, while remaining alight, in order to create further spot fires.

After the catastrophic bushfire that almost destroyed Hobart in 1967 the volunteer and professional fire-fighters were reorganised and substantially reequipped, a move that increased both their status and the desirability for new recruits. From then on, in peripheral city locations and rural districts, to be a fire-fighter became a very different proposition. It included sophisticated new vehicles, communications technology, more training and liaison with the professional services, better fire stations, and greater responsibility for fire prevention by controlling the build-up of fuel loads and fire-watching. A new era of fire-fighting emerged, one that now allowed the new policy of encouraging property owners to stay on their property and be assisted by these crews as fires threatened properties in turn. As a result, many districts were regularly saved from fires that would otherwise have been calamitous, and as a result of that fire-fighters were better supported by their communities and given more prestige within them.

As a result of being in closer touch with the trees themselves the volunteers began to appreciate the trees, agency, and the language of describing them changed as a result. For example, one of Hay's respondents, David Foster, a volunteer fire-fighter from a brigade in Wingello, told her that:

> The eucalypts are *cunning* – they've got the situation sussed. In winter they won't burn; two weeks later, you'll find yourself in high fire danger and you can't [back-] burn. The fuel builds up and builds up – and they seem to work the climate well so they don't burn when its convenient to you. (Hay, 2002: 212)

Several of his fire-fighting friends were horrifically burned and one was killed in 1998 when several trees with white stringybark exploded. He told

Hay that he 'hates stringybark with a passion'. Here in the thick of it, the fire-fighters begin to see that they are in a battle, or dance of agency with eucalypts, not with that abstract and much-romanticised thing called fire.

Suburbanisation into the bush has created an interesting homogeneity of experience for Australians of all ages, namely a semi-rural life in the city. This life has also involved everyone in the fiery dance with gum trees. This is as serious and as dangerous as it sounds in a country that favours wooden homes. Although humans still start most fires, these fires are now also related to the exigencies of suburban life (weekend barbecues or camp fires; a cigarette tossed out of a car window; teenagers playing with lighters) or to contemporary machinic farming where sparks generated between metal and rock can easily start a blaze. However, there are also more complex and intriguing causes of ignition that point towards the more *interpellative* qualities that fire has within a fire landscape. In Eastern Australia fire seems to draw people into its own self-perpetuating regime. While most Australians might admit to enjoying a fire around a camp or a log fire at home, there is absolutely no doubt that some people are attracted to fire, or more properly bushfires, and when fires fail to occur naturally or by accident on extreme fire-risk days, it is thought that many are now helped on their way by such enthusiasts. In an ABC documentary shown in February 2003 it was revealed that the number of arson-started fires, had grown from 30% to between 50 and 60% of all bushfires in the past ten years. According to Willis (2004), deliberately lit fires were between 25 and 50% of all bushfires. Whereas in the late 1980s there were approximately 60 deliberately lit fires per 100,000 people, by the 1990s there were 170 per 100,000 people. In the 1980s there were around 300 bush fires per annum, but by the 1990s this had grown to 4400. The ABC documentary also suggested that the voluntary fire-fighting brigades either attracted or produced 'firebugs' since the starting of fires produced huge thrills, the feeling of accomplishment, power and, in the Australian semi-bush and bush context, enhanced status from a nervous but appreciative community. According to Willis, the reasons behind the rise in bush fire arson in recent years reduce to five key factors: hero worship, to impress others, praise, excitement and self-esteem. Paradoxically, fire-fighters have been enrolled into the gum tree's fire world.

Bushfires that threaten communities produce great excitement, communitas and thrill, and have a certain deadly appeal, not dissimilar to war or mimetic contests such as sport.[4] However, I want to underline the fact that fire-fighting *is* a fight, not a mimetic contest. A lot hangs on winning each bout and it is this combined with the largely embodied nature of the fight that contributes to its gravitas, elevating its fighters above even sports celebrities, if only briefly and less remuneratively. The point is we really do *fight trees*, not a separate element. It seems that once experienced the thrill often leads to further thrill-seeking. Seventeen volunteer fire-fighters have been convicted of starting bushfires in the past five years, which is a startling number given the extreme difficulties of proving a crime the chief characteristic of which is the destruction of its own evidence. The *Sydney Morning Herald* of 30 November 2002 ran an article based on a soon to be published study by criminal profiler Dr Richard Kocsis, on serial bushfire arson:

> Most of the serial bushfire arsonists in the sample fell into the 'thrill' category, which Kocsis describes as 'the most malignant'. 'Thrill' arsonists associate random destruction with gratification of some kind – not sexual in nature, and not to do with personalised anger or resentment. The thrill seems to be centred on the power the fire gives them, or the attention they gain. (www.smh.com.au/articles/2002/11/29/1038386313851.html)

The key point here, the reason why I use the term interpellation, is that the factors that are so obviously at play here are neither human nor natural but both. The complex intertwining of trees constantly acting in such a way as to create fire, with a settlement and forest management pattern that exacerbates the risk of disaster, creates around country areas and suburbs alike a powerful tension that speaks directly to people and pulls them into its gravity. Peter Burgess was convicted of starting fifteen bushfires across New South Wales. Clearly he had pinned his life project on being a respected and superior fireman. He told police that he was excited by fire and that he got emotional satisfaction from the praise heaped on volunteer fire-fighters. Fire gave him a feeling of accomplishment.

Wildfires in the USA

The nature–culture of bushfires in Australia is not the same as the nature–culture of wildfires in California. To begin with, the anthropology of those who live among or near trees is very different. The rural fringes of Australian cities are typically and historically lower status areas and the rural small towns are frequently characterised as socially problematic. In most cities it is the central suburbs that command the most prestige. In California, Davis (1998: 142) reminds us that:

> the suburbanisation of Southern California's remaining wild landscapes has accelerated in the face of a perceived deterioration of the metropolitan core. As middle- and upper-class families flee Los Angeles (especially its older 'urbanized suburbs' like the San Fernando Valley), they seek sanctuaries ever deeper in the rugged contours of the chaparral fire belt.

Whereas the Australian bush cultures have developed a strong self-help ethos and where their own fire brigades are a focal point of community life and prestige, in the Californian case the wealthy hill-dwellers expect the state fire services to protect them absolutely and completely, regardless of the cost and without any input from themselves. So in Australia residents are organisationally and personally related to the forests around them, while the American residents are divorced and insulated. In the two areas these social and cultural factors lie behind two completely different policies on fire-fighting. In California the policy is for a complete fire ban in the most dangerous areas. While this might well succeed in reducing ignition among responsible middle class residents, it fails to do anything about fuel levels, and as each year passes the fuel accumulates, resulting in much hotter and destructive fires than was ever the case in the past. In Australia, by comparison, the local nature of fire-fighting and responsibility for prevention means that in cooler times of the year a great deal of back-burning takes place to reduce the fuel loads around residential areas. However, because the local brigades rely on fighting fires to maintain their status and income, individuals are now more prone to deliberately light fires.

Ironically, the wildfires of California are something of a misnomer in that the trees responsible for most of their ferocity are not wild native trees but introduced *Australian* eucalypts. For example, in the Oakland/Berkeley Hills the native dominant trees were native oaks but these were all logged in the 1880s and replaced by plantations of eucalypts which then seeded easily across the entire region/state. They now comprise 70% of the vegetation fuelling contemporary wildfires.[5] Again, here we have eucalypts with yet another dance partner and yet another fire regime – that Davis (1998: 143) has called the '"postsuburban" fire regime'. In this dance the trees are subject to no regime of regular burning, and the pattern of dispersed settlement makes it highly difficult to back-burn safely. The dance of fire-fighting in the Malibu area comprises a house-by-house defence strategy and now involves the use of new technologies: the CL-415 'Super Scooper' is a 'gigantic amphibious aircraft capable of skimming the surface of the ocean and loading up to 14,000 gallons of water per fire drop'.

It is perhaps only fitting that in such exclusive areas fire-fighting has become such an expensive, luxurious affair. The cost of mobilising the 15,000 fire-fighters alone during Halloween week in 1993 was $100 million, but in the wildfires of October 2007 the total insured cost was $1.9 billion.[6]

The total cost of natural disasters, most of it impacting on the built cityscapes of the world, was estimated at $75 billion in 2007, an increase of 50% on the previous year, but even this is as nothing compared to the total cost in 2005 of $220 billion, the year Hurricane Katrina slammed into New

Orleans. The cost of that underestimation of the relationship between nature and the city was $99 billion in New Orleans alone.

Conclusion

These last examples from the USA and Australia might be considered extreme, but as scholarship into what sociologists now call 'risk society' proceeds, it has become clear that in fact the modern metropolis is often, by virtue of its very advantageous position as a human centre, subject to highly structuring natural forces (Clark, 2000). These differentiate cities one from another and contribute to their political, institutional and cultural specificity. Thus, the politics and economy, space and natures of New Orleans are structured by water in a way that in San Francisco or Naples they are structured by plate tectonics, or in Moscow by snow and ice.

Similarly, by virtue of their unprecedented human population and their position as hubs of unprecedented global flows of things and people, cities have become intertwined with a dance with infectious disease. The 2009 Swine Flu pandemic is a good illustration of the (rapid) ways in which a potentially lethal virus or bacteria can penetrate a city's defences but it also illustrates how much non-threatening 'other natures' transit, spread and settle in the major city hubs. Some natural species 'discover' a natural affinity with cities and become newly emblematic: the buddleia plant I began this book with, the falcons that found nest sites on skyscrapers, the fruit bats of Melbourne and Sydney who found their city botanic gardens a safe haven in a hostile outer world; the badgers, foxes and dormice of the English suburbs who found protectors in the city as their habitat was destroyed in the country by more profit-hungry agribusiness. Even the short-tailed deer of Bambi fame has its stronghold in the North American city.

It seems we do not wish to make the city an other to the natural world and it also seems as though living in the city can sharpen our sense of our relationship with the environment and nature rather than the opposite. This is certainly the case with the newly emerging green political movements in most nations, but it does not necessarily reflect the fact that cities hold a disproportionate population of the educated middle classes who have become concerned about the natural world beyond the urban fringes.

As I emphasised at the beginning of this chapter, it is the 'nature' of cities to appear to its inhabitants to have a *life* of their own; that by being the confluence of a great many flows of people, materials, objects, plants and animals and by being more than a sum of the parts *and* by being uniquely London, Paris, Toronto or Tokyo, cities can present themselves as powerful, structuring environments in which our lives must be played out. We leave traces of ourselves and our lives in their streets and lanes, rivers and parks and our writers acknowledge this in their poetry, prose and novels.

It is thus puzzling that despite all of the profound consequences of this intertwining, urban studies remains resolutely humanist. Without singling out any works in particular, it is instructive that books that identify the subject proper of urban studies, such as Bridge and Watson's *A Companion to the City* (2000) (or their *Blackwell City Reader* of 2002) or Bounds's (2004) *Urban Social Theory* make barely any reference to this. However, it is not enough to merely *include* nature in the city. The project that this book supports is one that moves away from a humanist ontology as the guiding principle of urban scholarship, and that means reinvestigating the way in which people, machines and other non-humans combine and intertwine to create the cities we *actually* live in. It is this (urban) branch of sociology, social history, geography and anthropology that demands this most, since it is in cities where it most evident and where it is most vital, literally, in its consequences.

NOTES

1 Andrew Pickering's *Mangle of Practice* (1995) is instructive here.
2 National Nest Box Week is 14–21 February. www.bto.org/nnbw/index.htm
3 see www.gardenature.co.uk/downloads/FeedingGardenBirds.pdf. Accessed 3 November 2007.
4 see Elias and Dunning, *The Quest for Excitement* (1986).
5 see www.firewise.org/pubs/theOaklandBerkeleyHillsFire/vegetation.html. Accessed 16 February 2005.
6 The figures come from CNN Money 27 December 2007. http://money.cnn.com/2007/12/27/news/international/bc.germany.munichre.disa.ap/

10 Rites de Renaissance

City Life has tried to avoid the traps of the humanist ontology, that is, viewing cities as if they are merely humans among themselves and that humans are the only actors that do anything of significance. The reader who begins at the beginning and ends up here will already be disabused of this error, particularly after reading the section in the last chapter on city bushfires in Australia and the USA. The agency of trees, and by that I mean what trees actually *do*, has been systematically ignored in trying to understand the increasing threat (and cost) they pose to major cities. A posthumanist approach that investigates fires as an artefact of the *relationship* between trees and cities (a long-standing and ongoing relationship at that) is the *only* way in which we can understand why fires are more frequent and more deadly. I am quite sure that if the authorities in New Orleans had taken notice and taken seriously what the posthumanist sociologist Andrew Pickering was saying about the relationship between the Mississippi and the Corps of Engineers at New Orleans, a disaster might have been averted.

This and other examples scattered throughout the book provide a new way of figuring the city not as achievement, monolith and citadel, not as a modernist blueprint for living, but as a becoming in which the agency of more than just humans *matters*. I have described most cities as works in progress towards something else, and there are many manifestations of city life that are important to grasp because all iterations are dependent on past and even parallel cities. Paris under Napoleon III was in part a response to London's leafy, countrified parks and squares. A century later, most British cities were responding to the blueprints of the architect-king, Le Corbusier, and his machines for living. In both, the ramifications and relationships between humans and non-humans twist and turn, never without consequence; always with intertwined complexity. Today we speak of *city forests* being the amalgamation of all the tree species in their specific configuration and their implications for human and other species as habitats. They were barely noticed ten years ago; they did not matter.

But this book has also taken seriously all of the many people who have observed that cities appear to be alive, have a particular rhythm and pulse, are more than a sum of their parts and create excitement, redemption, change and interpellations. I have tried to get at what they mean by this, its particular anthropological, anthrozoological and anthrobotanical and cyborg states and manifestations. I have taken a look at such things as jazz, gardening, buying fashion clothes, the mysteries of street markets and the recodings and theatricality of second-hand markets and collecting. And, I have tried to relate things as widely and normally separated as birding, cafés, festivals, art galleries, reclamation yards and doing up old machines to contemporary conditions of liquid modernity, which is the metaphorical description of most Western social formations. Individualism, consumerism, risk, loneliness, the absence of bonds, the rise of mobility and the touristification of everyday life produce new iterations of modernity that have had a profound impact on the mobile, shapeless liquid life of cities. Just because we break up with partners more often and are lonelier more often, means that we need to perform the business of meeting and courtship more often, and for that we need the ritual spaces for these and other *rites de passage* more often and in greater variety, for different age groups develop their own tastes and styles.

Except, city life is no longer about *passage*, from a beginning to an end. Rather it has become a continuous round or series of new beginnings so it ought to be called something like *rites de renaissance*. Rituals of transformation, redemption and change lie at the heart of city life for humans in liquid modernity. My argument here is that this has had a profound bearing on the city and its *spectacularisation* in the past twenty years. We no longer merely shop or sight-see in cities, we want far more than this. We want to be challenged, entertained, educated, thrown alternatives, have the zeitgeist revealed. But most of all we want involvement; we sense our belonging and place in the world through performance and cities offer that experience more than any other spaces (although as I have argued, they did borrow this service from the resort).

It is hardly likely that the supercities and smaller cities considered in this book will be abandoned in favour of entirely different structures/human habitations, but this is not to say that redesign, redevelopment and change have not been on the agenda and will not continue to be so. As Inoguchi et al. (1999) point out, there are environmental grounds alone that will justify this long into the future. The fact that we have recently discovered so much nature in cities as well as the *permeability* and *vulnerability* of cities to the wider natures of which they are a part will mean that questions will continue to be posed about managing the benefits of a more promiscuous interweaving of human and non-human life as well as managing risks. Vasishth and Sloane (2002) also make the point that environmental decision-making is always at the same time an ecological question, not one that can be confined to the city boundaries. In their examination of rain and water issues in

Los Angeles we can see how it is the connections and the consequences of actions over a range of spatial scales that matter rather than merely the management of a city. As they say, from an ecological view, which may require drawing different boundaries, what does it mean to speak of 'the city'?

I have suggested that the ecological sensibility that now seeks to find solutions to such things as waste management, pollution, water shortages and quality, more effective and efficient transportation (alternative to the automobile) and better resource and energy conservation needs to be understood as emerging from a broader, more tolerant and experimental counter-culture that is ecological in the way it imagines *most* of its relationships. According to this ideal, relating to all objects and beings should be considerate, should seek to understand and find ways of compatibility and cohabitation. This is a form of ordering with a strong tendency to fail, and failure will be normative in the city because the problems are hard and the conflicts endemic. But this is a different sensibility to that which dominated the earlier half of the twentieth century where such compromises and complexities were part of a less tolerant ontology, one that sought to standardise, rather than cohabit and replace, rather than coevolve.

Equally, other ecological considerations and relationships concern the complex networks of relationships between human and non-human cultures in the city, and as we have seen these are both important and often neglected elements of city life. Poverty continues to be a spectre of the city and the increased pace of migration and mobility means that it is often hard to grasp who is living around you let alone come to a good working relationship and understanding. Often poverty and complex networks of migration and mobility figure significantly in some of the more vital stories we have told in this book. In the Mission district of San Francisco, Notting Hill in London, as in the bohemian quarter of Montmartre, Paris, many years ago, it was the brimming vitality, cultural vortices and tolerance of difference and pleasure that drew crowds, new settlers and subsequently new investment. Without wishing to condone poverty in any way, we might however note that the great cities have tolerated a great number of people who have problems and who find it difficult to find a niche elsewhere. I recall the case of an elderly woman who lived in a van close to Camden Lock market who figured for a while in Alan Bennett's biography *Writing Home*. This fearful, difficult and smelly person was looked after by Bennett and others in the most touching of ways, ways that I am sure would not have been forthcoming in the smarter or the respectable suburbs of the middle classes or in the country, for that matter. It is no accident that so many people with problems end up on the streets of London, but as Tony Biebuyck found when he did participant observation of single homeless men there the city does accommodate large numbers of them, there is something of a labour market for them and they even constitute a sub-culture right in the heart of the West End. As he remarked: 'The make up of the group is so heterogenous that I think almost anybody can be accommodated' (Biebuyck, 1982: 17).

This ethical approach first found expression in the efflorescence of cultural tolerance and experimentation. Culture was not a permanent point of difference (to be defended and maintained) but merely a set of practices that could be borrowed, fused with others and changed. Escaping the chains and boredom of 'establishment' or even 'suburban' ways of thinking and living (from a number of cultural origins) became the permanent revolution that the counter-culture set in train, and as Ley showed in respect of gentrification, it focused on those spaces that fell vacant, that were under less surveillance or control. These spaces of experimentation were strictly limited but as industrial capitalism waned in the city such a space opened up, and not just in one city.

As I have tried to argue, these spaces of change have become one of the main coordinates of urban renewal and odd partnerships have emerged between these cultural currents and corporate and municipal capital. The redesign of space and finance reshaped central areas of the city so that this more vibrant culture could take root and flourish; encouraging more investment, more settlers, more life. It too was experimental. In some places it worked well in others less so. It was never a solution to urban poverty and it rarely became one, but it did make the life of cities more fun for more people.

City life today and into the future will have many architects, not the architect-kings of the eighteenth, nineteenth and early to mid-twentieth centuries. This is also because there is a more ecological frame of reference and lifestyle, and tolerance of more diversity and difference of living arrangements. From the 1980s the broken rooflines of postmodern inner cityscapes, whether new or renewed, were somehow comforting after several decades of churning, and cultural rejection. It is unlikely that they will return, or need to, and if Rogers and Power (2000) are correct in their assessment of 'Cities for Small Countries', involving people in the process of development and change will ensure their success over esoteric blueprints.

Of course this will not and should not stop other architects from further experimentation, and this seems to be taking many forms. Paolo Soleri's long-running experiment in 'arcology' (the fusion between architecture and ecology) at Arcosanti, near Phoenix, Arizona, seeks to build an ecologically sustainable city as a showcase for the rest of the world. Planned to house 5000 eventually, this very slow growing project started in 1970 and has so far been most successful in educating and keeping alive these ideas among a new generation. The choice of one of the most difficult sites and regions to demonstrate its viability has been a problem because to date there is not a lot to showcase. However, as technologies proceed apace the variables are given a new shake and in recent years breakthroughs in industrial production of high quality prefabricated building units are beginning to offer incredible cost-effectiveness and flexibility. What might have been prohibitive building costs in central locations can now be affordable and these sorts of benefits can flow on to less affluent groups. They can also provide the inspiration for other utopian imaginings.

If cities have begun to lose their meaning (and importance) in the ecological grand scheme, requiring more joined-up and wider partnership-type approaches to their ecological management and consequences, then they certainly have not in terms of their place in the cultural zeitgeist. Whatever claims were made for the possibility of a complete decentralisation of modern life as a result of computer connectivity, a sort of return to the country good-life seems to have disappeared with a renewed enthusiasm for city life. Not for a quiet life in the suburbs but, increasingly, a more involved life in the centre of cities. Even in those cities that do not gravitate to a central city cultural area but are more distributed in what Garreau (1992) called *Edge Cities*, city life seems to be gathering around familiar sorts of configurations of building and activities, all with a strong cultural, playful and transformative content that choreographs change and the new. It is almost as if in a world of individualism and consumerism where our identity is fragile and never completed, always becoming something else, and where social bonds are, as Bauman argues, loose and 'until further notice', that we need cultural centres to our lives. Religion and ritual used to occupy this space in our collective existence, and, as we saw in Chapter 1, these were also located in centre-stage locations in Roman and medieval cities. Even into the beginning of the nineteenth century many of the dimensions of traditional city life were intact, from the more formal everyday presence of chapel life to the more episodic carnivalesque events. Through the proliferation of non-conformist sects, Protestantism introduced an ascetic new order to life in the producerist city, and this asceticism continued to assert pressure on many of the remaining areas of traditional city life, beginning with carnival, Spring and May Day festivals and even carnivalesque spaces and sensibilities of the everyday: the pubs and beer drinking itself. Much of city life had been lived on the street and in semi-public spaces of the working class courts. Streets were places of gaming, sports, exchange and retailing, partying and dancing, dalliances and sexuality, even Sabbath-breaking. Byelaws identified these as incompatible with the new city order and police forces were enacted to enforce them. As a result cities lost much of their life to a more privatised self-absorbed life that was so strongly entrenched that it took the best part of the twentieth century for it to unravel. Wars and post-war periods were times when it could be and was challenged culminating in a counter-culture that re-imagined the city both by looking to other cultures as well as reviving the past, tradition and ritual.

In many ways the significance of culture to modern city life is that it locates new centres for the consideration of what it is to be modern. It is not a question of putting in place the right buildings (although buildings can interpellate and inspire) or the 'right' events so much as encouraging, investing in, facilitating people's performative involvement in the city. It is a question of trusting that city life is what we are trying to produce, that it is an end in itself. There are no secrets to this knowledge though there have been areas of it that were hidden by other paradigms. The joy of dancing with others, of planting a garden, of being known in a quarter or a café or pub, of being challenged or interpellated by a reflexive and robust art scene or excited by a local soccer team and stumbling on ways to make ourselves anew – all these are the point of city life.

There is a long way to go before cities will offer an even and equitable experience to all people and maybe that point will never be reached as cities provide space for those individuals and groups who have fallen off the rails or who have been held back for a while. As with Canterbury, which embraced, homed, fed and inspired everyone who needed the magic dust of the cult of saints, everyone who sought rejuvenation, salvation and redemption, so too the contemporary city will continue to provide a place to come to; a place that offers dreams and futures.

References and Further Reading

Ackroyd, P. (2001) *London: The Biography*. London: Viking.

Adorno, T.W. (1967) *Prisms*. Cambridge, MA: MIT University Press.

Agamben, G. (2005) *State of Exception*. Chicago: University of Chicago Press.

Alexander, A., Phillips, S. and Shaw, G. (2007) 'Retail innovation and shopping practices: consumers' reactions to self-service retailing', *Environment and Planning A* doi:10.1068/a39117.

Amin, A. and Thrift, N. (2002) *Cities – Reimagining the Urban*. Cambridge: Polity Press.

Amis, M. (1984) *Money*. Harmondsworth: Penguin.

Amis, M. (1989) *London Fields*. Harmondsworth: Penguin.

Amis, M. (1995) *The Information*. London: Flamingo.

Atkin, R. (2003) 'A tale of cool cities', *The Christian Science Monitor*, October.

Atkinson, R. and Helms, G. (2007) *Securing an Urban Renaissance*. Bristol: Policy Press.

Baldassave, M. and Katz, C. (1992) 'The personal threat of environmental problems as predictor of environmental practices', *Environment and Behavior* 24: 602–16.

Bauman, Z. (1992) *Intimations of Postmodernity*. London: Routledge.

Bauman, Z. (1998) *Globalisation*. Cambridge: Polity Press.

Bauman, Z. (2000) *Liquid Modernity*. Cambridge: Polity Press.

Bauman, Z. (2002) *Society under Siege*. Cambridge: Polity Press.

Bauman, Z. (2003a) *City of Fears, City of Hopes*. London: Goldsmith College, University of London.

Bauman, Z. (2003b) *Liquid Love*. Cambridge: Polity Press.

Bauman, Z. (2005) *Liquid Life*. Cambridge: Polity Press.

Beck, U. (1992) *Risk Society*. London: Sage.

Becker, H.S. (1973) *The Outsiders*. New York: The Free Press.

Begnal, M. (ed.) (2002) *Joyce and the City*. New York: Syracuse University Press.

Bell, C. and Lyall, J. (2001a) 'The Accelerated Sublime: Thrill seeking adventure heroes in the commodified landscape', in S. Coleman and M. Crang (eds), *Tourism: Between Place and Performance*. Oxford: Berghahn.

Bell, C. and Lyall, J. (2001b) *The Accelerated Sublime*. London: Praeger.

Bennet, T. (1983) 'A thousand and one troubles: Blackpool Pleasure Beach', in H. Carby, L. Curti, I. Chambers and N. King (eds), *Formations of Pleasure*. London: Routledge and Kegan Paul.

Benjamin, W., McLaughlin, K. and Eiland, H. (2002) *The Arcades Projects*. Cambridge, MA: Harvard University Press.

Berger, B.M. (1960) *Working Class Suburb: A Study of Auto Workers in Suburbia*. Los Angeles: University of California Press.

Berman, M. (1988) *All That Is Solid Melts into Air*. Harmondsworth: Penguin.

Betjeman, J. (2003) *Collected Poems*. London: John Murray.

Betsky, A. and Adigard, E. (2000) *Architecture Must Burn*. New York: Ginko Press.

Biebuyck, T. (1982) *Single and Homeless: A Participant Observation Study of the Single Homeless. Working Paper 3 Single and Homeless Study*. London: Department of Environment.

Bogue, Donald J. (1955) 'Urbanism in the United States, 1950', *American Journal of Sociology* 60: 471–86.

Bolin, R.C. and Stanford, L. (1998) *The Northridge Earthquake: Vulnerability and Disaster*. London: Routledge.

Bounds, M. (2004) *Urban Social Theory: City, Self and Society*. Oxford: Oxford University Press.

Bourdieu, P. (1984) *Distinction*. Cambridge, MA: Harvard University Press.

Braun, B. and Castree, N. (1998) *Remaking Reality: Nature at the Millennium*. London: Routledge.

Bridge, G. (2000) 'Rationality, ethics and space: on situated universalism and the self-interested acknowledgement of "difference"', *Environment and Planning D: Society and Space* 12: 31–51.

Bridge, G. and Watson, S. (eds), (2000) *A Companion to the City*. Oxford: Blackwell.

Bridge, G. and Watson, S. (eds), (2002) *The Blackwell City Reader*. Oxford: Blackwell.

Brinkley, S. (2007) 'Governmentality and lifestyle studies', *Sociology Compass* 1(1): 111–26.

Brown, A., O'Connor, J. and Cohen, S. (2000) 'Local music policies within a global music industry: cultural quarters in Manchester and Sheffield', *Geoforum* 31(4): 437–51.

Brownlee, L. (2008) 'Growing up', *Guardian* Weekend, 28 June 98–101.

Bruce, S. (2001) 'Christianity in Britain, R.I.P.', *Sociology of Religion* 62(2): 191–203.

Bruegmann, R. (2004) *Sprawl – A Compact History*. Chicago: University of Chicago Press.

Bryson, B. (2007) *Shakespeare: The World as a Stage*. London: Harper Press.

Buck-Morss, S. (2002) *Dialectics of Seeing: Walter Benjamin and the Arcades Projects*, cited in G. Bridge and S. Watson (eds), *The Blackwell City Reader*. Oxford: Blackwell.

Burnett, J. (1978) *A Social History of Housing, 1815–1970*. London: Methuen.

Butler, T. (1997) *Gentrification and the Middle Classes*. Aldershot: Ashgate.

Butler, T. and Robson, G. (2003) *London Calling*. Oxford: Berg.

Callaghan, G. (2008) 'Green skins', *The Weekend Australian Magazine*, 21–22 June: 36–40.

Cartmill, M. (1993) *View to a Death in the Morning*. Cambridge, MA: Harvard University Press.

Cashmore, E. (1990) *Making Sense of Sports*. London: Routledge.

Castells, M. (1970) *The Urban Question*. London: Edward Arnold.

Castells, M. (1983) *The City and the Grassroots*. Berkeley, CA: University of California Press.

Castells, M. (1996) *The Information Age – The Rise of Network Society*. Oxford: Blackwell.

Champion, Tony (1989) 'Counterurbanization in Europe', *The Geographical Journal*, 155(1): 52.

Chatwin, B. (1987) *The Songlines*. London: Jonathan Cape.

Church, C. and Gale, T. (2000) *Streets in the Sky*. London National Sustainable Tower Block Initiative. www.towerblocks.org.uk/streets_sky.pdf. (Accessed 12 August 2007.)

Clark, N. (2000) 'Botanizing on the asphalt? The complex life of cosmopolitan bodies', *Body and Society* 6(3–4): 12–33.
Clarke, J., Critcher, C. and Johnstone, R. (1979) *Working Class Culture: Studies in History and Theory.* London: Hutchinson.
Cloke, P. and Jones, O. (2001) 'Dwelling, place and landscape: an orchard in Somerset', *Environment and Planning A* 33: 649–66.
Cohen, S. (2002) *Folk Devils and Moral Panics.* London: Routledge.
Coleman, S. and Crang, M. (eds) (2002) *Tourism: Between Place and Performance.* Oxford: Berghahn.
Collings, M. (2000) *This Is Modern Art.* London: Weidenfeld & Nicolson.
Collins, A. (2006) 'Sexual dissidence, enterprise and assimilation: bedfellows in urban regeneration', in A. Collins (ed.), *Cities of Pleasure: Sex and the Urban Socialscape.* London: Routledge.
Collins, J. (1995) *Architectures of Excess.* London: Routledge.
Cox, I. (1951) *The South Bank Exhibition.* London: HMSO.
Crespa, C.J., Keteyian, S.J., Heath, G.W. and Sempos, C.T. (1996) 'Leisure time physical activity among US adults – results from the third National Health and Nutrition Examination Survey', *Archives of Internal Medicine* 156(1): 93–8.
Crook, S. (1999) 'Ordering risks', in D. Lupton (ed.), *Risk and Socio-cultural Theory.* Cambridge: Cambridge University Press.
Cross, G. (ed.) (1990) *Worktowners at Blackpool: Mass-Observation and Popular Leisure in the 1930s.* London: Routledge.
Crossick, G. (1978) *An Artisan Elite in Victorian Society.* London: Croom Helm.
Crouch, C., Leontidou, L. and Petschel-Held, G. (2007) *Urban Sprawl in Europe.* Oxford: Blackwell.
Cushing, H. (2005) *Beyond Organics – Gardening of the Future.* Sydney: ABC Books.
Darke, J., Ledwith, S. and Woods, R. (2000) *Women and the City: Visibility and Voice in Urban Space.* London: Palgrave Macmillan.
Daunton, M.J. (1983) *House and Home in the Victorian City, 1850–1914.* London: Edward Arnold.
Davis, J. (1973) *Land, Family and Marriage in Pisticci.* London: Athlone.
Davis, M. (1998) *City of Quartz.* London: Pimlico.
Davis, M. (2002) *Dead Cities: A Natural History.* New York: New Press.
Davison, A. (2003) 'Stuck in a cul-de-sac? Suburban history and urban sustainability in Australia', *Urban Policy and Research* 24(2): 201–16.
de Botton, A. (2002) *The Art of Travel.* London: Hamish Hamilton.
de Botton, A. (2006) *The Architecture of Happiness.* London: Hamish Hamilton.
Deleuze, G. and Guattari, F. (1999) *A Thousand Plateaus.* London: Athlone.
Derksen, L. and Gartrell, J. (1993) The social context of recycling', *American Review of Sociology* 58: 434–42.
Detsicus, P. (1983) *The Cantiaci.* Sutton: Sutton Publishing Ltd.
Dickens, C. (1971) *Our Mutual Friend.* Harmondsworth: Penguin.
Dickens, C. (1993) *Bleak House.* Harmondsworth: Penguin.
Dickens, P. (1992) *Society and Nature: Towards a Green Social Theory.* Hemel Hempstead: Harvester Wheatsheaf.
Dickens, P. (1996) *Reconstructing Nature.* London: Routledge.
Dickens, P. (2001) 'Linking the social and natural sciences: Is capital modifying human biology in its own image?', *Sociology* 35(1): 93–110.
Dresser, M. (1983) 'People's housing in Bristol 1870–1939', in I. Bild (ed.), *Bristol's Other History.* Bristol: Bristol Broadsides.

Dunlap, R. and Catton, W. (1979) 'Environmental sociology', *Annual Review of Sociology* 5: 243–73.

Dunlap, R. and Catton, W. (1994) 'Struggling with human exceptionalism: the rise, decline and revitalization of environmental sociology', *The American Sociologist* 25: 5–30.

Durant, H. (1938) *The Problem of Leisure*. London: George Routledge and Son.

Eco, U. (1987) *Faith in Fakes*. London: Secker and Warburg.

Elias, N. (1990) *The Civilising Process*. London: Routledge.

Elias, N. and Dunning, E. (1986) *The Quest for Excitement*. London: Routledge.

Elliott, A. (1999) *The Mourning of John Lennon*. Melbourne: University of Melbourne Press.

Erenberg, L.A. (1984) *Steppin' Out: New York Nightlife and the Formation of American Culture*, 1890–1930. New York: Greenwood Press.

Ewing, R., Schieber, R. and Zegeer, C. (2003) 'Urban sprawl as a risk factor in motor vehicle occupant and pedestrian fatalities', *American Journal of Public Health* 93(9): 1541–5.

Fainstein, S.S. (1999) (ed.), *The Tourist City*. New Haven, CT: Yale University Press.

Featherstone, M. (1987) 'Lifestyle and consumer culture', *Theory, Culture and Society* 4: 54–70.

Festinger, L., Schachter, S. and Back, K. (1950) *Social Pressure in Informal Groups*. New York: Harper.

Finkelstein, J. (2007) *The Art of Self Invention*. London: I.B. Tauris.

Finnegan, R. (1998) *Tales of the City: A Study of Narrative and Urban Life*. Cambridge: Cambridge University Press.

Florida, R. (2003a) *The Rise of the Creative Class*. London: Pluto.

Florida, R. (2003b) *Cities and the Creative Class*. London: Routledge.

Florida, R. (2008) *Who's Your City?* New York: Basic Books.

Franklin A.S. (1984) *Squatting in England: A Case Study of Social Conflict in Advanced Industrial Capitalism*. Working Paper 37, School for Advanced Urban Studies, University of Bristol.

Franklin, A.S. (1989) *Privatism, the Home and Working Class Culture*. PhD thesis, University of Bristol.

Franklin, A.S. (1996) 'Australian hunting and angling sports and the changing nature of human–animal relations in Australia', *Australian and New Zealand Journal of Sociology* 32(3): 39–56.

Franklin, A.S. (2006) 'Burning cities: a posthumanist account of cities and eucalypts', *Environment and Planning D: Society and Space* 24(4): 555–76.

Franklin, A.S. (2002) *Nature and Social Theory*. London: Sage.

Franklin, A.S. (2003) *Tourism*. London: Sage.

Franklin, A.S. (2008a) 'The "Animal Question" and the consumption of wildlife', in *Consumptive Wildlife Tourism – Hunting, Shooting and Sport Fishing*. London: Routledge.

Franklin, A.S. (2008b) 'A choreography of fire: a posthumanist account of Australians and forests', in A. Pickering and K. Guzik (eds), *The Mangle in Practice: Science, Society and Becoming*. Durham, NC: Duke University Press. pp. 17–45.

Franklin, A.S. (2009) 'On loneliness', *Geografiska Annaler: Series B, Human Geography* 91(3): 416–30.

Franklin, S. (2000) 'Life itself: global nature and the genetic imaginary', Department of Sociology, Lancaster University. Available at: www.comp.lancs.ac.uk/sociology/soc048sf.html.

Franklin, S. (2001) 'Are we post-genomic?', Department of Sociology, Lancaster University. Available at: www.comp.lancs.ac.uk/sociology/papers/Franklin-Are-we post-genomic.pdf

Franklin A.S., Haraway D., Emmison D.M. and Travers M.H. (2007) 'Investigating the therapeutic benefits of dogs', *Qualitative Sociology Research* 25(2): 42–58.

Frisby, D. (1994) 'The *flâneur* in social theory', in Keith Tester (ed.), *The Flâneur*. London: Routledge.

Frumkin, H. (2002) *Public Health Reports*, May–June 2002, vol. 117: 204.

Frumkin, H., Frank, L. and Jackson, R. (2004) *Urban Sprawl and Public Health*. London: Island Press.

Fullager, S. (2004) 'On restlessness and patience: Reading desire in Bruce Chatwin's narratives of travel', *Tourist Studies* 4(1): 5–20.

Furedi, F. (1998) *The Culture of Fear*. London: Cassell.

Furedi, F. (2005) *The Politics of Fear*. London: Continuum.

Gandy, M. (2005) 'Cyborg urbanization: complexity and monstrosity in the contemporary city', *International Journal for Urban and Regional Research* 291: 26–49.

Garreau, J. (1992) *Edge City*. New York: Anchor Books.

Gellner, E. (1983) *Nations and Nationalism*. Oxford: Blackwell.

Giddens, A. (1991) *Modernity and Self-Identity*. Cambridge: Polity Press.

Gill, N. and Anderson, K. (2005) 'Improvement in the inland: culture and nature in the Australian rangelands', *Australian Humanities Review* 34: Jan–Feb.

Glass, Ruth (1948) *The Social Background of a Plan*. London: Routledge.

Glendinning, M. and Muthesius, S. (1994) *Tower Block*. Newhaven, CT: Yale University Press.

Goffman, E. (1967) *Interaction Ritual: Essays in Face-to-Face Behavior*. New York: Doubleday, Anchor Books.

Gordon, M. (1963) *Sick Cities*. Harmondsworth: Penguin.

Gottdiener, M. (1994) *The New Urban Sociology*. New York: McGraw–Hill.

Govaerts, F. (1989) 'Belgium: Old trends, new contradictions' in A. Olszewska and K. Roberts (eds), *Leisure and Lifestyle*. London: Sage.

Grange, J. (1999) *The City: An Urban Cosmology*. New York: SUNY Press.

Greer, G. (1970) *The Female Eunuch*. London: MacGibbon and Key.

Gregson, N. and Crewe, L. (1997a) 'Excluded spaces of regulation: car-boot sales as an enterprise culture out of control?', *Environment and Planning A* 29: 1717–37.

Gregson, N. and Crewe, L. (1997b) 'Performance and possession: rethinking the act of purchase in the light of the car boot sale', Mimeo, from N. Gregson, Department of Geography, Sheffield University.

Gregson, N. and Crewe, L. (1997c) 'The bargain, the knowledge, and the spectacle: making sense of consumption in the space of the car-boot sale', *Environment and Planning D: Society and Space* 15: 87–112.

Gregson, N. and Crewe, L. (2003) *Second-Hand Cultures*. Oxford: Berg.

Grey, F. (1983) *Crawley: Old Town, New Town*. Occasional Paper 18: Centre for Continuing Education, University of Sussex.

Hall, C.M. (2004) 'Sports tourism and urban regeneration', in B. Ritchie and D. Adair (eds), *Sports Tourism: Interrelationships, Impacts and Issues*. Clevedon: Channelview Publications. pp. 148–59.

Hall, S. (1969) 'The hippies: an American "moment"', in J. Nadel (ed.), *Student Power*. New York: Merlin.

Hannigan, J. (1998) *Fantasy City*. London: Routledge.

Haraway, D. (1991) *Simions, Cyborgs and Women: The Reinvention of Nature*. New York: Routledge.

Haraway, D. (2003) *The Companion Species Manifesto*. Chicago: Prickly Paradigm Press.

Haraway, D. (2008) *When Species Meet*. Minneapolis: Minnesota University Press.

Harvey, D. (1989) *The Condition of Postmodernity*. Oxford: Blackwell.
Harvey D. (1997) *Justice, Nature and the Geography of Difference*. Oxford: Blackwell.
Hatt, P.K. and Reiss, A.J. (1957) *Cities and Society*. New York: Fress Press of Glencoe, Inc.
Hay, A. (2002) *Gum – The Story of Eucalypts and Their Champions*. Sydney: Duffy and Snellgrove.
Hinchliffe, S., Kearnes, M.B., Degen, M. and Whatmore, S. (2005) 'Urban wild things – a cosmopolitical experiment', *Environment and Planning D: Society and Space* 23(5): 643–58.
Hitchens, Christopher (2007) 'Pint-sized Jewish fireplug left his imprint on the post-war decades', *Weekend Australian*, 18 November 2007.
Hollinghurst, A. (2004) *The Line of Beauty*. London: Picador.
Howard, E. (1902) *Garden Cities of To-Morrow*. London: Swan Sonnenshein.
Hylland Eriksen, T. (2001) *Tyranny of the Moment*. London: Pluto Press.
IGD Food and Grocery Information (2007) www.igd.com/cir.asp?menuid=67&cirid=2042. (Accessed 15 December 2007)
Inglehart, R. (1997) *Modernization and Postmodernization: Cultural, Economic, and Political Change in 43 Societies*. Princeton, NJ: Princeton University Press.
Ingold, T. (1993) 'The temporality of the landscape', *World Archaeology*, 25(2): 152–74.
Ingold, T. (1995) 'Building, dwelling, living', in M. Strathern (ed.), *Transformations in Anthropological Knowledge*. London: Routledge.
Inoguchi, T., Newman, E. and Paoletto, G. (1999) *Cities and the Environment*. New York: United Nations University Press.
Jacobs, J. (1961) *The Death and Life of Great American Cities*. New York: Random House.
Jahoda, M., Lazarsfeld, P.F. and Zeisel, H. (1972) *Marienthal: The Sociography of an Unemployed Community*. London: Tavistock.
James, M. (ed.) (1940) *A Complete Guide to Gardening*. London: Associated Newspapers Ltd.
Jervis, J. (1998) *Exploring the Modern*. Oxford: Blackwell.
Johnson, P. (1991) *The Birth of the Modern*. London: Phoenix.
Jones, C. and Hoppe, L. (1969) *The Urban Crisis in America*. Washington, DC: Washington National Press.
Jones, K.R. and Wills, J. (2005) *The Invention of the Park*. Cambridge: Polity Press.
Jordison, S. and Kieran, D. (2003) *Crap Towns: The 50 Worst Places to Live in the UK*. London: Boxtree Ltd.
Judd, D.R. and Fainstein, S.S. (eds) (1999) *The Tourist City*. New Haven, CT: Yale University Press.
Keller, S. (1968) *The Urban Neighbourhood: A Sociologist's Perspective*. New York: Random House.
King, A.D. (1996) *Re-Presenting the City*. New York: New York University Press.
Kingston, B. (1994) *Basket, Bag and Trolley – The history of Shopping in Australia*. Melbourne: Oxford University Press.
Kirshenblatt-Gimblett, B. (1998) *Destination Culture*. Berkeley and Los Angeles: University of California Press.
Koseki, S. (1989) 'Japan Homo Ludens Japonicus', in A. Olszewska and K. Roberts (eds), *Leisure and Lifestyle*. London: Sage.
Koven, S. (2004) *Slumming: Sexual and Social Politics in London*. Princeton, NJ: Princeton, University Press.
Krippendorf, J. (1987) *The Holiday Makers*. Oxford: Heinemann.
Landry, C. (2001) *The Creative City*. London: Earthscan.

Larsen, T. (2000) 'Thomas Cook, Holy Land pilgrims, and the dawn of the modern tourist industry', in R.N. Swanson (ed.), *The Holy Land, Holy Lands and Christian History*. Woodbridge, Suffolk: Boydell Press. pp. 335–62.

Lash, S. (1990) *The Sociology of Postmodernism*. London: Routledge.

Latour, B. (1993) *We Have Never Been Modern*. New York: Harvester Wheatsheaf.

Laurier, E. (2004) 'Busy meeting grounds: the café, the scene and the business'. Paper for 'ICT: Mobilizing Persons, Places and Spaces'. Utrecht, November 2004.

Laurier, E. and Philo, C. (2007) 'The buzz of the "Cappuccino Community"'. *ESRC Society Today*, ESRC 20 November 2007.

Law, J. (1999) 'After ANT: complexity, naming and topology', in J. Law and J. Hassard (eds), *Actor Network Theory and After*. Oxford: Blackwell.

Law, J. (2003) 'Machinic pleasures and interpellations,' in Brita Brenna, John Law and Ingunn Moser (eds), *Machines, Agency and Desire*. Oslo: University of Oslo. 1998 pp. 23–48.

Law, J. and Mol, A. (2002) *Complexities*. Durham, NC: Duke University Press.

Lawless, P. (1989) *Britain's Inner Cities*. London: Paul Chapman Publishing.

Leisure Trends Group (1998) Leisure TRAK Research. www.leisuretrends.com.

Ley, D. (1996) *The New Middle Classes and the Remaking of the Central City*. Oxford: Oxford University Press.

Light, A. (2002) 'The urban blind spot in environmental ethics.' The Thingmount Working Paper Series on the Philosophy of Conservation, TWP 3–02.

Lopez, R. (1974) 'Urban sprawl and risk for being overweight or obese', *American Journal of Public Health* 94(9): 1574–9.

Loverling, J. (1983) *The Economic Development of Bristol*. SSRC Inner City in context Project Working Paper 1. School for Advanced Urban Studies, University of Bristol.

Lowe, Jeanne R. (1967) *Cities in a Race with Time: Progress and Poverty in America's Renewing Cities*. New York: Random House.

Lowerson, J. (1995) *Sport and the English Middle Class*. Manchester: Manchester University Press.

Lury, C. (1997) 'The objects of travel', in C. Rojek and J. Urry (eds), *Touring Cultures*. London: Routledge. pp. 75–95.

Lyle, M. (2002) *Canterbury – 2000 Years of History*. Stroud, Glos.: Tempus Publishing.

MacDonald, S. (1995) 'A people's story: heritage identity and authenticity', in C. Rojek and J. Urry (eds), *Touring Cultures*. London: Routledge. pp. 155–75.

MacInnes, Colin (1980 [1959]) *Absolute Beginners*. London: Allison and Busby.

MacInnes, Colin (1980 [1960]) *Mr Love and Mr Justice*. London: Allison and Busby.

MacIntyre, S., McKay, L., Cummins, S. and Burns, C. (2005) 'Out-of-home food outlets and area deprivation: case study of Glasgow, UK', *International Journal of Behavioral Nutrition* 2(16): 159–71.

Macnaghten, P. and Urry, J. (1995) 'Towards a sociology of nature', *Sociology* 29(2): 124–37.

Macnaghten, P. and Urry, J. (1998) *Contested Natures*. London: Sage.

MacPhee, G. (2002) *The Architecture of the Visible*. London: Continuum.

Martin, P.J. (1995) *Sounds and Society*. Manchester: Manchester University Press.

Martindale, D. (1958) 'Prefatory remarks: Theory of the city', in Max Weber, *The City*. London: Macmillan.

Mathews, A. (2001) *Wild Nights: Nature Returns to the City*. New York: North Point Press.

Meller, H. (1976) *Leisure and the Changing City: 1870–1914*. London: Routledge and Kegan Paul.

Merrifield, A. (2002) *Metromarxism*. London: Routledge.
Michael, M. (2000) *Reconnecting Culture, Technology and Nature: From Society to Heterogeneity*. London: Routledge.
Miles, M. (1997) *Art Space in the City: Public Arts and Urban Futures*. London: Routledge.
Miller, D. (2001) *Car Cultures*. Oxford: Berg.
Mortimer, J. (1982) *Clinging to the Wreckage*. London: Weidenfeld & Nicolson.
Mortimer, J. (2003) *Where There's a Will*. London: Viking/Penguin.
Mosley, S. (2001) *The Chimney of the World: A History of Smoke Pollution in Victorian and Edwardian Manchester*. Cambridge: Cambridge University Press.
Mumford, L. (1961) *The City in History*. New York: Harcourt Brace Jovanovich. [1966 edn, Harmondsworth: Penguin.]
Munro-Clark, M. (1986) *Communes in Rural Australia*. Sydney: Hale and Iremonger.
Murphy, R. (1995) 'Sociology as if nature did not matter: an ecological critique', *British Journal of Sociology* 46(4): 688–707.
National Resources Committee, USA (1951) 'The problems of urban America', in P. Hatt and A. Reiss (eds), *Cities and Society*. New York: The Free Press of Glencoe. pp. 743–58.
Newton, T. (2003a) 'Truly embodied sociology: marrying the social and the biological', *The Sociological Review* 51(1): 20–42.
Newton, T. (2003b) 'Crossing the great divide: time, nature and the social', *Sociology* 37(3): 433–57.
Nunberg, G. (2006) 'Commentary', *Fresh Air*. National Public Radio, 31 July 2006.
O'Connor, J. and Wynne, D. (eds) (2000) *From the Margins to the Centre: Cultural Production and Consumption in the Post-industrial City*. London: Arena.
O'Connor, J. (2000) *The Cultural Production Centre in Manchester*. Manchester: Manchester Institute for Popular Culture, MMU.
Office for National Statistics (1996) *Social Trends*, 26th edn. London: The Stationery Office.
Office for National Statistics (2007) *Social Trends*, 38th edn. London: The Stationery Office.
Pakulski, J. and Waters, M. (1995) *The Death of Class*. London: Sage.
Pahl, R. (1970) *Patterns of Urban Life*. London: Longman.
Pahl, R. (1984) *Divisions of Labour*. Oxford: Basil Blackwell.
Painter, C. (ed.) (2002) *Contemporary Art and the Home*. Oxford: Berg.
Parisnotes (2007) www.parisnotes.com. (Accessed 6 March 2007.)
Peel, M. (2005) 'The urban debate: from "Los Angeles" to the urban village', in Patrick Troy (ed.), *Australian Cities: Issues, Strategies and Policies for Urban Australia in the 1990s*. Melbourne: Cambridge University Press. pp. 83–93.
Pelan, R. (2005) 'Masking the carnival as subversion: Devry's Halloween Carnival', *Politics and Culture*, issue 4 (online).
Pickering, A. (1995) *The Mangle of Practice*. Chicago: University of Chicago Press.
Pickering, A. (2008) 'New ontologies', in A. Pickering and K. Guzik (eds), *The Mangle in Practice: Science, Society and Becoming*. Durham, NC: Duke University Press.
Pile, S. (2005) *Real Cities*. London: Sage.
Potts, W. (1979) *Portraits of the Artist in Exile: Recollections of James Joyce by a European*. Seattle, WA: University of Washington Press.
Pountain, D. and Robins, D. (2000) *Cool Rules: Anatomy of an Attitude*. London: Reaktion Books.
Prior, N. (2002) *Museums and Modernity*. Oxford: Berg.
Quiney, P. (1986) *House and Home – A History of the Small English House*. London: BBC Books.

Quinion, M. (2004) *World Wide Words*. www.worldwidewords.org/qa/qa-jaz1.htm.
Raban, R. (1974) *Soft City*. London: Harvill Press.
Raco, M. (2007) 'The planning, design and governance of sustainable communities', in R. Atkinson and G. Held (eds), *Securing an Urban Renaissance*. Bristol: Bristol University Press. pp. 305–20.
Redman, D. (2003) 'Playful deviance as an urban leisure activity, secret selves, self validation and entertaining performance', *Deviant Behaviour* 24(1): 27–51.
Riggio, Milla C. (1998) 'Origins of rituals and customs in the Trinidad Carnival: African or European?', *The Drama Review* 42 (3): 7–23.
Roberts, E. (1984) *A Woman's Place*. Oxford: Blackwell.
Roberts, L. (2004) 'An Arcadian apparatus: the introduction of the steam engine into the Dutch landscape,' *Technology and Culture* 45: 251–76.
Roberts, Robert (1974) *Classic Slum*. Harmondsworth: Pelican.
Rogers, R. and Power, A. (2000) *Cities for a Small Country*. London: Faber & Faber.
Rojek, C. (1993) *Ways of Escape*. London: Routledge.
Rojek, C. (1995) *Decentring Leisure: Rethinking Leisure Theory*. London: Sage.
Rojek, C. (1997) 'Indexing, dragging and the social construction of tourist sites', in C. Rojek and J. Urry (eds), *Touring Cultures*. London: Routledge. pp. 52–74.
Rojek, C. (2001) *Celebrity*. London: Reaktion Books.
Rolls, E. (2002) *Visions of Australia – Impressions of the Landscape*. South Melbourne: Lothian Books.
Rome, A. (2001) *The Bulldozer in the Countryside*. London: Cambridge University Press.
Rose, D. (1980) *Home Ownership and Industrial Change – a Struggle for a Separate Sphere*. Urban and Regional Studies Working Paper 25, University of Sussex.
Rose, N. (2001) 'The politics of life itself', in *Theory, Culture and Society* 18(6): 1–30.
Rose, N. (2005) *The Politics of Life Itself*. Princeton, NJ: Princeton University Press.
Roseland, M. (ed.) (1997) *Eco-City*. New Haven, CT.: New Society Publishers.
Rowley, T. (2006) *The English Landscape in the Twentieth Century*. London: Continuum.
Ryan, C. and Kinder, R. (1996) 'Sex, tourism and sex tourism: Fulfilling similar needs?', *Tourism Management* 17: 507–18.
Sabloff, A. (2001) *Reordering the Natural World: Humans and Animals in the City*. Toronto: University of Toronto Press.
Safer Bristol Partnership Executive (2006) *Tackling Anti-Social Behaviour in Bristol*. www.bristol.gov.uk/ccm/cms-service/download/asset/?asset_id=18736018. (Accessed 12 August 2007.)
Santoro, G. (2001) 'All that Jazz', *The Nation*, January 29.
Schumacher, E.F. (1973) *Small is Beautiful*. London: Blond & Briggs.
Seabrooke, J. (1973) *Loneliness*. London: Maurice Temple Smith.
Seeley, J.R., Sim, A. and Loosley, E. (1956) *Crestwood Heights: A Study of the Culture of Suburban Life*. New York: Basic Books.
Self, W. (1999) 'Big Dome', in *London – the Lives of the City*. *Granta* 65 (Spring): 115–28.
Sennett, R. (1994) *Flesh and Stone*. London: Faber & Faber.
Serres, M. (1992) *The Natural Contract*. Ann Arbor, MI: University of Michigan Press.
Sheldon, J.H. (1948). *The Social Medicine of Old Age*. Oxford University Press: Oxford.
Sheller, M. and Urry, J. (2000) 'The city and the car', *International Journal of Urban and Regional Research* 24: 737–57.
Shields, R. (1991) *Places on the Margin*. London: Routledge.
Simmel, G. (1997a) 'The Alpine journey', in D. Frisby and M. Featherstone (eds), *Simmel on Culture*. London: Sage.

Simmel, G. (1997b) 'The Adventure', in D. Frisby and M. Featherstone (eds), *Simmel on Culture*. London: Sage. pp. 219–21.
Simon, D. and Burns, E. (1998) *The Corner*. New York: Broadway Books.
Sinclair, E., Parker, R. and Parker, E. (1939) *The Gardener's Weekend Book*. London: Seeley Service and Co.
Smiers, J. (2000) 'European cities – first sow, then reap', in M. Miles, T. Hall and I. Bordan, (eds), *The City Cultures Reader*. London: Routledge. pp. 111–20.
Smith, N. (1996) *The New Urban Frontier*. London: Routledge.
Smith, R.G. (2003) 'World city actor-networks', *Progress in Human Geography* 27(1): 25–44.
Stockdale, J.E., Wells, A. and Rall, M. (1996) 'Participation rates in free-time activities: a comparison of London and New York', *Leisure Studies* 15: 1–16.
Taylor, C. (1982) *Village and Farmstead – A History of Rural Settlement in England*. London: George Philip.
Thomas, K. (1983) *Man and the Natural World: Changing Attitudes in England, 1500–1800*. London: Allen Lane.
Thrift, N. (2000) 'Non-representational theory', in D. Gregory, R.J. Johnston, G. Pratt, D. Smith and M. Watts (eds), *Dictionary of Human Geography,* (4th edn). Oxford: Blackwell. p. 556.
Thrift, N. (2001) 'Still life in nearly present time: the object of nature', in P. Macnaghten and J. Urry (eds), *Bodies of Nature*. London: Sage. pp. 34–57.
Touraine, A. (2000) *Can We Live Together?* Cambridge: Polity Press.
Townsend, P. (1973) *Isolation and Loneliness in the Aged*. In R. Weiss (ed.), *Loneliness: The Experience of Emotional and Social Isolation*. Cambridge, MA: The MIT Press.
Tranter, B. (1996) 'The social bases of environmentalism in Australia'. PhD thesis, Department of Sociology, University of Tasmania.
Tunstall, J. (1963) *Old and Alone*. London: Routledge and Kegan Paul.
Turner, V. and Turner, E. (1978) *Image and Pilgrimage in Christian Culture*. New York: Columbia University Press.
Uriely, N. and Belhassen, Y. (2006) 'Drugs and risk taking', *Annals of Tourism Research* 33(2): 339–59.
Urry, J. (2003a) *Global Complexity*. Cambridge: Polity Press.
Urry, J. (2003b) *Sociology Beyond Societies: Mobilities for the Twenty-First Century*. London: Routledge.
Vasishth, A. and Sloane, D.C. (2002) 'Returning to ecology: An Ecosystem approach to understanding the city', in M.J. Dear (ed.), *From Chicago to LA – Making Sense of Urban Theory.* London: Sage.
Wackernagel M. and Rees W.E. (1996) *Our Ecological Footprint*. Gabriola Island, BC: New Society Publishers.
Ward, B. (1976) *The Home of Man*. Harmondsworth: Pelican.
Warde, A., Wright, D. and Gayo-Cal, M. (2008) 'The omnivorous orientation in the UK', *Poetics* 36 (2/3):148–65.
Warren, R. (1997) *The Urban Oasis*. New York: McGraw–Hill.
Weber, M. (1946) 'Class, party, status', in *From Max Weber*, edited by H. Gerth and C. Wright Mills. New York: Oxford University Press. pp. 180–95.
Weber, M. (1958) *The City*. London: Macmillan.
Weiss, R.S. (1973) *Loneliness: The Experience of Emotional and Social Isolation*. Cambridge, MA: The MIT Press.
Welsch, Wolfgang (1997) *Undoing Aesthetics*. London: Sage.
Weldon, Fay (2002) *Auto Da Fay*. London: Flamingo.

Weldon, F. (2005) *Mantrapped*. London: Harper Perennial.

Whatmore, S. and Hinchliffe, S. (2003) 'Living cities: making space for urban nature', *Soundings: Journal of Politics and Culture* 22: 137–50.

Which? Magazine (2007) *Which? 50 years, 1957–2007*. www.which.couk/about-us/A/who_we_are/50th%20anniversary/50th_anniversary_481_122599.jsp. (Accessed 1 December 2007).

White, William (2001) *The Social Life of Small Spaces*. London: Routledge.

Wickens, E. and Sönmez, S. (2007) 'Casual sex in the sun makes the holiday: Young tourists' perspectives', in Y. Apostolopoulas and S. Sonmez (eds), *Population Mobility and Infectious Disease*. New York: Springer. pp. 200–14.

Williams, K, Burton, E. and Jenks, M. (2001) *Achieving Sustainable Urban Form*. London: Routledge.

Williams, R. (1972) 'Ideas of nature', in J. Benthall (ed.), *Ecology, The Shaping Enquiry*. London: Longman. pp. 146–64.

Williams, R. (1973) *The City and the Country*. London: Chatto and Windus.

Williams, R. (1983) *Keywords*. London: Fontana Paperbacks.

Williamson, B. (1982) *Class, Culture and Community*. London: Routledge and Kegan Paul.

Willis, M. (2004) 'The invisible hand – Bushfire arson in Australia', Sydney: Bushfire Cooperative Research Council. www.bushfirecrc.com/publications/downloads/C3_willis,m_perth04.pdf.

Wilson, A. (1992) *The Culture of Nature – North American Landscape from Disney to Exxon Valdez*. Cambridge, MA: Blackwell.

Willmott, P. (1963) *The Evolution of a Community. A Study of Dagenham after Forty Years*. London: Routledge and Kegan Paul.

Withey, L. (1997) *Grand Tours and Cook's Tours: A History of Lesiure Travel 1750 to 1915*. Berkeley: University of California Press.

Wolch, J., Pincetl, S. and Pulido, L. (2002) 'Urban nature and the nature of urbanism', in M.J. Dear (ed.), *From Chicago to L.A.: Making Sense of Urban Theory*. London: Sage.

Wood, M. (1974) 'Nostalgia or never: you can't go home again', *New Society* 7 (November): 343–6.

Wood, M. (2000) *In Search of England*. Harmondsworth: Penguin.

Wood, M. (2005) *In Search of Shakespeare*. London: Basic Books.

Wright, D. and Gayo-Cal, M. (2008) 'The omnivorous orientation in the UK', *Poetics* 36 (2–3): 148–65.

Wynne, B. (1996) 'May the sheep safely graze? A reflective view of the expert-lay knowledge divide', in S. Lash, B. Szersznski and B. Wynne (eds), *Risk, Environment and Modernity*. London: Sage.

Yorke, R.F.S. and Gibberd, F. (1938) *The Modern Flat*. London: Architectural Press.

Young, M. Willmott, P. (1957) *Family and Kinship in East London*. Harmondsworth: Penguin.

Young, M. and Willmott, P. (1973) *The Symmetrical Family*. London: Routledge and Kegan Paul.

Young, T. (2007) 'My father – the man who started Which?', in *Which? Magazine, Which? 50 Years, 1957–2007*.

Index

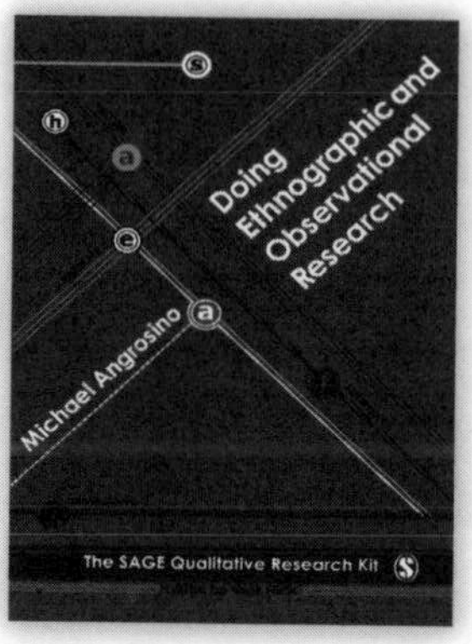

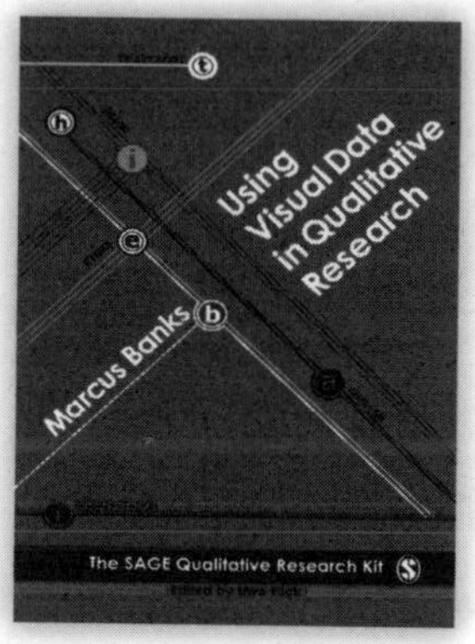

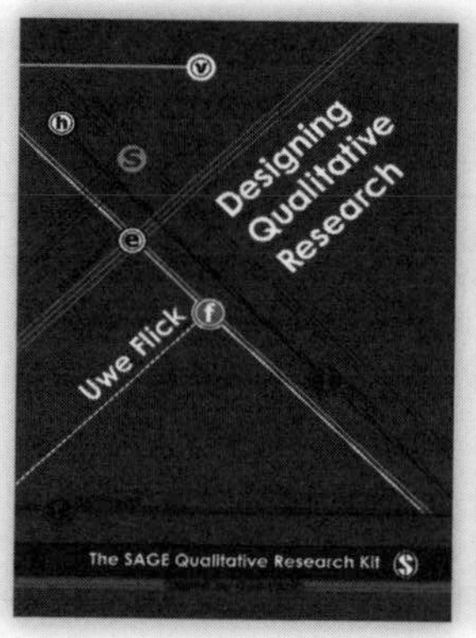

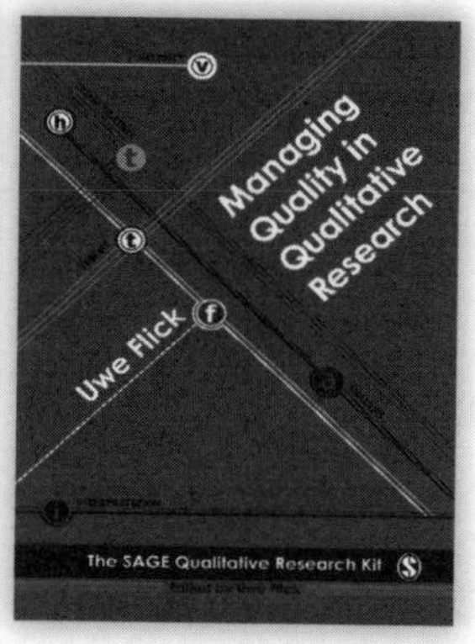

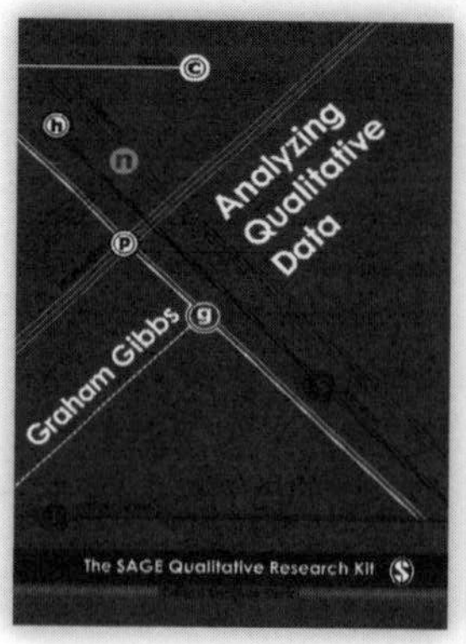

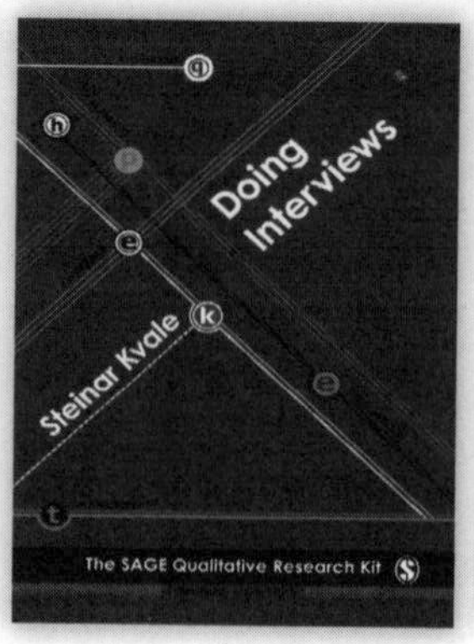

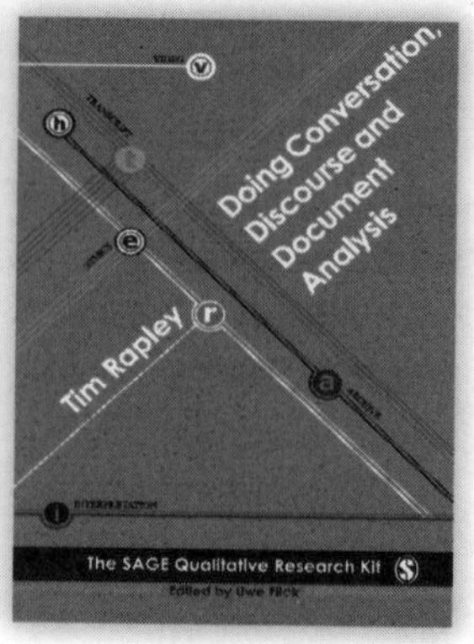